Reading Chinese Newspapers:

Tactics and Skills

Stanley Mickel

Far Eastern Publications
Yale University

Library of Congress Cataloging in Publications data:

READING CHINESE NEWSPAPERS: TACTICS AND SKILLS
Stanley L. Mickel
        1. Chinese language: reading (newspapers)
        2. Chinese language- Textbook for foreign speakers-
                English

ISBN 0-88710-165-8

10 9 8 7 6 5 4

To Karen,

my wife,

for her unlimited support and understanding,

while I wrote this book.

TABLE OF CONTENTS

Reading Chinese Newspapers:
Tactics and Skills

FOREWORD

Newspapers are important to your study of contemporary China for two reasons. First, and most obviously, they are primary sources of information about the country. Secondly, as advocated by the late 19th Century reformer Liáng Qǐchāo (梁啓超) and later championed by the eminent educator and literary figure Zhū Zìqīng (朱自清) in the 1940's, Chinese students have been urged to take the style of writing found in newspapers and journals as a model for their prose writing. Thus, it is essential for you to learn to read newspapers with the greatest possible efficiency and comprehension not only to be able to learn about current developments in China, but also to develop skill at reading the whole range of materials written in modern expository Chinese prose. To this end, this book is tightly focused on the goal of imparting tactics and skills that you will be able to use whenever you read Chinese. The first chapter discusses what specific skills are important when reading Chinese and how to go about developing them. The rest of the lessons in the book are designed to strengthen your ability to use these skills. When you are working with the texts and exercises in the lessons, concentrate on mastering the reading techniques discussed throughout this book.

Compiling a text such as this depends on the help of many people. First and foremost, Vivian Ling of Oberlin College made many important suggestions about format and content at the beginning of the project. She closely edited the first draft of the text and strengthened it immeasurably through her detailed and prompt comments. A suggestion from Shigeru Miyagawa of The Ohio State University resulted in the book having a much more readable tone. Appreciation is due to the many other professionals in the Chinese Language Teaching field who gave valuable time and energy to critique elements of this text. Thanks to the students at Wittenberg, Oberlin, and especially the third year crew at the 1991 Indiana University East Asian Summer Language Institute who worked with drafts of the book and gave comments which helped make the format more usable. Special gratitude goes to Bill Janeri for his work with the vocabulary indexes and to Professor Zheng Yide of the Beijing Language and Culture University for her rigorous critique of the Chinese language in the example sentences and the grammatical exercises. A sincere word of thanks is in order for the broad collection of Chinese newspapers at the East Asian Library at the University of Pittsburgh and their policy of open accessibility. The East Asian Libraries at The Ohio State University and Indiana University have also been most helpful, as were several people who sent some materials from China. Finally, crucial financial support for development of this book was provided by the Faculty Research Fund and the Faculty Development Organization at Wittenberg University.

Stan Mickel
June, 1995

A NOTE TO TEACHERS (with Suggestions on How to Use This Book)

1. You are urged to lead students to read and think about Lesson One. If students understand and use the concepts outlined there, their work with subsequent lessons will be much more efficient and effective.

2. Lessons 2 through 11 have similar formats. The main text is first presented as it was found in the newspaper. Structure notes keyed to that text immediately follow. A re-typed version of the text with facing vocabulary glosses is then given. Grammatical exercises come next. Lessons 7, 8 and 9 also give a simplified character version of the original full form character text. Two sight reading exercises end most lessons. Lesson 12, which focuses on newspapers from Taiwan, presents texts on subject matter found in earlier lessons (see item 6 below for further comments on the importance of Lesson 12). Lesson 13 presents a range of brief ads, schedules and announcements.

3. Since the major focus of the reading pedagogy employed in this textbook is to guide students towards recognition of structural and punctuation markers, it is most effective to have students read the structural notes for each main text and do the grammar exercises in advance of working with the main text itself.

4. All of the texts can be read extensively and/or intensively, though field trials of this book suggest that at least the main text should be read intensively. The sight readings can be handled either way to fit the needs of individual classes and students. You may have the students read the sight readings silently to themselves and then discuss them, but it seems to help everybody stay focused if you or they read the text out loud and then respond to the questions. It is best if they look at the questions before reading the sight reading. To build their scanning and skimming skills, have students read a sight reading text and then, without looking at it, use three to five minutes to write out a synopsis. Have them do this in English to avoid confusing tasks.

5. Lessons build in level of difficulty, but any one lesson can be skipped with no particular ill effect on work with subsequent lessons. It is a good idea to have your students work with the grammar structures in the skipped lessons.

6. Articles from newspapers in Taiwan are grouped together in Lesson 12 for a pedagogical reason; the differences in format and language style they present are challenges to students best met by concentrated study. The texts were chosen to mesh with the

contents of earlier lessons, so while Lesson 12 might be best used independently to work with vocabulary, structures and themes presented in a different form with a differing viewpoint, sub-sections of it can be used as supplemental materials when studying earlier lessons. Whichever way you decide is the most appropriate, it is important to work with this lesson to give students a full understanding of the two basic styles of contemporary Chinese newspapers.

7. Frequent vocabulary quizzes calling for both recognition and recall of the materials, especially of the Word Groups, are useful. Similarly, frequent review quizzes, when practicable, are also an effective means of helping students deepen their control of the vocabulary. The format and frequency of tests of course depends on your personal teaching style.

8. You should help students develop the practice of frequently going back to lessons studied earlier and reading the original texts presented at the head of each lesson. Urge them to read them for content, and for pleasure, just as they do with articles written in English.

9. The audio tapes contain the main texts of each lesson. You can use the tapes to train your students to "hear" and internalize the phrasing and flow of modern prose as well as help them with achieving accurate pronunciation of discrete vocabulary items. Working with tapes will also prepare students to better understand live radio and TV broadcasts. You can also select small segments of the tapes for dictation exercises.

10. The grammatical exercise sections of the accompanying workbook are grouped into three units: Lessons 2-4, 5-7, and 8-11. Each unit of the Workbook can best be used to review structures and vocabulary from the various texts. Workbook exercises are designed to reinforce control of grammar and to strengthen the students' understanding of some of the subtleties of Chinese prose. The reading exercises in the Workbook presents five examples of unannotated texts for each lesson, progressing in level of difficulty. Teachers may choose the level appropriate for further work in each lesson.

中國之窗

Reading Chinese Newspapers:
Tactics and Skills

Lesson One:
Strategy and Tactics for Reading
Chinese Prose

STRATEGY AND TACTICS FOR READING CHINESE PROSE

This book was compiled with the goal of helping you learn how to read modern Chinese prose with the greatest possible efficiency and understanding. Texts, structural explanations, vocabulary glosses, and sight reading passages were all selected to help you learn how to skim and scan Chinese texts for basic content as well as how to read intensively for complete comprehension. You are urged to read this lesson carefully as it first discusses the theory of reading that stimulated compilation of the book and then suggests various tactics which are helpful in developing the ability to read Chinese efficiently and effectively.

Reading Strategy

Research indicates that people generally take the strategies and tactics they use to read in their native language to their reading of foreign language materials. Thus, it is useful for you to be aware of how English speakers go about reading in their own language when you are working with Chinese texts. English readers first identify grammatical markers and vocabulary, then break texts into segments based on length, grammatical structures, and I suspect, punctuation markers. Units are generally sentence length, though complex sentences may be broken into several units for processing. After segments are understood by matching grammatical structures and vocabulary against language information kept in the brain, they are stored in short term memory. Segments are processed one after the other until the whole text has been read. When short term memory is filled, the contents are sent on to long term memory for retention.

Using this theoretical model as a pedagogical guide, this text focuses on presenting a reading strategy and supporting tactics which Chinese language students at the "beginning of the reading strategy instruction phase" (1) can use to read original Chinese materials most effectively. Initially, your control of these processes will be slow and laborious, but as you practice, utilize the various techniques described below and gain experience and confidence, your Chinese reading skills will become stronger, faster, and ultimately, second nature. At that point, you will be able to cease being concerned with the language of the materials and concentrate on the contents. In other words, you will be able to read Chinese for what it says, not how it says it.

There are many tactical skills to be developed in order to reach the level wherein you can read Chinese solely for content. Understanding how to read quickly and effectively by recognizing the grammatical markers that flag grammatical structures is the first and most important skill, but other skills must also be developed. You need to know how to recognize vocabulary by using word group affiliations and by analyzing the constituent elements in individual characters, how to use a dictionary efficiently, and how to employ prediction techniques (i.e., educated guessing) when reading. Understanding Chinese punctuation practices is another tactical skill constantly useful in making segmenting and grammatical decisions. Control of all these skills is necessary whether you are simply skimming a text or are reading it for complete comprehension.

Speaking on the function of journalistic writing as a model for modern expository prose, the important literary figure and influential educator Zhū Zìqīng (朱自清) said in the 1940's, "Middle school students should take the style of writing in newspapers and magazines as their main inspiration while practising writing." (2) Newspapers continue to be written in the style of expository writing you will most commonly encounter in your everyday work with the Chinese language and culture, so their contents are a good medium for practicing reading skills. The articles in this book were selected from newspapers such as 人民日报, 法制日报, 经济日报, 光明日报, 文汇报, 中央日報, 成都晚报 and 北京晚报 first and foremost for the language learning opportunities they present, but they were also chosen for thematic content that will be of lasting value in helping you understand contemporary Chinese culture. The texts range from straight news articles, to interviews, to letters to the editors, to advertisements. They are written in a variety of styles ranging from the colloquial to some clearly influenced by Neo-classical prose. Some of them are written with more skill and clarity than others. Most are in simplified characters, but several are in full form characters. The many different topics and sources result in a variety of vocabulary which will prove useful to your future work with Chinese texts.

Tactical Reading Skills: Text Organization

Chinese newspaper articles are generally organized around presenting one main event or theme and its supporting information. The main idea is first presented as the major headline and then expanded upon in the first paragraphs. Secondary but related information is frequently announced in the form of physically smaller headlines. These themes are usually addressed in the article after the main topic has been treated. There are of course numerous possible permutations on this structure, especially when the article does not deal with "hard news," but journalistic articles generally follow this layout.

These organizational principles mean that grammatical structures and vocabulary items tend to be repeated in articles. This not only makes the task of identifying the structures and learning the vocabulary easier, it also enhances your chances for successfully using contextually based prediction techniques as you skim, scan and read articles intensively. Keep this basic organizational structure in mind as you practice.

Tactical Reading Skills: Recognizing Grammatical Markers

English speakers apparently rely heavily on grammatical markers in the reading process. Markers such as [of], [and], [-ed], [-er], [-ing], etc. are identified, understood and then combined with vocabulary to enable the reader to understand the meaning of a text. Years of language experience and reading practice allow you to recognize and process English grammatical structures very quickly, usually without conscious effort. But as a student at the middle stage of Chinese language study, you probably do not have automatic control of most Chinese grammatical structures and must work hard to identify and process them. Grammatical markers such as [的], [地], [了], [还是], [才], etc. are especially important in the reading process since many Chinese words can have multiple grammatical functions differentiated only by markers such as these. Recognising these markers and understanding the structures they represent governs the speed and level of comprehension of your reading in Chinese.

A main feature of this book is its presentation of reading methods which you can use over and over to recognize and process Chinese sentence structures with ever increasing speed and certainty. Each lesson focuses on specific grammatical structures which you must firmly control in order to read Chinese efficiently. Attention is drawn to these structures by the structure notes placed next to the original texts. That is done to help you get in the habit of automatically looking for, recognizing and processing grammatical structures before you begin to work with the vocabulary. You should emphasize recognizing the markers and understanding the structures as you prepare the lessons for classroom work. Careful attention to the example sentences which accompany the structure notes plus work with the grammar exercises which follow each main text will help you strengthen your control of the grammatical patterns to the point that you will come to recognize and use them automatically.

Tactical Reading Skills: Steps for Approaching a Text

The first step in approaching a newspaper text is to look at the headlines (see the comments in the second lesson on how to read headlines), after which you should skim through the entire article. You will almost certainly feel very nervous about going past characters or compounds you don't immediately understand, but you will find skimming a text really is a valuable reading tactic which will save you a lot of time and energy in the end. Skimming allows you to begin to see the grammatical markers in relation to the rest of the sentence and the overall text in which they occur, it allows you to see which vocabulary is used repeatedly, and it helps you to get a feel for the basic ideas and layout of the piece.

After skimming the entire piece, or if it is very long, at least skimming the first several paragraphs, you should then go back to the beginning and skim it a second time. This time you should concentrate on analyzing it into meaningful grammatical units. These segments will sometimes be of sentence length, but since Chinese seem to like to write very long sentences, the initial grammatical units you will work with will very frequently be of sub-sentence length. Punctuation markers, especially commas, can be important guides to breaking sentences into processable units, so you are urged to pay particular attention to punctuation usages as they are described in the next section and in the structure notes in the lessons.

The third step involves scanning the text for specific bits of information. Scanning is similar to skimming in that you go quickly over the text, but while scanning you should concentrate on recognising key words or phrases and gain an overall idea of the basic informational content of the piece. The questions given at the end of each sight reading passage are designed to help you develop skill at looking through a text and locating specific information.

Finally, if you are working towards having a complete understanding of a text, re-read each line making sure you thoroughly understand each structure, each vocabulary item, and the flow of information within the article. Students tend to start with the vocabulary and often quickly bog down in a maze of unrecognized grammar and vocabulary. Hours are spent inefficiently and results are disappointing. Following the sequence of steps described here will train you to read Chinese efficiently and with greater understanding.

The sight reading texts which accompany each lesson were chosen to strengthen your skill at skimming and scanning Chinese prose. You will get the most out of these texts if you concentrate on using the skimming and scanning techniques discussed above and do not worry about the vocabulary. The questions asked at the end of each sight reading are designed to help you focus on these skills. Since most of the structures and vocabulary will already be familiar to you from your work with the main texts, you will find the sight readings helpful in practicing these extensive reading techniques. You should use the sight reading passages to build confidence at reading for speed and content, and to this end it is most profitable for class coverage to concentrate on reading and discussing the contents of the sight readings, preferrably in Chinese, rather than focusing on either structural or lexical items per se. The selections of headlines given with each lesson will also be helpful in developing your ability to skim and scan a newspaper page.

After you are confident that you understand the grammar, recognize the vocabulary and know what information is being presented in a text, put it aside for an hour, or a day, and then come back and re-read the whole thing. This time approach the text as something to be read simply for information and enjoyment. Approach it with the attitude that the text is no longer a language learning tool, but rather as something you want to read for its contents. As you progress through the book, go back and re-read the texts from previous lessons with the same intent of gaining information and pleasure from them.

Tactical Reading Skills: Punctuation Usages

China's contemporary punctuation system has markers which are unique to Chinese (of which #6, 7 & 8 below are only rarely used in newspaper texts), markers which are similar in written shape and function to English punctuation markers, and five punctuation markers which are written identically in English and Chinese texts, but which have both similar and dissimilar functions in the two languages. Knowledge of the values of all three types of markers will be very helpful in strengthening your reading ability. For example, focusing on   [丶] is extremely helpful because [丶] is used to mark lists of things, see 2:5. You can rely on familiar markers such as [?] and [!] to function in the same manner as they do in English. But understanding the usages of those markers which look the same but are used differently, especially the very frequently used comma [,] is particularly important for an accurate and efficient understanding of Chinese texts.

UNIQUELY CHINESE PUNCTUATION MARKERS

1. [。] Sentence Period   Marks the end of sentences.
   这是中国队第六次登上亚洲冠军宝坐。 2:32

2. [丶] Listing Comma   Marks items in lists.
   我认为，应采取"早、少、小"的三字措施来控制吸烟。 11:28

3. [《 》],[〈 〉],[「」] and [＿] in traditional texts   Title Markers   Mark literary titles.
   ……发出了《关于围绕"世界无烟日"积极开展劝阻吸烟活动的

通知》 ‥‥‥ 11:14

4. [「 」],[『 』] Quotation Markers Mark quotes and use of materials with special meanings; comparable with the Western style [" "].

‥‥‥他告诉「西藏自治区主席」多吉才让说:「如果‥‥‥」 12.3:10

5. [‥‥‥] Ellipsis Marker Marks the omission of text.

这种新型器件寿命长、重量轻‥‥‥ 5:23

6. [〔〕],[【】],[〖〗]Parentheses Markers Mark parenthetical material

7. [.], [＿] Emphasis Markers (N.B. [＿] marks literary titles in traditional texts) Placed under or besides characters to mark emphasis.

8. [□] Lost Character Marker Marks characters lost in transmission

GRAPHEMICALLY IDENTICAL, FUNCTIONALLY DIFFERENT MARKERS

1. [＿] Proper Name Marker Placed under or beside characters in traditional texts to mark the names of individuals.

2. [X],[O] Taboo Markers Used in to mark deleted taboo words.

3. [·] Sub-division Marker Placed mid level in the line to mark sub-sections of foreign names, literary titles, dates, and addresses.

4. [，] Comma Used in Chinese sentences to separate and thus emphasize materials. You must avoid automatically transferring your understanding of how commas are used in English to your reading of Chinese. It is crucial to be aware that Chinese commas can

separate grammatical structures which English commas do not. For example Chinese commas routinely separate subjects from verbs, e.g. 北方重工业城市沈阳,近年来采取有效的措施…… 4:5; verbs from objects, e.g. 航天工业部副部长、著名宇航专家孙家栋认为,这颗卫星发射成功…… 5:4; and place from subject and verb as in 在今天的射击比赛中，广东刘海英、解放军苏冰、湖南张秋萍四次超过两项亚洲记录。 2:8 To assume Chinese commas are always the same as English commas and dismiss these usages as mistakes is to be unclear about what is going on in the Chinese. If you understand how commas function in Chinese texts, you will be able to make those all important segmenting decisions more accurately, and you will be more aware of the extra-textual, connotative content of the materials. See 2:8, 4:10, 4:42, 5:8, 7:9, and 12.1:5 for further discussion of Chinese comma usages.

Markers which are graphemically and functionally similar are: [?] Question Mark; [！] Exclamation Mark; [" "] and [' '] Quote, Title and Special Usage Markers; [:] Colon; [;] Semi-colon; [-] Dash; [--] Hyphen; [[]] and [()] Parentheses; and infrequently used miscellaneous markers such as [‖], [〜], and [/], etc. (See Stan Mickel, "Modern Chinese Punctuation and CSL Reading Pedagogy," JCLTA, Vol XXIII: No. 1, Feb 1988, pp. 21-39 for further discussion of the punctuation system.)

Whether written with a shape familiar to you or with a form you have not seen before, skillful use of punctuation markers can be as helpful to your development of reading skills as the other tactical skills discussed in this book. Be careful and attentive to these 'traffic signs' when working with Chinese texts.

Tactical Reading Skills: Working with Vocabulary

Working with Chinese vocabulary is complicated by the fact that words can be used for several different grammatical functions without change in pronunciation or written form. This leads to a need for flexibility when thinking of the English equivalents for Chinese words, or otherwise you will have unnecessary difficulties when working with them.

For example, if you find 革命 translated as 'revolution' in a dictionary and then only think of it as a noun, you may have trouble understanding a sentence in which 革命 is used as the verb 'revolt', or the adjective 'revolutionary', or as the adverb 革命地, which does not have a direct English equivalent. If you accept that a Chinese word appearing in a particular grammatical position must be translated with an English equivalent reflecting that specific grammatical function, you will not be confused when something you saw as a noun in the dictionary is used as a verb, adjective, adverb, or vice versa. You should learn words for core meanings, almost without concern for the grammatical form of their English equivalent, and then understand and interpret them in terms of the grammatical slots in which they appear.

In addition to understanding the role of grammatical function in working with vocabulary, there are other techniques which will increase your efficiency with vocabulary, and ultimately with reading in general. Vocabulary should never be learned in a vacuum, every vocabulary item should be learned as part of a matrix of meanings, graphic shapes and phonetic values. For example, be alert to the existence of radicals and phonetics as clues to meaning and pronunciation. Radicals are helpful because they generally indicate the basic meaning associated with a character; e.g., the 'metal' radical in 铜、银、铂, etc. suggests they all have a meaning having to do with 'metal'. Phonetics also can be used to predict pronunciation and sometimes meanings; e.g., the phonetic 原 [yuán] 'original' gives a clue to the pronunciation and meaning of 源 [yuán] 'source, fountainhead'.

Use the idea of "Word Groups" as a way to fix vocabulary items in a matrix of conceptual relationships which will allow you to work with the vocabulary more efficiently. For example, if you are alert to the core meaning of 赛 [sài] 'compete' in the second lesson and combine that with your understanding of the meaning of the other part of the compounds in which 赛 is used, you will have a basic idea of the meaning of the words 比赛 'compare + compete' > 'competition', 赛事 'compete + affair' > 'competition' and 决赛 'decide + compete' > 'finals in a competition' without needing to look them up. Even if you do not recognize the other part of the compound, you can use your knowledge of radicals, phonetics and word group affiliations to predict the meaning of unfamiliar vocabulary; e.g., use 赛 and the 'boat' radical in 艇 to predict that the word 赛艇 has to do with 'sailing competition'. This tactic of contextualized guessing can sometimes result in hilarious misunderstandings, but the pleasure that you will experience when you find your guesses confirmed is very rewarding. You can also get many illuminating insights into how the Chinese understand the world around them from the elements used to construct words. Watch for this.

As you get better at implementing these techniques for working with vocabulary, not only will you be able to learn vocabulary more easily, you will improve your reading speed and comprehension.

Tactical Reading Skills: Dictionary Usage

Using a dictionary is unavoidable when reading in a foreign language, but you should take great care not to become chained to it. If you start out trying to read a Chinese text by looking up its vocabulary before you understand its grammatical structure, you will wind up spending hours decoding a puzzle instead of reading, and you will frequently still be unsure about just what the text means even though you may have spent lots of time hitting the dictionary. But there will inevitably be many times when you have to use a dictionary. So that you can more quickly move towards the central point of reading--working with and understanding the contents of texts--you should learn how to use dictionaries most efficiently and not spend undue time and energy finding words in them.

It is hard to learn how to use a dictionary expeditiously from written instructions, but knowing some basic principles is a good way to start. There are two ways to find vocabulary in most Chinese dictionaries: alphabetically and by graphemic analysis of the characters. If you know how to pronounce a Chinese word but are unsure of its meaning, the quickest and easiest thing to do is to look it up by its romanized spelling. A compound word is usually listed under its first character, so you can look it up by alphabetically locating the first character in the dictionary and then scanning the compounds listed under that character. In many dictionaries the compounds are also listed alphabetically. If you do not know the pronunciation of the rest of the compound, you can look at the listed compounds one by one until you find the word. Keeping the radical and/or phonetic of the unknown character in mind improves the speed with which the compound can be located.

When you do not know the pronunciation of the first character of a word, it is necessary to find it through graphic analysis of the character. The most common graphic organization of characters in dictionaries, indexes, phone books, etc., is by their radicals, though there is also the less commonly used four corner method. Radicals are listed in dictionaries (or in radical indexes) in order of ascending number of strokes. The first step is to identify the radical under which the character seems likely to be listed. Individual characters under each radical are also listed in order of ascending number of strokes, not including the strokes in the radical. Having counted the number of strokes, you should then go to the subdivision of the radical having that number of strokes and search out the character. (A good habit to cultivate when you are unable to find a character under the anticipated number of strokes is to look also under the next higher and then the next lower number of strokes.) In some dictionaries each individual character has its own assigned number, but usually just the page number where the character appears is given. Once you locate the first character of the compound in the dictionary, the search tactics discussed above for finding the compound should then be used.

As a general principle, it is worthwhile to poke around in the back and front parts of dictionaries. In addition to prefaces and radical indexes, lexicographers seem to delight in adding information such as lists of the names, regions, capitals, and currencies of countries; lists of governmental agencies; lists of measure words; and lists of common Chinese surnames, among other things, all of which can be interesting and unexpectedly useful.

Tactical Reading Skills: Cultural Knowledge

The Chinese write about the world around them, of course. Therefore, the more you know about their culture and how they view the world, the more likely you are to get the exhilarating "aha experience" of recognizing in Chinese texts things you already know, and the easier it will be for you to read what they write. For example, knowledge of Chinese social structure will give a clarifying background to the comments on the position of women in Chinese society given in Lesson Three. Knowing about the results of the 1945-49 Chinese civil war will give you a context for understanding the article on Taiwan in Lesson Eight more rapidly, as well as a context for understanding why comments are phrased as they are in the articles in newspapers from Taiwan in Lesson Twelve. Similarly, knowledge of Chinese foreign relations, especially those of the last 150 years, will make the Chinese foreign minister's comments in Lesson Seven clearer and help you see the covert as well as the overt messages being conveyed. What you learn about China in courses on Chinese history, religion, anthropology, literature and other disciplines, and from your own readings and experiences, will inevitably come in handy as you read.

DISCUSSION QUESTIONS

1. Outline the specific steps to be taken when preparing a Chinese text for class.

2. How does an active knowledge of grammatical markers help you read Chinese materials?

3. Why are grammatical markers discussed after the main text in each lesson?

4. What steps should you take to learn the vocabulary most efficiently?

5. What is the function of the sight reading texts?

6. How is a dictionary to be used when you are reading Chinese? Why do many people rely too much on dictionaries when reading in a foreign language?

7. What are the three groups of Chinese punctuation markers?

8. In what specific way does knowledge of the values of punctuation markers increase your ability to read Chinese?

9. What are some of the similarities and differences between Chinese and English comma usages?

10. How can classes taken in English be useful when reading Chinese language materials? What classes in traditional and modern Chinese culture have you taken?

11. What is your goal in learning to read Chinese? What level of proficiency do you wish to reach? Which of the strategies and tactics discussed in this book will be useful to you in reaching your goal?

FOOTNOTES

1. Galal Walker, "'Literacy' and 'Reading' in a Chinese Program," Journal of the Chinese Language Teacher's Association, (February 1984) vol. XIX: No. 1, 73-79.

2. Zhū Zìqīng 朱自清 Zhū Zìqīng lùn yǔwén jiàoyù (朱自清论语文教育), (China: Henan Educational Press, 1985), 22.

Reading Chinese Newspapers:
Strategies and Tactics

Lesson Two: Athletic Events

大沙河技术开发集团，由沙河市科委牵头，组织河北农大、河北林学院、省情报所及沙河市有关委、局参加，对大沙河12万亩滩地统一规划，布设开发基点。自今年3月成立至8月底，已开发河滩地5万亩，打井200眼，栽植各种果树和防护林200多万株，树下种植当年收益的经济作物，预计今年经济收益可达500多万元。

这些技术开发集团的建立，起到了技术开发示范、服务、扩散的作用。据统计，半年多来，各开发集团向山区提供技术服务40项、信息200多条、各种优良品种20多个。同时还使一些山区技术、生产、销售脱节的问题得到了较好的解决。

本报广州11月27日电 记者温子健、吴骅报道：自开幕以来持续高潮的第六届全运会在结束了今晚的争夺之后，赛事过半。游泳、体操、举重、花样游泳、击剑、赛艇、帆板、技巧和武术等九个项目结束了比赛。

在今天的射击比赛中，广东刘海英、解放军苏冰、湖南张秋萍四次超过两项亚洲纪录，前卫体协池行乐平了一项亚洲纪录。湖北陈菊英、广东王永华、河北赵存林今天下午在田径场，分别打破了女子400米栏和男子400米全国纪录。举重比赛的最后一个级别争夺中，辽宁选手才力以215公斤的成绩，打破了213公斤的挺举全国纪录。帆板比赛在海口进行的，辽宁张德春获冠军，广东张小冬获亚军。

目前，广东代表团以总分850分、金牌39枚的战绩，居各路健儿之首，上海队其次，总分728分，金牌26枚。第三名辽宁总分591分，金牌27枚。北京以508分名列第四。

本报曼谷11月27日电 中国男篮在丢掉亚洲桂冠1年11个月后，今天又重新把它夺回来。第14届亚洲男篮锦标赛决赛今天在这里举行，中国队经过延长期苦战，以86：79战胜老对手南朝鲜队。

这是中国队第6次登上亚洲冠军宝座。在本届亚洲锦标赛上，中国男篮共出战8场，获得全胜，但是夺冠道路并不平坦。对伊拉克队和菲律宾队，中国队都是在最后关头才以两三分优势险胜的。

六届全运会赛事过半

昨天射击又超过两项亚洲纪录

中国男篮夺回亚洲桂冠

经过苦战击败南朝鲜队

签署命令，任命迟浩田为中国人民解放军总参谋长，杨白冰为中国人民解放军总政治部主任，赵南起为中国人民解放军总后勤部部长。

他们今天已全部到职。

==============================

万里若思尺

星通信网开通

和互不相联历史宣告结束

、辽河、库尔
、胜利、长庆、
江、濮阳、深
卫星通信地面
等5座数字微
地面站设在固
星通信网，除
外，还可以开
数据传输等业

务，并备有全网性加密电路，传输保密文图。边远地区的地面站还可提供本地彩色电视信号的接收业务。此项工程于1982年由国家批准，引进国外先进设备，租用印度洋上空国际5号卫星，于1985年9月开始安装、入网验证测试。建设中克服了许多困难，取得了石油通信工作的重大进步和飞跃。

现代化通讯手段是现代石油工业建设的一个重要组成部分。这次建成的石油专用卫星通信网，标志着我国石油通信事业向现代化迈出了新的一步，对我国石油工业的生产将产生深远影响。

一万辆

reproduction of original text
(line numbers added)

STOP: Read Lesson One BEFORE working on this lesson!

HOW TO READ HEADLINES AND BY-LINES

Headlines with larger, thicker characters carry the principal information, and those with smaller characters carry secondary messages. Size of a headline is more important than its location; a main headline may be to the right, left, top, middle, or below smaller headlines. Headline information is always repeated in greater detail in the body of the article. The main headline is usually restated in the first paragraph or two, and the information given in the secondary headlines is elaborated upon somewhere later in the article. In this lesson, the main headline of line 1 is restated in lines 3 & 4 and that of line 24 in lines 26-28. Restatement of secondary headlines is generally in relation to their size and location. The sub-headline of line 2 is restated in lines 4 & 5, and that of line 25 in lines 28-31.

Grammatical principles are observed in headlines, but the omission of grammatical markers often makes headlines terse and more difficult to understand. When you do not understand a headline, it is often more efficient to read the first paragraph or two of the story and then come back to the headlines.

Being able to scan a newspaper page by looking at the headlines is an important reading skill. After you have studied the main texts and are familiar with the vocabulary and subject matter, work with the headline exercise in each lesson and continually build your ability to read Chinese headlines.

The usual order in by-lines is for the news agency or source to come first, here 本报 ('this newspaper'). The location of the news story follows, here 广州 (Guǎngzhōu, 'Canton'). The date generally comes next followed by the method of transmitting the text, here 电. Names of reporters usually follow that, and a verb meaning 'report', here 报道 (bàodào), often ends the by-line.

STRUCTURE NOTES (A tag definition is also given for each structure at its line occurrence in the Vocabulary. Structure notes line numbers refer to the original text. Vocabulary line numbers refer to the re-typed text and may differ slightly.)

2: Time 又 Verb = 'Verb again at a time' Distinguish between the two 'again' markers 又 and 再: T 又 V marks the completed repetition or continuation of an earlier verb action (be alert for other values when 又 is not preceded by Time); (T) 再 V marks a continuation or repetition yet to come of a verb action. Consider the use of 又 in line 28 below and 8:23. Use 又 as a way to locate the core verb of a structure, since the verb will come after it. Two examples of this use of 又 are:

> a. 我们昨天又考了生词。
> b. 辽宁女篮队是全国第一。她们又战胜了广东队。

4-5: 在 Clause 之后, Y = 'After clause, (then) Y' 之后 (and its synonyms 以后 and 后) followed by a comma marks the material in the structure before it as a dependent time clause. Keep in mind that the English equivalent for 之后 marks the head of the clause rather than the end. See also l. 26-27 below. (See 3:7 for comments on 之时 time clauses.) Examples are:

> a. 他昨天拜访了白先生以后，就到书店去了。
> b. 她打破了女子400米全国记录之后感到很高兴。

5: 了 When used within a sentence or comma unit, 了 marks completion of the core verb action. Thus 了 is highly useful in locating the main verb in a sentence or comma unit. See l. 10, 12, and 14 below. See also the discussion at 6:11. Do not confuse this function with the use of 了 as part of a verb-potential complement such as 吃不了 or 走得了, or with its use in vocabulary items such as 了解, 好极了, etc.

5-8: 、 = 'enumerative comma' The presence of enumerative commas identifies a series of roughly equal grammatical structures; usually nouns, but sometimes phrases or even clauses. Use 、 to locate grammatical structures which have multiple subjects or objects. The last two items in the series are usually marked by the conjunctions 和 or 以及, see l. 8-9, 11 and 19 below. Writers are not always careful to maintain the distinctions between enumerative and regular comma usages, see Lesson 7. Two examples are:

a. 书、笔、纸和墨水你们学生都应该买。
b. 击剑、田径、举重和体操的记录都分别被打破了。

8-10: ，　When you begin working with a text, it is important that you notice the placement of the punctuation markers, especially the commas. You will find that while Chinese use commas to mark grammatical structures within sentences, commas are very often used to indicate pauses and emphases in ways which English comma usages do not allow. It is common to find sentences such as S, VO, SV, O, ST, PVO, SP, V among others in which a comma separates the subject from its core verb, the core verb from its object, etc. The key to working with Chinese comma usages is to analyze the grammatical structures of each unit of material end-marked by a comma. If there is no core verb within one of these "comma units", the materials within that unit will be part of a grammatical structure which extends across the comma, and you will need to go into the next comma unit to locate the core verb. For example, do not see something such as 劳动 in 正在装线上紧张劳动的工人，... as the core verb of this comma unit. The 的 marks 劳动 as modification of the noun 工人, so even though 劳动 is frequently used as the main verb of structures, it is part of a modification clause here and therefore not the core verb of the comma unit. If there is a core verb within a comma unit, as there is in l. 9 and 10, that unit will be a clause to be processed before you go on to the next comma unit. If you keep in mind that core verbs are usually preceeded or followed by markers such as 还, 了, 着, etc., you will find it easier to locate them.

　　When a location phrase comes before the subject of a clause or sentence, as it does here in l. 8, it must be end-marked with a comma, and you will find its subject, verb, etc. after the comma. See also l. 13, 33 and 35-36 below. Similarly, adverbial phrases placed before the subject must be end-marked by a comma to indicate they are out of the usual adverbial position directly before the verb phrase, see 4:42. On the other hand, time phrases preceeding the subject may or may not be end-marked by a comma, see l. 18. Additionally, location, time and adverbial phrases in their normal position between the subject and the verb can be separated from the verb by a comma for emphasis, as happens in l. 12 and 14.

Commas can be very useful reading tools which help you recognize the parameters of grammatical structures, if you understand how Chinese use them. They can be very confusing if you assume they function just as they do in English.

14: S 以 X, Verb phrase = 'Subject does the verb using/by means of X' Notice that a comma separates the constituent elements of this pattern in this sentence. A literary synonym of 用, 以 is also frequently used in the structure Verb 以 X = 'verb by means of X'. Recognise 以 as the marker of a common prose structure. See also l. 18, 22, 30-31, and 36-37 below. Examples are:

> a. 谢文石同学以99分考得全校第一名。
> b. 我们上星期四以三比一击败了第五十五中学队。

15: The structure S 是 T P V O 的 is used to mark emphasis on when (T), where (P), or why a verb action occurred. Here the structure marks emphasis on the place (海口) where the verb action (进行) happened. 是 is usually found after the subject in this structure, but it is omitted here. See also l. 36-37 below. Examples of S 是 T P V O 的 are:

> a. 我们是三、四年以前开始学习中文的。
> b. 中国男篮是去年一月在东京丢掉亚洲桂冠的。

28: 把 marks placement of the object before the verb in a S(T)(P) 把O1 V (O2) structure. Keep in mind that the transposed object may be heavily modified and thus come many characters after the 把 marker. Recognising 把 (and its synonym 将 jiāng, see 5:32) is an important step towards locating the object, and thus the following core verb of a sentence or comma unit. For example:

> a. 真奇怪，他常把"十"字看作"千"字！
> b. 在六届全运会上运动员差不多把所有的记录都打破了。

35: 并 negative Verb = 'definitely negative verb' 并 intensifies the negative nature of a verb situation and signals a setting straight of the record by marking that contrary to what may have been said earlier, the expected verb action did not, is not, or will not occur. Compare this with its synonym 决 jué which simply emphasises the negative state of the verb; see 9:13. Note the very different use of 并 as a conjunction in 4:22. Two examples of its use with negatives are:

  a. 你个人的事情我并没告诉他！
  b. 他们并不能再一次超过亚洲的射击记录。

VOCABULARY

So that you can devote more energy to mastering the skills needed to recognize the grammatical structures while reading, vocabulary beyond the second year level is glossed and placed next to the text for easy reference. As a way of helping you see the inter-connections between some vocabulary items and to make learning the vocabulary easier, particular attention is given in the Vocabulary to groups of words found within a lesson which have one or more characters in common. These "Word Group" (词组) members are glossed at the occurrence of the first member of the group in the format WG>4:'gloss'. This indicates that the word being glossed is part of a Word Group and first appears and is defined at the fourth line of the text. As a stimulus to you to recognize and use these Word Groups, subsequent members of WG are listed at their line positions in the text and reference to membership in a Word Group given in the format '?' 字:1. This means that the English equivalent is not shown and that it is a member of the 字 Word Group glossed in line 1. If you do not remember the meaning of a WG member from its initial glossing, you should use your understanding of its Word Group connections to predict its meaning before looking up the gloss given earlier.

Words are glossed in the lessons according to their function in the grammatical structures and contexts in which they occur. You need to keep in mind that because many Chinese words can be used in different places for different grammatical values, they can be correctly translated with a variety of English equivalents. When learning vocabulary, you should memorize a core, almost a-grammatical value for words, and select a correct English equivalent based on how the words are used in the Chinese text before you when you translate.

1   六届全运会赛事过半

2   昨天射击又超过两项亚洲纪录

3   本报广州11月27日电   记者温子健，吴骅
4   报道：自开幕以来持续高潮的第六届全运会在
5   结束了今晚的争夺之后，赛事过半。游泳、体
6   操、举重、花样游泳、击剑、赛艇、帆板、技
7   巧和武术等九个项目结束了比赛。

VOCABULARY

1: 届   [jiè] '(measure for periodic events)'

1: 全运会 [quányùnhuì] 'athletic event'

1: 赛事 [sàishì] 'competition' WG>6:赛艇 [sàitǐng] 'boat races';
     WG>7:比赛 [bǐsài] 'competition'; WG>29:决赛 [juésài]
     'finals (in a tournament)'; WG>29:锦标赛 [jǐnbiāosài]
     'championship game'

2: 射击 [shèjī] 'shooting' WG>6:击剑 [jījiàn] 'fencing'; WG>24:击败
     [jībài] 'defeat'

2: 又 V [yòu] Verb '(verb action repeated) again' (SN)*

2: 超过 [chāoguò] 'surpass'

2: 项   [xiàng] '(measure for items)' WG>7:项目 [xiàngmù] 'item'

2: 亚洲 [Yàzhōu] 'Asia' See 1. 16 for different usage of 亚.

2: 纪录 [jìlù] 'record' (Note: 纪录 is sometimes written as 记录.)

*(SN) marks that this item is discussed in the Structural Notes.

3: 温子健 [Wēn Zǐjiàn]、吴骅 [Wú Huá] '(names of two reporters)'
    See the discussion at the end of Vocabulary for comments on how
        to recognize Chinese names.

4: 自 [zì] 'from'

4: 开幕 [kāimù] 'start an event'

4: 持续 [chíxù] 'continue, sustain'

4: 高潮 [gāocháo] 'high tide'

5: 在X之后 [zài X zhīhòu] 'after X' (SN)

5: 结束 [jiéshù] 'conclude'

5: V 了 [Verb lê] 'marks verb completion' (SN)

5: 争夺 [zhēngduó] 'competition' WG>28:夺回 [duóhuí] 'seize back';
    WG>35:夺冠 [duó guān] 'seize back first place'

5: 游泳 [yóuyǒng] 'swimming' WG>6:花样游泳 [huāyàng yóuyǒng]
    'synchronized swimming'

5: 、 [dùnhào] 'enumerative comma' (SN)

5: 体操 [tǐcāo] 'gymnastics'

6: 举重 [jǔzhòng] 'weight lifting'; WG>15:挺举 [tǐngjǔ] 'clean and jerk';
    WG>29:举行 [jǔxíng] 'hold (a meeting, ceremony, etc.)'

6: 花样游泳 [huāyàng yóuyǒng] '?' 游 WG:5

6: 击剑 [jījiàn] '?' 击 WG:2

6: 赛艇 [sàitǐng] '?' 赛 WG:1

6: 帆板 [fānbǎn] 'sailing'

6: 技巧 [jìqiǎo] 'acrobatics'

7: 武术 [wǔshù] 'martial arts (swordplay, shadow boxing, etc.)'

7: 等 [děng] 'etc.' (summarizes the noun series)

7: 项目 [xiàngmù] '?' 项 WG:2

7: 比赛 [bǐsài] '?' 赛 WG:1

8   在今天的射击比赛中，广东刘海英、解放
9   军苏冰、湖南张秋萍四次超过两项亚洲纪录，
10 前卫体协池行乐平了一项亚洲纪录。湖北陈菊
11 英、广东王永华、河北赵存林今天下午在田径
12 场，分别打破了女子400米栏和男子400米全国
13 纪录。举重比赛的最后一个级别争夺中，辽宁
14 选手才力以215公斤的成绩，打破了213公斤的
15 挺举全国纪录。帆板比赛在海口进行的，辽宁
16 张德春获冠军，广东张小冬获亚军。

17   目前，广东代表团以总分850分、金牌39
18 枚的战绩，居各路健儿之首，上海队其次，总
19 分728分，金牌26枚。第三名辽宁总分591分，
20 金牌27枚。北京以508分名列第四。

VOCABULARY

8: ， [dòuhào] 'comma' (SN)

8: 刘海英 [Líu Hǎiyīng]、苏冰 [Sū Bīng]、张秋萍 [Zhāng Qiūpíng]
    '(names of people)'

8: 解放军 [Jiěfàngjūn] 'People's Liberation Army'

10: 前卫体协 [Qiánwèi tǐxié] '(abbr. for 前卫体育协会) Vanguard
    Athletics Association'

10: 池行乐 [Chí Xínglè] '(name of a person)'

10: 平 [píng] 'tie, even' WG>35: 平坦 [píngtǎn] 'level, smooth'

10: 陈菊英 [Chén Júyīng]、王永华 [Wáng Yǒnghuá]、赵存林 [Zhào
    Cúnlín] '(names of people)'

11: 田径场 [tiánjìngchǎng] 'field for track and field events'

12: 分别 [fēnbié] 'separately' WG>13: 级别 [jíbié] 'flight, rank'

12: 打破 [dǎpò] 'smash, break'

12: 米 [mǐ] 'meter (length)'

12: 栏 [lán] 'hurdle'

13: 级别 [jíbié] '?' 别 WG:12

13: 辽宁 [Liáoníng] 'Liaoning (province)'

14: 选手 [xuǎnshǒu] 'participant' WG>31:对手 [duìshǒu] 'opponent'

14: 才力 [Cái Lì] '(name of a person)'

14: 以X,Vp [yǐ X, Vp] 'verb phrase by means of X' (SN)

14: 公斤 [gōngjīn] 'kilograms'

14: 成绩 [chéngjī] 'achievement' WG>18:战绩 [zhànjī] 'success in competition'

15: 挺举 [tíngjǔ] '?' 举 WG:6

15: S是PV的 [S shì PV de] 'stresses past verb action location' (SN)

15: 海口 [hǎikǒu] 'harbor'

15: 进行 [jìnxíng] 'carry out' WG>29:举行 [jǔxíng] 'hold (an event etc.)'

16: 张德春 [Zhāng Déchūn]、张小冬 [Zhāng Xiǎodōng] '(names of people)'

16: 获 [huò] 'attain, win'

16: 冠军 [guànjūn] 'first place (in competition)' WG>25:桂冠 [guìguān] '(victory) laurel'; WG>35:夺冠 [duóguān] 'seize back first place'

16: 亚军 [yàjūn] 'second place (in a competition)'

17: 目前 [mùqián] 'right now, at present'

17: 代表团 [dàibiǎotuán] 'delegation, team'

17: 总分 [zǒngfēn] 'total points' WG>17:分 [fēn] 'points' 分 WG:12

17: 分 [fēn] '?' 分 WG:17

17: 金牌 [jīnpái] 'gold medal for first place'

18: 枚 [méi] '(measure for medals)'

18: 战绩 [zhànjī] '?' 绩 WG:14

18: 居 X [jū X] 'be situated at X' (e.g. 居各路健儿之首 [jū gè lù jiàn'ér zhīshǒu] 'be at the head of all of the athletes')

18: 健儿 [jiàn'ér] 'good athlete'

18: 队 [duì] 'team'

18: 其次 [qícì] 'next, second'

20: 名列 [míngliè] 'rank as'

24   经过苦战击败南朝鲜队
25   中国男篮夺回亚洲桂冠

26   本报曼谷11月27日电　中国男
27   篮在丢掉亚洲桂冠1年11个月后，
28   今天又重新把它夺回来。第14届亚
29   洲男篮锦标赛决赛今天在这里举行，
30   中国队经过延长期苦战，以86:79战
31   胜老对手南朝鲜队。
32   这是中国队第6次登上亚洲冠
33   军宝座。在本届亚洲锦标赛上，中
34   国男篮共出战8场，获得全胜，但
35   是夺冠道路并不平坦。对伊拉克队
36   和菲律宾队，中国队都是在最后关
37   头才以两三分优势险胜的。

VOCABULARY

24: 苦战 [kǔzhàn] 'bitter fighting' WG>30:战胜 [zhànshèng] 'defeat';
　　　WG>34:出战 [chūzhàn] 'go forth to combat'

24: 击败 [jībài] '?' 击 WG:2

24: 南朝鲜 [Nán Cháoxiǎn] 'South Korea' (See below for comments on
　　　foreign place names.)

25: 男篮 [nánlán] '(abbr. for 男子篮球) men's basketball'

25: 桂冠 [guìguān] '?' 冠 WG:16

26: 曼谷 [Màngǔ] 'Bangkok'

27: 丢掉 [diūdiào] 'lose'

28: 重新 [chóngxīn] 'again, anew' (Note that 重 is [chóng] when it means 'again' and [zhòng] when it means 'heavy'. See 举重 in l. 6)

28: 把OV [bǎ OV] 'marks object placed before verb' (SN)

28: 夺回 [duó huí] '?' 夺 WG:5

29: 锦标赛 [jǐnbiāosài] '?' 赛 WG:1

29: 决赛 [juésài] '?' 赛 WG:1

29: 举行 [jǔxíng] '?' 举 WG:6; 行 WG:15

30: 延长期 [yánchángqī] 'overtime period'

30: 战胜 [zhànshèng] '?' 战 WG:24; 胜 WG:37

31: 对手 [duìshǒu] '?' 手 WG:14

32: 登上 [dēngshàng] 'mount, get up on'

32: 宝座 [bǎozuò] 'precious throne, coveted position'

34: 出战 [chūzhàn] '?' 战 WG:24

35: 夺冠 [duó guān] '?' 夺 WG:5; 冠 WG:16

35: 并 Neg [bìng negative verb] 'definitely negative verb' (SN)

35: 平坦 [píngtǎn] '?' 平 WG:10

35: 伊拉克 [Yīlākè] 'Iraq'

36: 菲律宾 [Fēilǜbīn] 'Philippines'

36: 关头 [guāntóu] '(crucial) moment'

37: 优势 [yōushì] 'favorable position'

37: 险胜 [xiǎn shèng] 'win by a narrow margin' WG>30:战胜 [zhànshèng] 'defeat (an opponent)'

(Did you notice a military flavor to much of this vocabulary?)

NOTE ON CHINESE NAMING PRACTICES

   Recognizing names in Chinese is a constant problem, but if you are aware of the structural principles behind names it will be easier. The names of Chinese people may be two (陈明) or four characters long (司马文生), but the majority of them are three characters long (余志坚). The family name, 90% of the time one character (李, 张, 王, 何), but occasionally two characters long (欧阳, 司徒), always comes first. The given name, usually two characters (友坤, 汉忠), but often only one (冰, 萍), always comes after the family name. The meaning of the family name is not important for naming purposes, while the meaning of the given name is. The name as a whole rarely makes sense, which along with its two to four character length and its grammatical function as a noun are solid clues to it being a name. Chinese personal names come after the names of their units and positions (中国国务委员兼外交部长吴学谦), but names come before titles (吴学谦外长). What does this reflect about Chinese cultural values?

   Names of foreigners are usually transliterated and have as many characters as it takes to render the name (杰克·肯普). A solid dot [·] is placed at mid-level in the line to mark the sub-divisions of foreign names. The [·], the lack of meaning to the character string, its length, and its grammatical function are good clues to the presence of a foreign name.

   There are several patterns behind how the names of countries are rendered into Chinese. They are most often transliterated based on how the citizens of the countries pronounce the names: e.g.美国 'America', 德国 'Deutschland', 西班牙 'España'. The combinations of characters most often do not make sense by themselves, but occasionally the whole names of countries are translated: e.g.冰岛 'Iceland', 象牙海岸 'Ivory Coast', in which case the character combinations make sense. Sometimes names of countries are a combination of transliteration and translation: e.g.新西兰 [Xīn Xīlán] 'New Zealand', 苏联 [Sūlián] 'Soviet Union'. Alphabetically arranged tables of country names can be found in the back of many dictionaries.

GRAMMAR EXERCISES

1. Identify the grammar of the following headlines and translate them into English:

第二届世界室内田径锦标赛成绩喜人
一天刷新 4 项世界纪录

两"虎"相争 头球建功
广东队胜辽宁队获足球金牌

奥运会女篮预选赛在即
中国女篮将西征参加角逐

不幸运的美国女篮球员

网球名将和棋坛高手昨立下战功
上海金牌总数跃居第二

中国男女羽毛球队双获小组第一

中国选手国际比赛创新绩 世界青年足球赛分组确定

全英羽毛球赛開戰

2. Fill in the blanks using the correct structural marker from those in

   parentheses at the end of each sentence and translate:

一) 四个田径运动员分别打破＿＿＿一些全国记录。(着、了、把)

二) 温子健、吴骅＿＿＿第六届全运会的赛事给我们作报道。(又、把、了)

三) 陈萏英打破了女子400米栏＿＿＿不是小事。(并、了、是...的)

四) 中国男篮是＿＿＿两分优势险胜的。(又、以、把)

五) 中国男篮战胜了南朝鲜队，＿＿＿亚洲桂冠夺回来了。(并、以、把)

六) 这届运动会的比赛项目有击剑＿＿＿技巧＿＿＿体操和武术等等。

   (。、;、、)

3. Use the correct structural marker to fill in the blank and then translate: 以、

   了、又、之后、是...的 and 、.

一) 中国男篮＿＿＿登上了亚洲冠军宝座。

二) 第十四届亚洲男篮锦标赛＿＿＿11月27日在广州举行＿＿＿。

三) 辽宁队＿＿＿591分的总成绩名列第三。

四) 广东代表团以总分850分获得＿＿＿39枚金牌。

五) 明天的比赛结束了＿＿＿，选手们都要回国了。

六) 张秋萍＿＿＿张德春＿＿＿张小冬以及王永华都不是体操运动员。

4. Rewrite and translate the following sentences using the markers given at the

   end of each sentence:

一) 苏冰在射击比赛中打破了一项亚洲记录。(是...的)

二) 才力打破了挺举记录，就登上了全国举重冠军的宝座。(之后)

三) 刘海英打破了一项全国记录。(又)

四) 中国男篮虽然赢了这场比赛，但是成功的道路不很平坦。(并)

SIGHT READINGS

Sight reading passages are chosen for topics and grammatical structures similar to those found in the primary text. You can either read them silently to yourself, or out loud as a class. While familiarity with the vocabulary from the primary text is assumed, further glossing is done for the sight readings so that you may concentrate on practicing the reading strategy and tactics learned from working with the primary text without concern for looking up vocabulary. Glossing is done immediately next to the passages to maximize reading ease and speed. Words Groups are not indicated here because the goal is to nurture the skimming skills needed to read for general comprehension; but as a vocabulary building exercise, try developing WG with the vocabulary items from the sight reading texts and then connect them with the vocabulary from the main text.

Try answering the questions posed at the end of each sight reading after skimming the text once or twice. Keep re-reading the texts until you can answer all of the questions. Form the habit of recognizing and retaining crucial bits of information as you practise skim reading.

#1   ALL ENGLAND BADMINTON OPEN CONCLUDES

1   全英羽毛球公开赛结束
2   我国选手获女单、混双、男双冠军

3   本报伦敦 20 日电 （记者彭惕强）   1988 年全英羽毛
4   球公开赛决赛今天下午在伦敦温伯利体育馆举行。我国选
5   手辜家明轻取南朝鲜选手李英淑获女单冠军，两局的比分
6   都是11:2。王明仁与史方静以15:9，18:13击败丹麦选手努森
7   和尼尔森获混双冠军。男双比赛是这次公开赛的高潮，李
8   永波和田秉毅抵住了马来西亚的西迪克兄弟的轮番重扣并
9   猛烈反击，以15:6，15:7的战绩蝉联这个项目的冠军。

VOCABULARY

1: 公开 [gōngkāi] 'open'

2: 女单 [nǚ dān] 'women's singles'

2: 混双 [hùn shuāng] 'mixed doubles'

3: 伦敦 [Lúndūn] 'London'

3: 彭惕强 [Péng Tìqiáng] '(name of a person)'

4: 温伯利 [Wēnbólì] 'Wembly Stadium'

5: 辜家明 [Gū Jiāmíng] '(name of a person)'

5: 轻取 [qīngqǔ] 'win an easy victory'

5: 李英淑 [Lǐ Yīngshū] '(name of a person)'

5: 局 [jú] '(measure for games)'

6: 王明仁 [Wáng Míngrén] '(name of a person)'

6: 与 [yǔ] 'and, with'

6: 史方静 [Shǐ Fāngjìng] '(name of a person)'

6: 丹麦 [Dānmài] 'Denmark'

6: 努森 [Nǔsēn] '(name of a person)'

7: 尼尔森 [Ní'ěrsēn] '(name of a person)'

7: 李永波 [Lǐ Yǒngbō] '(name of a person)'

8: 田秉毅 [Tián Bǐngyì] '(name of a person)'

8: 抵住 [dǐzhù] 'withstand'

8: 马来西亚 [Mǎláixīyà] 'Malaysia'

8: 西迪克 [Xīdíkè] '(name of a person)'

8: 兄弟 [xiōngdì] 'brothers'

8: 轮番 [lúnfān] 'take turns'

8: 重扣 [zhòng kòu] 'heavy blows'

9: 猛烈 [měngliè] 'fiercely'

9: 反击 [fǎnjī] 'counter attack'

9: 蝉联 [chánlián] 'continue to win'

QUESTIONS

A. How many championships did the Chinese athletes win?

B. How many single championships did they win?

C. What nationality were the opponents in men's doubles?

D. Were most of the matches close, or were they walkovers?

E. What mistake was made in reporting the scores?

F. Who won the mixed doubles championship?

#2 CHINA WILL HOST WOMEN'S INTERNATIONAL VOLLEYBALL CHAMPIONSHIP

1   中国将主办世界女排锦标赛
2   签字仪式在北京举行

3   据新华社北京 3 月 22 日电 （记者薛剑英） 1990 年世界
4   女排锦标赛将在北京、上海、沈阳等 4 个城市举行。
5   今天下午，国际排联和中国排球协会在这里举行了举
6   办这次锦标赛的议定书签字仪式。国际排联主席阿科斯塔
7   和中国排球协会副主席魏纪中在议定书上签了字。
8   在简短的签字仪式之后，举行了记者招待会。阿科斯
9   塔高度评价了北京、沈阳等地的体育场馆，称这些场馆是
10   "世界第一流"的。他向关心排球事业发展的中国人民表
11   示感谢，并希望这次锦标赛获得成功。

VOCABULARY

1: 主办 [zhǔbàn] 'sponsor'
1: 世界 [shìjiè] 'world'
1: 女排 [nǚpái] 'women's volleyball'
2: 签字仪式 [qiānzì yíshì] 'signing ceremony'
4: 沈阳 [Shěnyáng] 'Shenyang'
5: 国际排联 [Guójì páilián] 'International Volleyball Federation'
5: 举办 [jǔbàn] 'hold (a competition, meeting, etc.)'
6: 议定书 [yìdìngshū] 'protocol'
8: 招待会 [zhāodàihuì] 'reception, conference'
9: 高度 [gāodù] 'high degree'

9: 评价 [píngjià] 'evaluate'

9: 称　 [chēng] 'state, declare'

10: 流　 [liú] 'level, class'

QUESTIONS

A. How many Chinese cities will host the 1990 International Volleyball Championship?

B. What event happened today?

C. What did the chair of the International Volleyball Federation say about the Chinese facilities?

D. What group of people did he thank in particular?

李建華繪

Reading Chinese Newspapers:
Tactics and Skills

Lesson Three: Women in China

轻视歧视妇女带来严重社会问题

我国男女比例开始失调

男的比女的多两千余万

新华社北京3月4日电 全国人大常委会副委员长、全国妇联主席陈慕华日前在接受《党建》记者采访时透露，由于歧视妇女，目前我国已开始出现男女比例失调，女的占人口的48.9%，男的占51.1%。这样发展下去，意味着将来会有几千万娶不上妻子的男光棍。

陈慕华说，这是一个严重的社会问题，可是现在不少人还没有认识到。

陈慕华是在谈到妇女参政议政以及就业、教育等方面的问题时讲到这一情况的。陈慕华说，在受教育问题上，轻视、歧视妇女的现象也较突出。

陈慕华说，妇女参政议政的情况不如过去。现在全国人大代表，妇女约占21%，人大常委，妇女占9%，从中央到地方各级部门领导岗位上的女干部极少。妇女的政治地位同我们10多亿人口的社会主义国家中妇女应有的地位不大相称。

陈慕华说，现在企业实行优化劳动组合，搞承包，不少女工被从岗位上"优化"下来。这有经济上的原因，但也有观念上的原因。她说，妇女华说，生育孩子不是妇女个人的事，而是为繁衍后代尽社会责任。妇女为此在生理上、精神上都要付出重大代价，应该得到社会的理解承认和支持，而不应视为包袱，更不应成为歧视妇女的理由。

陈慕华说，妇联组织是党联系群众的纽带她说，为了适应新的历史时期的需要，妇联工作也要改革，要把妇女解放运动提高到新水平。

资金增长过快
资金收不抵支

全大局完成调节基金征收任务

近几年我国预算内资金增缓慢，收不抵支，连年出现财赤字，与预算外资金大幅度长形成鲜明对照。同时，由于力过于分散，财政收入占国收入的比重连年下降，由78年的37.2%下降到1988年的19.3%，国家预算内财力严重不足，削弱了对经济的宏观调控能力。

最近，国务院决定征集国家预算调节资金，从预算外资金中集中一部分财力，为改革和建设的顺利进行创造条件，也有利于合理引导预算外资金流向，紧缩一般，加强重点，压缩社会总需求，控制盲目建设和消费膨胀。但由于总的资金紧张，开征调节基金有一定难度，任务艰巨。财政部要求各地区、各部门顾全大局，及时足额地完成今年调节基金的征收任务。

建设资金
集783亿

漏交情况严重

锑锑报道：我国从1983年开年，6年累计已征集783亿部分资金的集中使用，促进解了国民经济发展中的"卡预算，弥补财政赤字，调节起到了积极作用。据悉，今

——◁✱▷——

各式各样的美养和美品，引诱着孩子们的侥幸心理。这几个摸奖的孩子花完了压岁钱，连一个末等奖也没捞着。

乔石强调重视党的自身建设

越是大转变时期越是对党的考验

据新华社北京3月4日电 3月5日出版的《党建》杂志发表了中共中央政治局常委乔石关于加强党的建设的讲话。他指出，在大转变时期更要重视和加强党的自身建设。

乔石在中央党的建设研究班上的这篇讲话，联系新形势，谈了加强党的建设的问题。他说，我们党正处在一个历史性的大转变时期。这是建党以来党的又一次巨大而深刻的转变。越是大转变时期，越是对党的考验，也越需要重视和加强党的自身建设。

乔石指出，过去几十年中，我们为加强党的建设积累了许多好经验、好传统，对于今天仍然适用的，当然要继承和发扬。同时，我们又必须运用马克思主义的基本观点和方法，研究新的历史条件下加强执政党建设的理论和实践，逐步改变不适应新形势要求的观念和做法，不断创造新经验、新做法。在党的自身建设方面，过去哪些做法是必须坚持的，不坚持就会削弱党的建设，削弱党的领导，哪些做法是必须改革的，不改革就同样会削弱党的建设，削弱党的领导，这是需要很好研究的。坚持和改革都要从实际出发，实事求是。坚持要坚持在点子上，

(reproduction of original text)

STRUCTURE NOTES (Line numbers here refer to the original text.)

3: 万 Large numbers, numbers over 10,000, are counted in terms of how many units of 10,000 there are. To arrive at the correct amount, multiply the number before the 万 by 10,000; here 2000 X 10,000 = 20,000,000. In line 12 there is the indefinite 几千万 = 'several tens of millions'. Line 28 has 十多万, so multiply 10,000 by ten plus = 'over 100,000'.

7: ⟨⟩ are used to mark the name of a literary work.

7: Clause 时 时 used at the end of a structure marks all the material before it as part of a dependent time clause. In this usage, 时 may also be written as 之时 or with the less formal 的时候. It is most often end-marked with a comma. Process the grammatical structures which precede the 时 and only then process those after it. Remember that 'when', the English equivalent to 时, comes at the head of the equivalent English clause, not at the end as it does in Chinese. Note lines 17-19 where the 时 structure is the time element in the S 是 T P V O 的 pattern discussed in 2:15. Examples of 时 using vocabulary from past lessons are:

a. 我看书的时候，很不喜欢有人找我谈话。
b. 六届全运会开幕时，所有运动员全部都到场。

10: 48.9% 51.1% Though written in the Western format, these per cent figures are still read in the Chinese style: [bǎi fēn zhī sìshibā diǎn jiǔ, bǎi fēn zhī wǔshiyī diǎn yī]. See also l. 24, 25.

11: Verb 着 = 'verbing' When you see the continuing action marker 着, expect a main verb to be directly before it. 着 can be very helpful in locating the verb heart of sentences. See also 8:13 for the V1 着 V2 pattern. Examples are:

a. 母亲常告诉我不应该吃着饭说话。
b. 糟糕，我们今天都忙着考试，不能去看电影了。

12: 娶[qǔ]不上 Verb-potential complements (also called "resultative verbs") are usually three (娶不上), sometimes four (代表不了), or rarely, five (研究得出来) syllables long. They are always marked by either 得 or 不 in the middle. They should be translated as "able to/can verb" or "unable/cannot verb". Examples are:

a. 老对手南朝鲜队今年比不上我国男篮队。

b. 陈慕华主席指出，解放以前中国妇女得不到社会的理解、承认和支持。

12: 的 It is extremely important that you recognize that the primary function of 的 in contemporary Chinese prose is to mark modification of a noun. If you keep this principle in mind, it will help you quickly and accurately identify the noun acting as a subject, object, indirect object, or location name, even in very lengthy structures. Noun modification structures can be either very simple or very involved, but they are always formed according to the rules of Chinese grammar. For example, if you notice the 的 towards the end of the sentence in l. 11-13, you can then see that the object 男光棍 is modified by a number-measure (几千万) Verb(娶不上) Object (妻子) structure. Keep in mind that these modifying structures generally come after the noun in English: "...tens of millions of bachelors who are unable to get wives." Similarly, in l. 40-41 the object 理由 is modified by a V(歧视) O(妇女) "...the reason for discriminating against women" structure. Lines 17-19 appear more complicated, but the 的 in the 时 clause similarly indicates that the object (问题) is modified by S(妇女) V (参政) O(...等方面) "...problems of women participating in the various aspects of..." On the other hand, modification structures marked by 的 may be as simple as a Sv(严重) in l. 14-15 "...a social problem which is serious" or a Place(经济上) "...a reason which is based on economics" in l. 33. Sometimes the modified noun is so clear from the context it is omitted as it is in l. 9 (女的) and l. 10 (男的). When processing lengthy comma units always be alert to the presence and position of the 的, they are of crucial importance to your ability to read accurately and quickly. See 5:11-13 for comments on more complicated 的 structures. (Context distinguishes this major function from the use of 的 in vocabulary words such as 目的, 的确, etc, and patterns such as S 是 T P V O 的, O 是 S V 的, S 是 V的, etc.)

17-19: What is the meaning of this S 是 T P V O 的 structure? See 2:15.

20-21: Why must there be a comma after the 在 structure here and after 地方 in l. 25? See 2:8.

32: S [bèi] (X) Verb = 'S is being / was Verbed (by X)' The passive marker 被 focuses attention on the subject as the recipient of what is usually an unpleasant, or at best, neutral verb action. Examples are:

　　a. 在这次决赛中，日本队被打败了。
　　b. 张伟先又被历史期末考试考住了。

32: "　" What do the quote marks bracketing 优化 suggest?

34-36: X 为 [wèi] Y Verb phrase = 'X verbs for Y' This structure focuses on X doing a verb action was done for the benefit of Y. Y may be a complex structure such as the V (繁衍) O (后代) in this line, or it may as simple as a single noun. Distinguish between this use of 为 as a formal prose synonym of 给 and the usage discussed in l. 43-44 below. Note the different use of 为 [wéi] as a verb complement in l. 40: V 为 X = 'Verb (it) to be X'. Examples are:

　　a. 我国政府为适应新历史时期的需要，将改革妇联工作。
　　b. 为人民服务！

40: Verb 为 [wéi] = 'Verb to be' When used as a verb complement, 为 indicates that something verbs to be/as something else. Note that 为 has the second tone in this usage. The two uses here are 看为 'regard as' and 成为 'become'. See also 8:12 where wéi is a formal prose synonym of 是.

　　a. 体操决赛会变为全运会的最重要的一次比赛。
　　b. 男女比例失调已成为极大的社会问题。

43-44: 为[wèi] （了） X Verb phrase = 'Do the verb phrase for the purpose of X'
了 (or sometimes 着) often follows 为 when X expresses a reason or goal. X will usually be more complex than a single noun. Here it has the structure V (适应) O (需要). When a 为了 structure comes before the subject, the focus is on X, and it must be end marked by a comma, which makes it easy to define where it ends. Examples of this usage are:

 a. 为了学会中国话，我每天听中文广播。

 b. 为了夺回去年丢掉了的桂冠，中国男篮参加了很多比赛。

45: 把 O What is the function of 把 here? See 2:28.

1   轻视歧视妇女带来严重社会问题
2   我国男女比例开始失调
3   男的比女的多两千余万

4   新华社北京3月4日电
5   全国人大常委会副委员长、全
6   国妇联主席陈慕华日前在接受
7   《党建》记者采访时透露，由
8   于歧视妇女，目前我国已开始
9   出现男女比例失调，女的占人
10   口的 48.9%，男的占 51.1%。
11   这样发展下去,意味着将来会
12   有几千万娶不上妻子的男光棍。
13   陈慕华说，这是一个严重
14   的社会问题，可是现在不少人
15   还没有认识到。
16   陈慕华是在谈到妇女参政
17   议政以及就业、教育等方面的
18   问题时讲到这一情况的。陈慕
19   华说,在受教育问题上,轻视、
20   歧视妇女的现象也较突出。

VOCABULARY

1: 轻视 [qīngshì] 'look down on' WG>1:歧视 [qíshì] 'discriminate
   against'

1: 严重 [yánzhòng] 'serious'

2: 比例 [bǐlì] 'ratio, proportion'

2: 失调 [shītiáo] 'imbalance'

3: 余 [yú] 'more than, in excess of'

3: 万 [wàn] '10,000' (SN)

5: 人大 [Réndà] '(abbr. for 人民代表大会) National People's Congress'

5: 常委会 [chángwěihuì] '(abbr. for 常务委员会) Standing Committee'

5: 副 X [fù X] 'assistant X, vice-X'

6: 妇联 [Fùlián] '(abbr. for 妇女联合会) Women's Federation'

6: 主席 [zhǔxí] 'chairperson'

6: 陈慕华 [Chén Mùhuá] '(person's name)'

7: 《 》 [shūmínghào] "marks name of literary work" (SN)

7: 党建 [Dǎngjiàn] '(newspaper name)'

7: 采访 [cǎifǎng] 'interview'

7: 时 [shí] 'when' (SN)

7: 透露 [tòulù] 'divulge, reveal'

8: 目前 [mùqián] 'right now, at present'

9: 占 [zhàn] 'make up, constitute'

10: % "Use Chinese to read per cent figure" (SN)

11: 意味 [yìwèi] 'imply, suggest'

11: V 着 [Verb zhě] "verbing" (SN)

12: 娶不上 [qǔbúshàng] 'unable to take a wife' (SN)

12: 的 [dě] "modification marker" (SN)

12: 光棍 [guānggùr] 'bachelor'

16: 参政 [cān zhèng] 'participate in government' WG>18:议政 [yì zhèng] 'discuss government and politics'; WG>27:政治 [zhèngzhì] 'politics'

17: 议政 [yìzhèng] '?' 政 WG:17

17: 就业 [jiùyè] 'gain employment' WG>30:企业 [qǐyè] 'enterprise'

17: 教育 [jiàoyù] 'education' WG>33:生育 [shēngyù] 'give birth to'

20: 现象 [xiànxiàng] 'phenomena'

20: 突出 [tūchū] 'prominent'

21　　　陈慕华说，妇女参政议政
22　的情况不如过去。现在全国人
23　大代表，妇女约占21%，人大常
24　委，妇女占9%，从中央到地方，
25　各级部门领导岗位上的女干部
26　极少。妇女的政治地位同我们
27　10多亿人口的社会主义国家中
28　妇女应有的地位不大相称。
29　　　　陈慕华说，现在企业实行
30　优化劳动组合，搞承包，不少
31　女工被从岗位上"优化"下来。
32　这有经济上的原因，但也有观
33　念上的原因。她说，妇女生育
34　孩子不是妇女个人的事，而是
35　为繁衍后代尽社会责任。妇女
36　为此在生理上、精神上都要付
37　出重大代价，应该得到社会的
38　理解承认和支持，而不应视为
39　包袱，更不应成为歧视妇女的
40　理由。

VOCABULARY

22: 不如　[bùrú] 'not the equal of'
24: 中央　[zhōngyāng] 'Central Committee'
24: 地方　[dìfāng] 'local'
25: 部门　[bùmén] 'department, branch'
25: 岗位　[gǎngwèi] 'post, station'
26: 政治　[zhèngzhì] '?'　政 WG:16

27: 亿　[yì] 'hundred million'

28: 相称　[xiāngchèn] 'match up, suit'

29: 企业　[qǐyè] '?' 业 WG:17

30: 优化　[yōuhuà] 'make excellent, improve'

30: 劳动　[láodòng] 'physical labor'

30: 组合　[zǔhé] 'groupings'

30: 搞　[gǎo] 'engage in, work at'

30: 承包　[chéngbāo] 'contract' WG>38:承认 [chéngrèn]
　　　'acknowledgement'; WG>39: 包袱 [bāofu] 'burden, millstone'

31: 被　[bèi] "passive marker" (SN)

32: 原因　[yuányīn] 'reason, cause'

32: 观念　[guānniàn] 'concept, idea'

33: 生育　[shēngyù] '?' 育 WG:17, 生 WG:36

35: X, 为 Y Vp　[X,wèi Y Vp] "X, verbs for Y" (SN)

35: 繁衍　[fányǎn] 'gradually increase in numbers'

35: 后代　[hòudài] 'following generations'

35: 尽　[jìn] 'complete, finish'

36: 生理　[shēnglǐ] 'physiology' 生 WG:33; WG>38:理解 [lǐjiě]
　　　'comprehension'; WG>40: 理由 [lǐyóu] 'reason, ground'

36: 精神　[jīngshén] 'spirit'

37: 代价　[dàijià] 'cost, price'

38: 理解　[lǐjiě] '?' 理 WG:36

38: 承认　[chéngrèn] '?' 承 WG:30

38: 支持　[zhīchí] 'support'

38: V 为　[Verb wéi] "verb it to be" (SN)

39: 包袱　[bāofu] '?' 包 WG:30

40: 理由　[lǐyóu] '?' 理 WG:36

41   陈慕华说，妇联组织是党
42   联系群众的纽带。她说，为了
43   适应新的历史时期的需要，妇
44   联工作也要改革，要把妇女解
45   放运动提高到新水平。

VOCABULARY

42: 联系 [liánxì] 'connect'

42: 纽带 [niǔdài] 'tie, link'

42: 为了 X Vp [wèile] X Vp "Verb phrase for the purpose of X" (SN)

43: 适应 [shìyìng] 'fit, suit'

43: 需要 [xūyào] 'needs, requirement'

45: 提高 [tígāo] 'raise, elevate'

45: 水平 [shuǐpíng] 'level, standard'

GRAMMAR EXERCISES

1. Choose the correct structural marker from those in parentheses and

translate the following into natural English:

一) 男女比例失调＿＿，很多男人娶不上妻子。(上、着、时)

二) 改革妇联工作是＿＿提高妇女社会地位。(为、被、把)

三) ＿＿满足《党建》记者的要求，全国妇联主席介绍了中国妇女目前的情况。 (被、为了、把)

四) 陈慕华告诉采访她＿＿记者，中国妇女的政治地位同她们应有＿＿地位不大相称。(的、得、地)

2. Use the sentences below to practice locating and translating 的 modification

structures:

一) 中国妇女在精神上、生理上付出的代价极大。

二) 在今天的射击比赛中超过两项亚洲记录的广东人叫刘海英。

三) 当全国人大常委会副委员长、全国妇联主席的人姓什么？

四) 我上星期三在图书馆借的中英词典不大好用。

3. Rewrite the following using the markers given in parentheses at the end and

then translate:

一) 中国妇女生育孩子的目的是繁衍后代，并不是她们个人的事。(为)

二) 听说在东北有很多企业正在把女工"优化"下来。(被)

三) 她谈到了妇女教育和就业方面问题，也谈到了她们参政以及议政的困难。 (时)

四) 记者一个一个地写下了陈主席提出来的问题。(把)

4. To continue developing skill at processing "comma units", analyze the grammatical structures of each comma unit in the reading texts. Start with the first paragraph of each text and do as many paragraphs as time allows.

SIGHT READINGS

#1   IT'S HARD TO STOP EARLY MARRIAGE FOR FEMALES

1   女子早婚难禁

2   一　男女性别比例失调。1985 年的人口统计资料表明，
3   我地区 240 多万人口中，男性公民约为 130 万，女性公民
4   约为 110 万。已经到达或超过法定结婚年龄的男子需寻求
5   配偶，而同一年龄层次女子的数量却存在较大的缺口，人
6   们的目光自然转向下一个年龄层次的女子，于是，形成了
7   这个地区特有的大丈夫、小媳妇的婚姻格局。

VOCABULARY

1: 禁　[jìn] 'prohibit'

2: 统计　[tǒngjì] 'statistical'

4: 寻求　[xúnqiú] 'seek'

5: 配偶　[pèi'ǒu] 'mate, spouse'

5: 层次　[céngcì] 'level, stage'

5: 缺口　[quēkǒu] 'shortage'

6: 转向　[zhuǎnxiàng] 'turn towards'

7: 格局　[géjú] 'situation'

QUESTIONS

A. What is the ratio of male to female in this article?

B. What source of information is used for this article?

C. What reason does the piece give for older males marrying younger
    females?

D. What phrase does the article use to describe the resulting marital
    condition?

#2   MORE FEMALE CADRE SOUGHT IN HUBEI

1   湖北招干部女性入选过半

2   据新华社武汉 3 月 3 日电 （记者方政军、通讯员鲁
3 知炳) 记者从湖北省人事厅获悉: 在刚刚结束的全省招考
4 干部工作中被录取的3268人，女性达1780人，占录取总数
5 的54%。这一结果，显示了女性在竞争中的潜力。从1988
6 年下半年开始,湖北省人事部门在政法、银行、工商、税
7 务系统公开招考干部，并规定，不定男女比例,按考试成
8 绩择优录取。

VOCABULARY

1: 招 [zhāo] 'recruit, enlist'
1: 入选 [rùxuǎn] 'be selected'
4: 录取 [lùqǔ] 'enroll, recruit'
5: 潜力 [qiánlì] 'potential'
6: 税务 [shuìwù] 'tax bureau'
7: 规定 [guīdìng] 'rule'
8: 择优 [zéyōu] 'select the best'

QUESTIONS

A. What does the headline specifically say?

B. How many new cadre were chosen altogether in Hubei?

C. What statement is made about the percentage of women selected?

D. What was the stated basic criterion for selection of new cadre?

#3 FIVE FEMALE OFFICERS PROMOTED TO MAJOR GENERAL

1   五名女军官被授予少将军衔

2   新华社北京9月16日电 (记者易俭如、杨民青) 记者
3   从全军军衔办公室获悉，人民解放军实行新的军衔制，有
4   5名女军官被中央军委授予少将军衔。 这5名女将军是国
5   防科工委科学技术委员会副主任聂力、解放军总医院副院
6   长廖文海、第一军医大学副校长吴晓恒、第三军医大学副
7   校长李希楷、解放军洛阳外语学院副院长胡斐佩。
8   我军在 1955 年首次实行军衔制时，全军只有一名女将
9   军。她是参加过长征，身经百战的李贞。当时，她被授予
10   少将军衔。她是我军历史上第一位女将军。
11   据资料记载，世界上的女将军为数寥寥。美军自60年
12   代以来有34名女将军，其中25名已退役，服现役的9人中
13   有2名少将，7名准将。瑞士有一名女准将。

VOCABULARY

1: 军衔 [jūnxián] 'military rank'

3: 获悉 [huòxī] 'get news'

3: 制   [zhì] 'system'

4: 国防 [guófáng] 'national defense'

5: 总医院 [zǒngyīyuàn] 'Chief Hospital'

9: 长征 [Chángzhēng] 'Long March'

9: 身经百战 [shēn jīng bǎi zhàn] 'has fought a hundred battles'

11: 记载 [jìzǎi] 'record'

11: 寥寥 [liáoliáo] 'very few'

12: 退役 [tuìyì] 'retired from the military'

13: 准将 [zhǔnjiàng] 'brigadier'

QUESTIONS

A. Where does this information come from?
B. What organization authorized these promotions? 中央军委
C. What are the specialities of the new generals, and what does that suggest?
D. What was the background of the first Chinese woman general?
E. What two other countries does this article mention?
F. What does the number 9 refer to in the last paragraph?

GRAMMAR EXERCISE

Identify the grammar of the following headlines and translate them into English:

妇女人才在改革中脱颖而出
我国女干部超过870万

首都各界妇女集会庆"三八"
妇联表彰千余"三八"红旗手五百多优秀妇联干部

六次全国妇代会在京开幕

不出家门也能挣大钱
辽宁新金县10万妇女在庭院经济中大显身手

Reading Chinese Newspapers:
Tactics and Skills

Lesson Four: Environmental Pollution

沈阳市全面治理环境

工业产值上升　污染负荷下降

　　本报讯　中国环境报记者陈福民、本报记者杨涌报道：北方重工业城市沈阳，近年来采取有效的措施，治理污染，工业总产值虽增加一倍以上，污染却有所下降，不少污染物排放指标已达国家规定标准。

　　过去，沈阳市是我国有名的污染城市，大气中颗粒物和二氧化硫浓度高。沈阳市政府、环保局对这一潜在的危害十分重视，对各种不同类型的污染，分别采取措施，进行综合治理。

　　煤烟型大气污染过去一直是这个市较突出的问题。近年，该市先后发布实施了6个法规性的文件，在全市范围内建立起专兼职结合的烟尘监督管理队伍，组成市、区、街三级管理网络，并在市区16个制高点上设立烟尘瞭望哨，监视烟尘排放清况。皇姑区环保局成立了服务小组，帮助冒黑烟的单位对锅炉设备进行技术改造，使这个区锅炉治理率达到98.5%以上。去年，这个区同沈河区成为东北最早的烟尘控制区。

　　工业污水是沈阳市全方位环境管理的一项重要内容。沈阳有工业企业5118家，年排放污水2.3亿吨。市环保部门在综合整治中，实施计划管理和目标管理。一方面整治排水管道系统，兴建大型污水处理厂，另一方面，坚持严格的审批制度，超前治理，以控制新污染源的产生。

　　机械行业含油废水排放是这个市水质污染的重要原因。对这一污染源，沈阳市实行了污染物流失总量控制管理办法。

　　到目前止，全市40家排油大户每年自行处理含油废水已达852吨，占全部排油废水的28%。

　　对乡镇企业发展带来的污染问题，该市因地制宜，使这一污染源基本得到控制。

个体采金矿混乱大量黄金走私外流

国家损失严重　社会治安受扰

　　本报讯　记者刘燮阳报道：当前　各地个体户采矿秩序十分混乱，大量黄金被走私，倒卖、藏匿，国家蒙受重大损失，已引起有关部门的高度重视。

　　据有关部门对14个个体采矿比较集中的省区调查，这些省区采金人数高峰季节高达40万人，常年人数在25万人左右，估计年生产黄金在40万两左右，其中交售给国家的不到10%，绝大部分都被走私和藏匿了。去年，公安部门破获黄金走私案件高达4000多起，缴获黄金2.3万多两。

　　在河南、陕西、黑龙江盛产黄金的地方，一些专事倒卖走私黄金的不法分子，活动十分猖獗。他们或携带巨款从私藏者手中直接收购，或内外勾结，多次倒手，搞成购、运、销"一条龙"，使大量矿产黄金从产金地和国内流失。湖南省原是我国主要产金省之一，由于黄金大量外流，黄金产量急剧下降。

　　黄金倒卖走私严重，已影响社会的治安秩序。内蒙古、河北都出现了蒙面人持刀抢劫私人藏金的事件。在一些矿区，黄金贩挥金如土，聚众赌博、私窝暗娼、看黄色录像，这些地方被人们称为"五毒俱全"的地方。

　　造成黄金走私严重，主要是一些地区对黄金贩打击不力，有的干部错误认为金子是个人劳动所得，谁出高价就卖给谁。有的干部和黄金贩，内外勾结，置国家利益而不顾，一些银

闻喜玻璃器皿-

音乐酒具独佳

　　本报讯　山西省闻喜县玻璃器皿一厂金星分厂起步不凡，3个月创出"闻花牌"音乐酒具，进厂1年，就完成产值250万元，实现利润35万元，相当于投资总额2倍。

　　金星分厂是闻喜玻璃器皿一厂与旅关镇王村合办的一个联营企业，拥有350名职工。去年9月建厂初期，由于技术人员短缺，设备不配套，产品型号陈旧单一，加之缺乏管理经验，企业开张就不很景气，在去年年底的两次订货会上只订了2万多元的货，引起职工

厂长李怀存下去，于是，在长沙海关同，一面获悉电子市场十分动，联技术人员张的攻坚了音乐酒多方改进明桃形灯浅绿等具造型有

(reproduction of original text)

STRUCTURE NOTES (Line numbers here refer to the original text.)

8: Verb phrase 1, 却 [què] Verb phrase 2 = 'Contrary to what you might expect from the information given in Vp 1, it is actually Vp 2'. 却 (also written 卻), is easy to overlook, but it is a very important signal of the flow of information. 却 is usually translatable as 'however, but', though they do not convey 却's connotative flavor of "regardless of what earlier information led you to expect, the situation is actually..." Examples of 却 are:

> a. 美国妇女联合会虽然建立了很长时间，但是美国妇女的社会地位却一直不高。
>
> b. 张华光病了三个多星期，但他历史大考却考得好极了。

10: ， When a time phrase is placed at sentence head for emphasis, it is often end-marked by a comma as it is here and in l. 17 and 28.

10-11: X 是 Y = 'X is Y' The presence of 是 in a comma unit (except as part of vocabulary items such as 还是, 可是, 尤其是, etc. and in grammatical patterns such as S 是 T P Vp 的, O 是 S V 的, etc.) simplifies your job of identifying the basic grammatical structure since 是 is a reliable indicator that the heart of the structure is the verb 是. Elements on either side of the 是 may be grammatically simple or complex, but the 是 is the core of the structure. All four 是 sentences in this lesson: l. 10-11, 16-17, 30-31, and 40-41, are all simple Noun 是 Noun 'Noun is noun' structures. See 5:11-13, 7:10-11, and 9:9-11 for comments on 是 structures wherein the preceding and following elements are grammatically complex. Always focus on 是 when it occurs in a sentence; it is an obvious and useful indicator of the basic grammatical structure. Examples of Noun 是 Noun sentences are:

> a. 解放军篮球队目前是中国最好的篮球队。
> b. 环境污染是我国突出的问题。

12-15: S1、S2 对 X Vp1, 对 Y Vp2, Vp3 = 'Subjects 1 and 2 did verb 1 concerning X and verb phrases 2 and 3 regarding Y' The most difficult thing to deal with in working with a complicated 对 phrase is to remember that its English equivalent comes at the end of the sentence. Form the habit of noticing the 对 phrase and holding it in your mind until you have completed translating the verb(s) and object(s). Notice similar, but less complicated 对 phrases in l. 42 and 49 below. Examples are:

    a. 全国妇联主席对男女比例失调表示关心。

    b. 沈阳市对含油废水排放已经进行了综合治理。

22: 并 [bìng] When used as a conjunction, 并 (and its full form 并且) are very helpful in locating the head of a grammatical structure. This is particularly useful when you are looking at a sentence composed of numerous comma units. Compare this with its use in 2:35 to emphasize a negative. Examples of 并 used as a conjunction are:

    a. 陈主席谈到了妇女参政的困难，并提到她们就业的问题。

    b. 我的朋友不但获得了击剑比赛的冠军,并且超过亚洲记录。

26:   X，使[shǐ] Y Verb phrase = 'X, caused Y to Verb phrase' Unless used as part of a word (e.g.,大使,使用, etc.), the presence of 使 in a clause is a reliable indicator of a causative grammatical structure. The X here is the two comma units S V1 了 O1, V2 O2 (V O 的 S P V O), before the 使, Y is 治理率, the Verb is 达到, and the Object is the remainder: "The Huanggu Environmental Protection Office establshed service groups and helped units emitting black smoke implement technological reform of the boilers which caused the boiler control ratio in this area to reach over 98.5%." See l. 50-51 for a similar structure. Be alert to the presence of 使, it can be a very useful boost to your reading efficiency. See the synonymous yet different 让 at 8:39. Two examples are:

    a. 空气污染使大气中的颗粒物和二氧化硫浓度提高了。

    b. 男女比例失调使几千万男人娶不上妻子。

35-39: 一方面 X, (另)一方面 Y = 'On one hand X, on the other hand Y' This structure either links two aspects of one activity or it stresses the existence of two related activities, which may occur sequentially. Examples are:

    a. 工厂设计人员一方面提高了产值，一方面减少了废水排放。

    b. 女工被 "优化" 下来一方面有经济上的原因，另一方面也有
       观念上的原因。

38: <u>Verb phrase 1 以 Verb phrase 2</u>   When 以 is used to connect two verb phrases, it conveys the idea of goal or intent and can be translated as 'do verb phrase 1 in order to do verb phrase 2'. The comma seen in this line is optional and probably expresses emphasis. Compare this with the 以 usage seen in 2:14. Examples of this usage of 以 are:

a. 中国队训练了几个月以提高队员的实战能力。

b. 我国大学生深入工厂和农村以了解社会上的问题。

42:   ，   When an adverbial structure precedes the subject of a sentence, it must be end-marked by a comma. See another instance of this usage in l. 49-50. See l. 14 where an adverbial phrase placed after the subject is separated from its following verb phrase by a comma, probably for emphasis. Further examples are:

a. 为了满足学生的要求，学校取消了今天的考试了。

b. 对歧视妇女的问题，不少人还没意识到。

45: 到 X 止 [zhǐ] = 'Stop at X' X is generally a time phrase. This structure is also written 到X为止.

1　　　　　沈阳市全面治理环境
2　　工业产值上升　污染负荷下降

3　　　　本报讯　中国环境报记者
4　陈福民、本报记者杨涌报道：
5　北方重工业城市沈阳，近年来
6　采取有效的措施，治理污染，
7　工业总产值虽增加一倍以上，
8　污染却有所下降，不少污染物
9　排放指标已达国家规定标准。
10　　过去，沈阳市是我国有名
11　的污染城市，大气中颗粒物和
12　二氧化硫浓度高。沈阳市政府
13　、环保局对这一潜在的危害十
14　分重视，对各种不同类型的污
15　染，分别采取措施，进行综合
16　治理。

VOCABULARY

1: 沈阳 [Shěnyáng] '(name of a city)'

1: 治理 [zhìlǐ] 'bring under control' WG>21:管理 [guǎnlǐ] 'manage, supervise'; WG>36:整治 [zhěngzhì] 'work, fix'; WG>38:处理 [chǔlǐ] 'dispose, process'

1: 环境 [huánjìng] 'environment' WG>13:环保局 [Huánbǎojú]
    'Environmental Protection Office'

2: 污染 [wūrǎn] 'pollution'

2: 负荷 [fùhé] 'burden, load'

2: 下降 [xiàjiàng] 'decrease, decline'

6: 有效 [yǒuxiào] 'effective'

8: 却V2 [què] Verb 2 "contrary to what you expect, it's a different situation"
    (SN)

9: 排放 [páifàng] 'discharge' WG>47: 排油 [páiyóu] 'discharge oil'

9: 指标 [zhǐbiāo] 'index' WG>9: 标准 [biāozhǔn] 'standard';
    WG>36: 目标 [mùbiāo] 'target'

9: 规定 [guīdìng] 'rules, standards' WG>19: 法规性 [fǎguīxìng] 'legalistic'

10: X是Y [X shì Y] 'X is Y' (SN)

11: 颗粒物 [kēlìwù] 'particulate matter'

12: 二氧化硫 [èryǎnghuàliú] 'sulfur dioxide'

12: 浓度 [nóngdù] 'density, concentration'

13: 环保局 [Huánbǎojú] '?' 环 WG:1

13. 对 [duì] "towards (note placement of English equivalent)" (SN)

13: 潜在 [qiánzài] 'latent'

13: 危害 [wēihài] 'danger, harm'

14: 类型 [lèixíng] 'kind, type' WG>17: 煤烟型 [méiyānxíng] 'coal smoke
    type'

15: 综合 [zōnghé] 'comprehensive'

17   煤烟型大气污染过去一直
18 是这个市较突出的问题。近年，
19 该市先后发布实施了6个法规
20 性的文件，在全市范围内建立
21 起专兼职结合的烟尘监督管理
22 队伍，组成市、区、街三级管
23 理网络，并在市区16个制高点
24 上设立烟尘瞭望哨，监视烟尘
25 排放情况。皇姑区环保局成立
26 了服务小组，帮助冒黑烟的单
27 位对锅炉设备进行技术改造，
28 使这个区锅炉治理率达到
29 98.5% 以上。去年，这个区同
30 沈河区成为东北最早的烟尘控
31 制区。

VOCABULARY

17: 煤烟型 [méiyānxíng] '?' 型 WG:14, 烟 WG:21

18: 突出 [tūchū] 'prominent'

19: 该 [gāi] 'that'

19: 发布 [fābù] 'announce'

19: 实施 [shíshī] 'implement, carry out'

19: 法规性 [fǎguīxìng] '?' 规 WG:9

20: 范围 [fànwéi] 'range, limits'

21: 专兼职 [zhuān jiānzhí] (combines 专职 and 兼职) 'holding one
    position with different duties or simultaneously holding
    different positions with overlapping duties' (See Lesson 9:30)

21: 烟尘 [yānchén] 'smoke particulates' WG>17:煤烟 [méiyān] 'coal smoke'

21: 监督 [jiāndū] 'supervisory' WG>24:监视 [jiānshì] 'keep watch on'

21: 管理 [guǎnlǐ] '?' 理 WG:1, 管 WG:37

22: 队伍 [duìwù] 'contingent, troops'

22: 区 [qū] 'district'

23: 网络 [wǎngluò] 'network'

23: 并 [bìng] 'moreover' (SN)

23: 制高点 [zhìgāodiǎn] 'commanding elevations' WG>30:控制区
    [kòngzhìqū] 'control zones'

24: 瞭望哨 [liàowàngshào] 'post for watching over distant spots'

24: 监视 [jiānshì] '?' 坚 WG:21

25: 皇姑 [Huánggū] '(district name)'

27: 单位 [dānwèi] 'work unit'

27: 锅炉 [guōlú] 'boiler'

27: 设备 [shèbèi] 'equipment'

28: X 使 YVO [X shǐ Y V O] 'X makes Y verb the object' (SN)

28: X 率 X [lǜ] 'rate of X, ratio for X'

29: 同 [tóng] 'and, along with'

30: 控制 [kòngzhì] '?' 制 WG:23

32   工业污水是沈阳市全方位
33 环境管理的一项重要内容。沈
34 阳有工业企业5118家，年排放
35 污水2.3亿吨。市环保部门在综
36 合整治中，实施计划管理和目
37 标管理。一方面整治排水管道
38 系统，兴建大型污水处理厂；
39 另一方面，坚持严格的审批制
40 度，超前治理，以控制新污染
41 源的产生。
42   机械行业含油废水排放是
43 这个市水质污染的重要原因。
44 对这一污染源，沈阳市实行了
45 污染物流失总量控制管理办法。
46   到目前止，全市40家排油
47 大户每年自行处理含油废水已
48 达852吨，占全部排油废水的
49 28%。
50   对乡镇企业发展带来的污
51 染问题，该市因地制宜，使这
52 一污染源基本得到控制。

VOCABULARY

34: 企业 [qǐyè] 'enterprise' WG>42:行业 [hángyè] 'trade, industry'

35: 吨   [dūn] 'tons'

36: 整治 [zhěngzhì] '?' 治 WG:1

36: 目标 [mùbiāo] '?' 标 WG:9

37: 一方面X, 一方面Y [yì fāngmiàn X, yì fāngmiàn Y] 'one one hand X, on the other Y' (SN)

37: 管道 [guǎndào] 'piping, conduit', 管 WG:21

38: 系统 [xìtǒng] 'system'

38: 兴建 [xīngjiàn] 'construct'

38: 处理 [chǔlǐ] '?' 理 WG:1

39: 坚持 [jiānchí] 'persist in'

39: 严格 [yángé] 'strict'

39: 审批 [shěnpī] 'examination and approval'

40: 超前 [chāoqián] 'before hand, in advance'

40: 以V2 [yǐ verb 2] 'in order to do verb 2' (SN)

40: 源 [yuán] 'source'

42: 机械 [jīxiè] 'machinery'

42: 行业 [hángyè] '?' 业 WG:34

42: 含油 [hányóu] 'oil bearing' WG>47:排油 [páiyóu] 'discharge oil'

42: 废水 [fèishuǐ] 'waste water' WG>43:水质 [shuǐzhì] 'water quality'

43: 水质 [shuǐzhì] '?' 水 WG:42

45: 流失 [liúshī] 'run off'

45: 总量 [zǒngliàng] 'overall amount'

46: 到X止 [dào X zhǐ] 'stop at X' (SN)

46: 排油 [páiyóu] '?' 排 WG:9, 油 WG:42

47: 大户 [dàhù] 'rich and influential entities'

47: 自行 [zìxíng] 'voluntarily'

50: 乡镇 [xiāngzhèn] 'villages and towns'

51: 因地制宜 [yīn dì zhì yí] 'suit measures to local conditions'

52: 基本 [jīběn] 'fundamentally'

GRAMMAR EXERCISE

1. Fill in the blanks using the correct grammatical marker from the following and translate: 却、是、并、以、，、、使

   一) 过去____妇女的政治地位同应有的社会地位不大相称。

   二) 该厂的总产量下降了，但排放的含油废水____增多了！

   三) 轻视妇女____一个严重的社会问题。

   四) 妇联进行的改革已____妇女解放运动达到新水平。

   五) 妇女占全国人大代表的21%，____在人大常委占9%。

   六) 沈阳市采取了一些措施____尽快地进行综合治理。

2. Rewrite each sentence using the marker in parentheses at the end of each sentence and then translate:

   一) 政府必须治理城市的污染，也要关心乡镇的环境问题。
      (一方面X，一方面Y)

   二) 去年十月，工业产值增加了两倍以上。(到 X 为止)

   三) 中国队虽经过了长期苦战，还是丢掉了桂冠。 (却)

   四) 由于有严重污染情况，上海市政府将要建立煤烟监督小组。(了)

3. Now that you have practised the grammar structures and become familiar with the vocabulary, turn back to the main texts of lessons 2-4 and enjoy reading them as newspaper articles conveying information, not as language learning texts.

SIGHT READINGS

#1 PROTECTION OF 10 MAJOR ENVIRONMENTAL RESOURCES
ASSIGNED

1
2
3

国务院决定
保护十大环境资源
各部门将分工合作

4　　新华社北京二月二十一日电　　自然资源的使用者、管理
5 者也要担负资源保护者的责任。根据这一原则，国务院最近
6 决定，对十大环境资源，由各部门分工合作，进行保护。
7　　这十大资源分别是矿产、土地、草原、森林、生物、野
8 生动植物、水、海洋、气候、风景。
9　　国务院确定的环境资源保护分工是：地质矿产部主管矿
10 产资源保护；农业部主管草原资源和生物资源保护；林业部
11 主管森林资源保护；林业部与农业部共同主管野生动植物资
12 源保护；水利部主管水源资源保护；国家海洋局主管海洋资
13 源保护；国家气象局主管气候资源保护；建设部主管风景资
14 源保护。国家环保局、能源部等是环境资源保护的协同部门。

VOCABULARY

1: 国务院　[Guówùyuàn] 'State Council'

3: 合作 [hézuò] 'co-operate'

4: 自然 [zìrán] 'natural'

5: 担负 [dānfù] 'be charged with'

5: 原则 [yuánzé] 'principle'

7: 矿产 [kuàngchǎn] 'mining'

7: 草原 [cǎoyuán] 'grasslands'

7: 森林 [sēnlín] 'forests'

7: 野生 [yěshēng] 'wild, feral'

8: 动植物 [dòng zhíwù] 'animals and plants'

9: 地质 [dìzhì] 'geological'

13: 气象 [qìxiàng] 'meterological'

14: 能源部 [néngyuánbù] 'Energy Ministry'

14: 协同 [xiétóng] 'cooperating'

QUESTIONS

A. What attitude is conveyed by the headline?

B. What is the nature of the change discussed in the first sentence of the text?

C. How did the State Council determine what the areas of responsibility were to be?

D. How many resources are identified?

E. What natural resource will be an area of joint responsibility?

F. What will be the role of the National EPA and the Ministry of Energy?

#2 SOUTHERN TAIWAN RIVERS AND STREAMS BADLY POLLUTED

1   台湾南部河川污染严重

2   本报讯 台湾"环境保护局"的一名研究员在一份调
3 查研究报告中说，台湾中南部 6 条主要河川受到中度及重
4 度污染的河段 280.6 公里，占总长度 38.6%，受到中度污染
5 的河段 154.5 公里，占总长度 21.3%，受到严重污染的河段
6 126.1 公里，占总长度 17.3%。
7   9 条主要河川是，朴子河、八掌河、急水河、曾久河、
8 盐水河、二仁河、高屏河、东港河和林边河。它们占台湾
9 全省 21 条主要河川的 42.9%。这 9 条河川是台湾南部自来
10 水源和牡蛎、虱目鱼的养殖区。值得注意的是供自来水水
11 源用的东港，其水质符合标准率仅 54.1%。

VOCABULARY

3: 报告 [bàogào] 'report'

4: 河段 [héduàn] 'section of river system'

10: 牡蛎 [mǔlì] 'oyster'

10: 虱目鱼 [shīmùyú] '(name of a fish)'

10: 养殖区 [yǎngzhíqū] 'spawning grounds'

11: 符合 [fúhé] 'meet, match up to'

11: 仅 [jǐn] 'only'

QUESTIONS

A. To whom is this report attributed?

B. What two degrees of pollution are described?

C. How many rivers are discussed? Are they a significant portion of the
   river system?

D. What particular significance do these rivers have to Taiwan?

E. Why is Dōnggǎng of specific importance?

Identify the grammar of the following headlines and translate them into English:

依法保护海洋环境

——吴钧谈《海洋环境保护法》实施五周年

预测 2000 年我国水资源污染
有关专家在京提出防治对策

国家环保局局长曲格平指出

保护饮用水源刻不容缓

第三次全国环保会议闭幕
环境污染在蔓延生态状况恶化
政府将以更有效措施坚决治理

Reading Chinese Newspapers:
Tactics and Skills

Lesson Five: Space Satellites

1988年3月24日 星期四 第三版

我国租星时代将结束

宇航专家孙家栋谈通信卫星定点意义

本报讯 航天报记者孙民强、本报记者何黄彪报道：我国3月22日定点成功的实用通信卫星与以往发射的卫星有什么不同？在技术和效果上有哪些改进？航天工业部副部长、著名宇航专家孙家栋认为，这颗卫星发射成功，标志我国租星时代将要过去，960万平方公里土地上的10亿人民可以分享自己国家航天技术的成果。

孙家栋对记者说：这颗卫星是我国自1984年4月以来用"长征三号"运载火箭发射成功的第3颗地球同步轨道通信卫星。这颗卫星与1986年2月1日发射的实用通信广播卫星比较，除卫星的定点精度和稳定精度都有提高以外，还显示出几大特点：

卫星的工作寿命增加了50%。上颗卫星的设计寿命是3年，这颗卫星增加到4年半。寿命的长短，主要靠卫星所带能源的多少来决定。为了解决卫星多带能源，设计人员研制出了一套全新的可靠性装置。

通信容量比以前增大了一倍。这是在技术上攻克了新型器件的难关后取得的。这种新型器件寿命长、重量轻，特别是线性好，由于解决这项关键技术，传输电话和电视的质量也有显著提高。这颗实用卫星完全可以满足目前我国内卫星电话通讯和中央电视台转播各套节目的需要。

孙家栋强调，"长征三号"运载火箭连续三次把我国三颗通信卫星送上太空，这说明"长征三号"运载火箭和它的发控技术已经完善与成熟，有很高的可靠性。这使我们增强了今后用它发射我国的各种应用卫星的信心；也更有利于我们将"长征三号"运载火箭投入国际市场，为国际用户服务。

辐射交联聚乙烯绝缘电缆研制成功

本报讯 一种长期依靠进口的飞机场专用照明电缆——辐射交联聚乙烯绝缘电缆由中国科学院辐射技术公司试制成功。

辐射聚乙烯绝缘电缆是一种通过加速器辐射处理后具有极高的防潮、抗压、阻燃和防老化性能的电缆，是高技术产品。我国每年都要从国外高价购买这种产品。新成立不久的中科院辐射技术公司凭借在加速器制造、辐射技术应用和辐射材料配方等方面的优势，经过一年的试制，在该公司下属的烟台电缆厂推出这种电缆。最近召开的鉴定会认为，该产品性能指标达到或超过同类产品的国际标准，完全能够替代进口产品以满足我国民航事业的需要。 （杨永田 王友恭）

同外地大专院校科研单位结

上虞乡镇企业产品靠

本报讯 浙江省上虞县乡镇企业与大专院校、科研单位结成科研生产联合体和科研、教育、生产、贸易四结合的经济实体，有33家乡镇企业发展成为骨干外向型企业，生产的40多种产品，出口和配套出口10多个国家和地区。

上虞县依靠科技进步发展外向型乡镇企业，最早是从村办厂上虞风机厂与上海交通大学横向联合的成功中受到启发的。到1986年，全县就有100多家乡镇企业与136所大专科研单位结成科研生产体。去年4月，县政府海交大签订协议，成火"联合集团，并且形开发"食品产地'冷藏及应用示范"、"风机新发及计算机应用研究"为重点的虞中机电"星集小区。这样，全县乡有了坚强的后盾。

且前，全县有52家业自己办科研，聘用专

农村小学不是"安置站

黄祖文 陈代平

笔者最近调查了公安县某镇22所村小学，发现所接受了近几年换下来的15名村干部，其中9名任校他们的文化程度分别是高中1人、初中5人、小学9能胜任教学工作的只有5人。学校简直成了照顾换部的"安置站"。

多数村小学的教师是定编的。换届村干部安插校，挤占了教师编制，进一个村干部就得出一名教一些有教学能力的教师明知不能拿鸡蛋去碰石头，告退。学校在村党支部的领导之下，支部拍了板，学不听？水月村一所小学，去冬来了一位换届干部当校撤了颇有教学经验的老校长，没过几天，新校长又排当干部，老校长再复职。如此这般竟折腾了三次后干脆学校没有校长。至于文化程度低的换届村拿起教鞭来手无策，教学质量直线下降，更是必然果了。

"坑豆一年一点，干部一年一选。"如今农村年有换届干部，而农村教师虽然清苦，多少还有点对分子的照顾政策。换届干部着上了这点"照顾"，却要以损害教育事业为代价，此风非割不可。当然，当

快

(reproduction of original text)

STRUCTURE NOTES (Line numbers here refer to the original text.)

2: 将 Verb = 'verb action will happen' When used before a verb, 将 marks that the verb action will or is about to take place. In this usage it is often followed by a reinforcing 要 or 会, see l. 8. Note the distinctly different 将 Noun structure discussed at l. 32 below. Examples are:

a. 我国男女比例将要失调。

b. 设计员将会研究出新型通信卫星器件。

4-5: The structure of this sentence is X(卫星) 与 Y(卫星) V(有) 什么 O(不同). This is the literary equivalent of X 跟 Y 怎么不一样. 与 is frequently used in writings as a literary synonym for 跟.

6: 些 Nouns is used when a writer wishes to indicate that there are more than one of the nouns being discussed but does not want to be specific about the exact number. It is usually better to translate 些 Nouns as "nouns" rather than "a few/some (i.e. 一些) nouns".

7: ， Note that this comma separates the verb (认为) from its object (the rest of the sentence.)

8: ， The first comma separates the subject(成功) from its verb (标志). See this usage also in l. 19. The second comma in this sentence would probably be a period in English, because the self-contained grammatical structure S (人民) V (分享) O(成果) follows.

11-13: 的 If you are alert to the function of 的, you can accurately understand sentences with very complicated modification structures. For example, if you see the 的 and the 是 in the unit after the colon in these lines, it will help you recognize the basic structure is X(卫星) 是 ...的 Y(第三颗地球同步轨道通信卫星). This will help you determine that <u>Y</u> has a <u>S(我国) T (自 X 以来) Cv(用) X(火箭) Vp(发射成功)</u> <u>的</u> modifying structure which should be translated as a relative clause in English: "The Y which the subject used X to verb with at a point in time." This will lead you to understand the whole structure as: "This satellite (X) is the 3rd geo-synchronous communications satellite (Y) which our country has launched using a 'Long March #3' carrier rocket since April, 1984." Similarly in l. 26-28, if you spot the 的 before the object (需要), you will then be able to determine that it is modified by a lengthy <u>X(通讯) 和 Y (S(电视台) V(转播) O(节目)) 的</u> structure and correctly translate it as '...the needs for X and Y.' The 的 in l. 31-33 marks that a <u>T Cv (用) X(它) V(发射) O(卫星) 的</u> structure modifies the object (信心). See 3:12 for earlier comments on 的 structures. If you remember that a noun usually follows a 的, you will be able to see that a word you may have learned as a verb is used as a noun. For example, in l. 19 多少 is 'amount, quantity', not 'how much'.

15-16: <u>除了 X 以外, 也 Y</u> = 'besides X, Y' When followed by a comma unit containing the adverbs <u>还</u>, <u>也</u>, or <u>又</u>, <u>除了 X 以外</u> means 'besides X'. When followed by 都 it means 'except for X'. <u>除了 X 以外</u> sometimes occurs without <u>除了</u> and sometimes without <u>以外</u>, but one element or the other must be present to mark the structure. <u>除</u> and/or <u>外</u> are sometimes used for a more formal prose tone. Examples using vocabulary from past lessons are:

   a. <u>除了</u>管理者<u>以外</u>，使用者也要担负起保护自然资源的责任。
   b. <u>除了</u>极少数人<u>以外</u>，大多数人都认识到我国妇女付出的代价。

18: <u>Verb 到</u> = 'verb to the point of' Verb complements such as <u>到</u>, <u>起</u>, <u>回</u>, etc. can be very helpful in finding the core verb of a sentence or comma unit. Examples are:

   a. 全国妇联主席又谈<u>到</u>了妇女受教育的问题。
   b. 请问，我们汉语课下星期要学习<u>到</u>第几课？

19: <u>所 Verb 的 Noun</u> 所 adds emphasis to a verb (here 带) modifying a noun (here 能源), but since it has no direct English equivalent, the <u>所 Verb 的</u> Noun structure is difficult to translate. This usage of 所 is very common in writings, but it is rarely used in everyday speech. Examples are:

    a. 沈阳市<u>所</u>兴建<u>的</u>是大型污水处理厂。

    b. 在广州<u>所</u>举行<u>的</u>第六届全运会已经结束了。

20: <u>为了 X Verb phrase</u> What is the function of <u>为了</u> X Vp here and of <u>(X) 为</u> Y Vp in l. 33? See 3:43-44.

22: <u>X 比 Y Vp</u> = 'X is more Vp than Y' Other than occasional use in words such as 比赛, 比例, etc., the major grammatical function of <u>比</u> is to mark a comparative structure. When you see <u>比</u> expect an <u>X 比 Y Vp</u> structure wherein <u>X</u> and <u>Y</u> may either be grammatically very simple or complex. Two examples of this common structure are:

    a. 中国八一男篮队<u>比</u>南朝鲜的男篮队打得好。

    b. 这次卫星发射的成果<u>比</u>以前的多得多。

22: <u>S 是 T V 的</u> What is the function of <u>是...的</u> here? See 2:15.

25-26: <u>由于 X, 也 Y</u> = 'because of X, Y' When you see words such as the formal prose <u>由于</u> or its more oral synonym <u>如果</u> head a comma unit, expect at least one following unit marked by a word such as <u>也</u>, <u>就</u>, <u>所以</u>, <u>还</u>, etc. These and other patterns such as <u>虽然</u> X, <u>可是</u> Y, <u>不但</u> X, <u>而且</u> Y, and <u>既</u> X, <u>也</u> Y, etc. mark a tandem relationship between comma units, so look for grammatical and thematic connections. English tends to mark the first unit but leave the second unmarked, so while <u>也</u>, <u>就</u>, and <u>还</u> are very useful in locating the second Chinese unit, they are generally not translated into English. The grammatical structures of the comma units may be very simple or very complicated, but in any case your reading should start with locating the core verb in each comma unit. Examples are:

    a. <u>由于</u>政府将要设立煤烟瞭望哨，那样，污染率<u>就</u>会下降。

    b. <u>由于</u>通信卫星3月22日定点成功，中国10亿人民<u>都</u>十分高兴。

31: <u>X 使 Y Verb phrase</u> What is the function of <u>使</u> here? See 4:26.

32: 将 Object Verb phrase = 'placement of the object before the verb for emphasis'
When followed by a noun, 将 functions in the same way 把 does to transpose the object before the verb, though 将 is more literary in tone than 把. Compare this with the 将 Verb usage discussed in line 2 above. Two examples of 将 Object are:

a. 陈幕华希望将中国妇女的参政议政重要性的认识提到新的阶段。

b. 中国以后要将"长征三号"运载火箭租给国际用户。

1   宇航专家孙家栋谈通信卫星定点意义
2   我国租星时代将结束

3   本报讯　航天报记者孙民强、本报记者
4   何黄彪报道：我国3月22日定点成功的实用
5   通信卫星与以往发射的卫星有什么不同？在
6   技术和效果上有哪些改进？航天工业部副部
7   长、著名宇航专家孙家栋认为，这颗卫星发
8   射成功，标志我国租星时代将要过去，　960
9   万平方公里土地上的10亿人民可以分享自己
10 国家航天技术的成果。
11   孙家栋对记者说，这颗卫星 是我国自
12 1984 年4月以来用"长征三号"运载火箭发
13 射成功的第3颗地球同步轨道通信卫星。这
14 颗卫星与1986 年2月1日发射的实用通信广
15 播卫星比较,除卫星的定点精度和稳定精度
16 都有提高以外，还显示出几大特点：

VOCABULARY

1: 宇航 [yǔháng] 'space navigation'
1: 孙家栋 [Sūn Jiādòng] '(name of a person)'
1: 通信 [tōngxìn] 'communication'
1: 卫星 [wèixīng] 'satellite'
1: 定点 [dìngdiǎn] 'achieve orbit'
2: 租星 [zūxīng] 'rent satellites'

2: 将 V [jiāng] Verb "verb will happen" (SN)

3: 航天报 [Hángtiān bào] 'Spaceflight Journal'

5: 与 [yǔ] 'and, with' (SN)

5: 以往 [yǐwǎng] 'previous, former'

5: 发射 [fāshè] 'launched'

6: 效果 [xiàoguǒ] 'results' WG>10:成果 [chéngguǒ] 'achievements'

7: 著名 [zhùmíng] 'famous' WG>26:显著 [xiǎnzhù] 'outstanding'

7: 颗 [kē] '(measure for satellites)'

8: 标志 [biāozhì] 'indicate, symbolize'

9: 960万 960 [wàn] '(960 X 10,000 =) 9,600,000'

9: 平方公里 [píngfāng gōnglǐ] 'square kilometers'

9: 10 亿 10 [yì] '(10 X 100,000,000 =) 'one billion'

9: 分享 [fēnxiǎng] 'share (in the enjoyment of)'

10: 成果 [chéngguǒ] '?' 果 WG:6

12: 的 [dě] "description marker" (SN)*

12: 长征三号 [Chángzhēng sānhào] 'Long March #3'

12: 运载火箭 [yùnzài huǒjiàn] 'carrier rocket'

13: 地球 [dìqiú] 'globe, world'

13: 同步 [tóngbù] 'synchronic'

13: 轨道 [guǐdào] 'orbit'

14: 广播 [guǎngbō] 'broadcast' WG>28:转播 [zhuǎnbō] 'relay (a broadcast)'

15: 除X以外 [chú X yǐwài] 'besides X' (SN)

15: 精度 [jīngdù] 'precision'

15: 稳定 [wěndìng] 'stability'

16: 显示 [xiǎnshì] 'show, display' 显 WG:26

*Remember that (SN) means that this item is discussed in the Structural Notes. Use (SN) to make your work with the texts more efficient.

17　　　卫星的工作寿命增加了 50%。上颗卫星
18　的设计寿命是 3年，这颗卫星增加到 4年半。
19　寿命的长短，主要靠卫星所带能源的多少来
20　决定。为了解决卫星多带能源，设计人员研
21　制出了一套全新的可靠性装置。
22　　　　通信容量比以前增大了一倍。这是在技
23　术上攻克了新型器件的难关后取得的。这种
24　新型器件寿命长、重量轻、特别是线性好，
25　由于解决这项关键技术，传输电话和电视的
26　质量也有显著提高。这颗实用卫星完全可以
27　满足目前我国内卫星电话通讯和中央电视台
28　转播各套节目的需要。

VOCABULARY

17: 寿命 [shòumìng] 'life-span'

17: 增加 [zēngjiā] 'increase' WG>22: 增大 [zēngdà] 'expand';
　　　　WG>32: 增强 [zēngqiáng] 'strengthen, enhance'

17: 上　[shàng] 'previous, former, last'

18: 设计 [shèjì] 'designed'

18: V 到 Verb [dào] "verb to the point of" (SN)

19: 靠　[kào] 'rely on'

20: 解决 [jiějué] 'work out a solution'

20: 研制 [yánzhì] 'design, develop'

21: 套 [tào] '(measure word for sets of things)'

21: 性 [X-xìng] '(suffix showing) nature or quality of X'
    WG>24: 线性 [xiànxìng] 'reception'

21: 装置 [zhuāngzhì] 'device'

22: 容量 [róngliàng] 'capacity' WG>24: 重量 [zhòngliàng] 'weight'
    WG>26: 质量 [zhìliàng] 'quality'

22: X 比 YVp [X bǐ Y Vp] 'X is more Vp than Y' (SN)

22: 增大 [zēngdà] '?' 增 WG:17

23: 攻克 [gōngkè] 'solve'

23: 新型 [xīnxíng] 'new model'

23: 器件 [qìjiàn] 'parts'

23: 难关 [nánguān] 'difficulty' WG>25: 关键 [guānjiàn] 'key point, crucial'

24: 重量 [zhòngliàng] '?' 量 WG:22

24: 线性 [xiànxìng] '?' 性 WG:21

25: 由于 X, 也 Y [yóuyú X, yě Y] 'because of X, Y' (SN)

25: 关键 [guānjiàn] '?' 关 WG:23

25: 传输 [chuánshū] 'transmit'

26: 质量 [zhìliàng] '?' 量 WG:22

26: 显著 [xiǎnzhù] '?' 著 WG:7, 显 WG:16

27: 满足 [mǎnzú] 'satisfy, fulfill'

27: 电视台 [diànshìtái] 'television station'

28: 转播 [zhuǎnbō] '?' 播 WG:14

28: 节目 [jiémù] 'program'

29   孙家栋强调，“长征三号”运载火箭连
30 续三次把我国三颗通信卫星送上太空，这说
31 明“长征三号”运载火箭和它的发控技术已
32 经完善与成熟，有很高的可靠性。这使我们
33 增强了今后用它发射我国的各种应用卫星的
34 信心；也更有利于我们将“长征三号”运载
35 火箭投入国际市场，为国际用户服务。

VOCABULARY

29: 强调 [qiángdiào] 'stress, emphasize' WG>32:增强 [zēngqiáng]
       'strengthen, enhance'

29: 连续 [liánxù] 'consecutively'

30: 太空 [tàikōng] '(outer) space'

31: 发控 [fākòng] '(abbr. for 发射控制) launch control'

31: 完善 [wánshàn] 'perfect'

32: 成熟 [chéngshú] 'mature'

32: 增强 [zēngqiáng] '?' 增 WG:17, 强 WG:29

34: 有利于 X [yǒulìyú X] 'be beneficial in the area of X'

34: 将 O [jiāng] Object "place object before verb for emphasis" (SN)

35: 投入 [tóurù] 'enter, "throw hat in the ring"'

35: 国际市场 [guójì shìchǎng] 'international market'

35: 用户 [yònghù] 'customer'

GRAMMAR EXERCISES

1. Please fill in the blanks (填空 tiánkòng) and translate (翻译 fānyì)
   the following:

一) 除了有新的装置___，这颗卫星的重量也较轻。(呢、了、以外)

二) 与以往发射的卫星不同____这颗通信卫星是3月22日定点成功的。
   (比、的、将)

三) ____提高电视机质量设计人员研制出了新型器件。(除了、由于、
   为了)

四) 中央电视台的需要____我们发射这颗卫星。(以外、使、比)

五) ____给我国人民说明这次发射成功的意义，孙家栋举行了一次记
   者招待会。(为了、由于、将)

六) 我国多年来的租星时代____要结束。(会、将、使)

2. Please 填空 using the correct marker from those listed and then translate:
   (为、使、除了、为了、的)

一) 这枚火箭的发射成功____我们增强了可以用它发射其他种类卫
   星的信心。

二) 这颗卫星____工作寿命增加了以外，通信容量也增大了一倍。

三) 连续三次把我国三颗通信卫星送上太空____"长征三号"运载
   火箭发控技术非常可靠。

四) ____满足国内的电话通讯需要，3月7日又发射了一颗通讯卫星。

五) 设计人员____通讯卫星研究出了特别好的线性。

3. Please rewrite the following sentences and then translate them:

一) 因为这颗卫星能多带能源，使用寿命就增长了。(由于)

二) 设计人员把传输电话的质量显著地提高了。(将)

三) 1986年发射的卫星没有这颗通信卫星的容量那么大。(比)

四) 由于"长征三号"的可靠性,我国能为更多的国际用户服务。(将)

Identify the grammar of the following headlines and translate them

中英港三公司合作發射衛星
明年初用"長征三號"火箭送入軌道

我石油专用卫星通信网开通

我首颗通信卫星超运行一年
星上三万电子器件工作正常

傅美方已經同意
委託中共發射商用衛星

新疆上空发现不明飞行物

我首次参与经营国际通信卫星
明年由「长征三号」火箭发射

中　央　日　報
星期二　中華民國七十七年八月九日
夏曆戊辰六月廿七日

以長征火箭發射人造衛星
中共否認將用於軍事用途

SIGHT READINGS

#1 OUR COMMUNICATIONS SATELLITE TRANSMITS CENTRAL TV PROGRAMS

1 　　　　　我通信卫星正式传送
2 　　　　　中央电视台三套节目

3 　　　　新华社上海4月15日电　　(记者冯亦珍)　我国通信卫
4 星于今天起正式传送中央电视台的三套节目，这标志着我
5 国卫星通信和电视传送进入新阶段。
6 　　　　国内卫星承担电视传送业务后，中央电视台节目发送
7 到印度洋上空的国际通信卫星上，由乌鲁木齐卫星地面站
8 接收后，可以发送到位于东经87.5度的我国通信卫星上，
9 再由我国的地面卫星站接收。
10 　　　　乌鲁木齐及上海卫星通信站的卫星电视发送和接收设
11 备都是邮电部第一研究所提供的。

VOCABULARY

1: 正式 [zhèngshì] 'formally, officially'
1: 传送 [chuánsòng] 'transmit'
2: 套　[tào] '(measure for sets of things)'
5: 阶段 [jiēduàn] 'stage'
6: 承担 [chéngdān] 'assume, undertake'
7: 印度洋 [Yìndùyáng] 'Indian Ocean'
7: 乌鲁木齐 [Wūlǔmùqí] 'Urümqi'
7: 地面站 [dìmiànzhàn] 'earth station'

8: 东经 [dōngjīng] 'east longitude'

10: 设备 [shèbèi] 'equipment'

11: 邮电部 [yóudiànbù] 'Ministry of Posts and Telecommunications'

11: 提供 [tígōng] 'supply'

QUESTIONS

A. Where did this story come from?

B. What is seen as the significance of this use of the satellite?

C. How many transmission steps are described for television transmissions using this new satellite?

D. After signals from the Indian Ocean satellite are received in Urümqi, where are they sent?

E. Why is the Ministry of Posts and Telecommunications mentioned?

F. What role does Shanghai play in the transmissions?

#2 WE WILL LAUNCH A SATELLITE FOR SWEDEN

1　　　　　我国将为瑞典发射一颗卫星

2　　　新华社北京 12 月 3 日电　（通讯员孙民强）　我国将为瑞
3　典发射卫星。 11 月 23 日，瑞典方面向中国长城公司交付第
4　一笔发射服务费，双方于 11 月 19 日签订的合同开始生效。
5　　　合同规定，中国长城公司于 1991 年秋天用"长征 2 号"
6　运载火箭将瑞典空间公司的"弗列亚"号科学探测及邮政
7　通信兼用卫星发射到地球预定轨道。

VOCABULARY

1: 瑞典 [Ruìdiǎn] 'Sweden'
3: 中国长城公司 [Zhōngguó chángchéng gōngsī] 'China Great Wall
　　　Company'
3: 交付 [jiāofù] 'pay'
4: X 费 [X-fèi] 'fee for X'
4: 签订 [qiāndìng] 'conclude and sign'
4: 合同 [hétóng] 'contract'
4: 生效 [shēngxiào] 'go into effect'
6: 空间 [kōngjiān] '(outer) Space'
6: 探测 [tàncè] 'survey, probe'
7: 兼用 [jiānyòng] 'dual function'
7: 预定 [yùdìng] 'pre-determined'

QUESTIONS

A. Who gave money to whom on November 23?

B. What happened on November 19?

C. What is the name of the rocket to be used in the launch?

D. What two functions will the satellite have?

E. Who owns the satellite?

Reading Chinese Newspapers:
Tactics and Skills

Lesson Six: Minorities in China

人民日报

RENMIN RIBAO

第14847期 （代号1—1）

人民日报社出版

夜间 晴间多云
风向 偏北
风力 四、五级
风向 偏北
风力 三、四级
温ど 最高 7℃
最低 —2℃

发展少数民族经济新构想
西北地区将双向开放
一向沿海海外　一向内陆邻国

据中新社北京2月20日电（记者**伟翔**）中国西部、北部民族地区将实行"双向开放"，一是向东向南对沿海及发达国家开放，二是向西向北对邻国及相近国家开放。

据称，中国西部、北部民族地区"双向开放"的构想已经由国家民委上报中央，并得到了中央一些高级领导人的赞赏。

国家民委副主任赵延年今天在此间的一个会议上披露了这一构想。

他说，内陆边境的对外开放，一是一般的边境贸易点、过货点；二是对邻国及该国相邻地区的重点贸易及经济技术交流合作的城市；三是可以通过向第三国乃至更大范围的铁路、公路、水路的重要口岸。

国家民委提出的这一构想要求，向西向北开放，应从陆地边境民族地区的实际情况出发，参考沿海开放地区的政策和作法。

由于中央实施沿海经济发展战略，位于中国西部、北部的少数民族地区感受到较大的压力。来自国家民委的消息说，去年东西部之间的经济差距仍在拉大。此番有关方面提出的"双向开放"构想，意在加速少数民族地区经济的发展，尽可能地缩小中国东西部之间现已存在的经济差距。

国家民委的一位高级官员认为，对于大多数民族地区来说，通过向西向北开放，能够由偏远变为前哨，由远离国内市场的劣势变为就近进入国际市场的优势。

赵延年说，这一构想的实施，可以有力地促进少数民族地区的产业结构产品结构的变化，促进商品经济的发展和人们精神面貌的改变。

据悉，这一构想的具体方案近日可望出台，内蒙古的满洲里和二连、新疆的喀什和伊犁、西藏的亚东、云南的德宏和西双版纳、吉林的延边等都极有可能成为中国西部、北部民族地区实行"双向开放"的先头地域。

赵紫阳等领导人会见第二届全国优秀企业家和荣获一九八八年度全国企业管理优秀奖的企业代表。
新华社记者　刘少山摄

海南大力肃　梁湘说歪

新华社海口3月2日电（记者**任小东**）海南省长梁湘今天在此间召开的一次会议上提出，海南将大力反贪污受贿，建立一个廉洁的特区政府。

梁湘今天在会上严厉批评海南一些干部，利用职权和工作便利，非法倒卖紧俏商品、炒卖土地、索贿受贿、贪污盗窃、滥发奖金、挥霍公款，其中尤以炒卖土地、受贿贪污最为严重。

梁湘说，外商反映，到海南有些部门办事，不花钱、不送礼、不请客

我投资亿元提高
今年将增连铸能力一

据新华社北京3月2日电（记者**陈新**）本社记者今天从冶金部获悉，面对国内能源供应和运输能力全面紧张的局面加速对引

说，今年钢铁工业预计1100万吨新建连铸能力产，国家为此投入了上金。这种从国外引进的产技术不仅有利于提高

(reproduction of original text)

STRUCTURE NOTES (Line numbers here refer to the original text.)

6: 将 What is the function of 将 here? See 5:2.

6: " " Quotation marks are used to indicate the words they enclose are being used for a special value. See 8:4-6 for extensive examples.

6: 向 Place 对 Place Remember that the English equivalents of place phrases headed by 向 or 对 usually come after the verb and object. See 4:12-15 for comments on how to handle these phrases.

7-9: 一是..., 二是... Technically a X 是 Y = 'X is Y' pattern, a number 是... structure (not number measure 是) marks a listing of conditions or stipulations. You should expect at least 二是..., and perhaps 三是... (l. 21 below), or even 四是... or 五是..., etc. to follow somewhere later in the sentence. Each one is usually a separate comma unit and may be either structurally simple or complex. Examples of this usage are:

  a. 全国妇联提出了重要建议：一是男女地位应当平等，二是妇女不该受任何歧视。
  b. 学习外语时必须极用功：一是练习口语，二是阅读课文，三是记住语法。

9: 及 [jí] If you remember that conjunctions such as 及, 和, 以及, 跟, 同 and 与 conjoin elements of roughly equal grammatical value, it will be easier for you to identify multiple subjects, objects and places whether they have complex or simple structures. For example, 及 joins two places in l. 8-9 (邻国及...国家) and l. 20-21 (邻国及...地区). In l. 19-20 及 links multiple objects (...的重点贸易及...的城市). 和 links multiple objects in l. 48-49 (...的发展和...的改变) and 5:27-28, and 和 joins two place names in l. 52 and 54. See 2:5-8 for comments on use of 和 and 以及 with the listing comma 、. Examples are:

  a. 我们这个星期要复习的是第三、第四、第七跟第十课。
  b. 含油废水排放和二氧化硫浓度高是我国环境污染的重要原因。

11:      X 由 Y Verb phrase = 'verb action is done to X by Y' In this pattern 由 marks that a verb action, generally having a neutral to beneficial impact on X, is done to something by someone. The focus is on Y. See 被 3:22 where the focus is on X. Note line 42 below where 由 is used as a synonym of 从 cóng to mark location structures. To tell which usage of 由 is before you in a text, see if there is a place name after it. Examples of its use to mark passive sentences are:

a. 沈阳市的环境治理由该市的环保局管理。

b. 女子400米栏记录由河北赵存林打破了。

11-14:   Verb 了 The marker 了 is very useful in finding the core verb of comma units and sentences since it comes immediately after a verb (also see 2:5). 了 marks the verb actions the writer views as completed: e.g., l. 11 得到了 "obtained Central Committee approval" and in l. 15 披露了 "divulged a plan". Absence of 了 after the other verbs in the article may suggest either that those actions are yet to be finished or that their completion is not the focal point of the discussion.

a. 企业实行了优化劳动组合以後，不少女工被"优化"下来了。

b. 沈阳市建立了服务小组，帮助冒黑烟单位进行技术改造。

37:      Adverb 地 [dě] marks the use of the word before it as an adverb modifying the verb which immediately follows. 地 is suffixed to words not generally used as adverbs:e.g., 热烈, 高兴，科学，详细，etc., though not all such adverbial uses are so marked. Recognizing 地 as an adverbial marker is very useful in locating the core verb of a unit, since the verb will come right after the 地, see 1. 46 below. Some examples of 地 are:

a. 孙副部长十分详细地谈了中国的航天工业。

b. 中国男篮很自然地又登上了亚洲冠军宝座。

42:      由 Place = 'from the place' 由 marks the starting point or origin of a verb action. In this usage it should be translated as "from," and as with 对 and 向, should be placed after the English verb and object. Refer to its different usage discussed in l. 11 above. Examples are:

a. 由美国到中国有一万多里路。

b. 我明天早晨八点半由虹桥机场起飞回国。

42:     Verb 为 what is the function of 为 as a verb complement here and in 43 and 55 below? Should it be pronounced [wéi] or [wèi]? See 3:40.

50-57   、   You can more easily analyze and process this 84 character long sentence if you take into notice the five 、 'list marking commas' it contains. The first four mark the list of place names in lines 51-55 which are the subject of the verb (成为) in l. 55. The fifth 、, in line 55, marks the listing of two more place names which are used to modify the object (先头地域). See 2:5.

1　　　　发展少数民族经济新构想
2　　　　西北地区将双向开放
3　一向沿海海外　一向内陆邻国

4　　　　据中新社北京 2 月 20 日电
5 （记者伟翔）　中国西部、北部
6 民族地区将实行"双向开放"，
7 一是向东向南对沿海及发达国
8 家开放，二是向西向北对邻国
9 及相近国家开放。
10　　　据称，中国西部、北部民
11 族地区"双向开放"的构想已
12 经由国家民委上报中央，并得
13 到了中央一些高级领导人的赞
14 赏。
15　　　国家民委副主任赵延年今
16 天在此间的一个会议上披露了
17 这一构想。
18　　　他说，内陆边境的对外开
19 放，一是一般的边境贸易点、
20 过货点；二是对邻国及该国相
21 邻地区的重点贸易及经济技术
22 交流合作的城市；三是可以通
23 过向第三国乃至更大范围的铁
24 路、公路、水路的重要口岸。
25　　　国家民委提出的这一构想
26 要求，向西向北开放，应从陆
27 地边境民族地区的实际情况出
28 发，参考沿海开放地区的政策
29 和作法。

VOCABULARY

1: 少数 [shǎoshù] 'minority'

1: 民族 [mínzú] 'nationality' WG>12:民委 [Mínwěi] '(abbr. for 国家民族事物委员会) State Nationalities Commission'

1: 构想 [gòuxiǎng] 'plan, scheme' WG>48:结构 [jiégòu] 'structure'

2: 双向开放 [shuāngxiàng kāifàng] 'develop in two directions'

3: 向/对place [xiàng/duì] place 'towards place' (SN)

3: 沿海 [yánhǎi] 'coastal'

3: 内陆 [nèilù] 'interior, hinterland'

3: 邻国 [línguó] 'neighboring countries' WG>19:相邻 [xiānglín] 'nearby'

7: 一是... [yīshì...] "marks lists of conditions or stipulations" (SN)

9: 及 [jí] "conjunctions" (SN)

10: 据称 [jùchēng] 'according to reports' WG>51:据悉 [jùxī] 'it is reported'

12: X 由 YV [X yóu Y verb] "verb done to X by Y" (SN)

12: 民委 [Mínwěi] '?' 民 WG:1

12: 上报 [shàngbào] 'report to a higher authority'

13: 赞赏 [zànshǎng] 'admiration'

16: 披露 [pīlù] 'reveal, divulge'

18: 边境 [biānjìng] 'border, frontier'

18: 贸易 [màoyì] 'trade'

20: 过货 [guò huò] 'transfer goods'

20: 相邻 [xiānglín] '?' 邻 WG:3

22: 交流 [jiāoliú] 'exchange, transfer'

22: 通过 [tōngguò] 'go through, make use of'

23: 乃至 [nǎizhì] 'and even'

24: 口岸 [kǒu'àn] 'port'

28: 参考 [cānkǎo] 'consult, refer to'

28: 政策 [zhèngcè] 'governmental policy'

30　　　　由于中央实施沿海经济发
31　展战略，位于中国西部、北部
32　的少数民族地区感受到较大的
33　压力。来自国家民委的消息说，
34　去年东西部之间的经济差距仍
35　在拉大。此番有关方面提出的
36　"双向开放"构想，意在加速
37　少数民族地区经济的发展，尽
38　可能地缩小中国东西部之间现
39　已存在的经济差距。
40　　　　国家民委的一位高级官员
41　认为，对于大多数民族地区来
42　说，通过向西向北开放，能够
43　由偏远变为前哨，由远离国内
44　市场的劣势变为就近进入国际
45　市场的优势。
46　　　　赵延年说，这一构想的实
47　施，可以有力地促进少数民族
48　地区的产业结构产品结构的变
49　化，促进商品经济的发展和人
50　们精神面貌的改变。

VOCABULARY

31: 战略 [zhànlüè] 'strategy'

31: 位于 [wèiyú] 'situated at'

31: 感受 [gǎnshòu] 'experience, be affected by'

33: 压力 [yālì] 'pressure'

34: 差距 [chājù] 'disparity'

35: 拉大 [lādà] 'expand, grow'

35: 此番 [cǐ fān] 'this occurrence'

35: 有关 [yǒuguān] 'relevant, appropriate'

36: 加速 [jiāsù] 'speed up, hasten'

38: 尽可能 [jìn kěnéng] 'as far as possible'

38: Adv 地 [adverb dě] "adverb marker" (SN)

38: 缩小 [suōxiǎo] 'shrink, diminish'

39: 存在 [cúnzài] 'exist'

43: 由 P [yóu] place 'from place' (SN)

43: 偏远 [piān yuǎn] 'remote' WG>43:远离 [yuǎnlí] 'far removed from'

43: 前哨 [qiánshào] 'vanguard'

43: 远离 [yuǎn lí] '?' 远 WG:43

44: 市场 [shìchǎng] 'markets'

44: 劣势 [lièshì] 'inferior position' WG>45:优势 [yōushì] 'superior position'

44: 就近 [jiùjìn] 'nearby'

45: 优势 [yōushì] '?' 势 WG:44

46: 实施 [shíshī] 'implementation'

47: 促进 [cùjìn] 'promote, accelerate'

48: 结构 [jiégòu] '?' 构 WG:1

48: 变化 [biànhuà] 'change' WG>50:改变 [gǎibiàn] 'transformation'

49: 商品 [shāngpǐn] 'products, goods'

50: 精神 [jīngshén] 'spirit, feeling'

50: 面貌 [miànmào] 'appearance, features'

50: 精神面貌 [jīngshén miànmào] 'mental outlook'

50: 改变 [gǎibiàn] '?' 变 WG:48

51   据悉，这一构想的具体方
52 案近日可望出台，内蒙古的满
53 洲里和二连、新疆的喀什和伊
54 犁、西藏的亚东、云南的德宏
55 和西双版纳、吉林的延边等都
56 极有可能成为中国西部、北部
57 民族地区实行"双向开放"的
58 先头地域。

VOCABULARY

51: 据悉 [jù xī] '?' 据 WG:10

51: 具体 [jùtǐ] 'concrete, specific'

51: 方案 [fāng'àn] 'program, scheme'

52: 出台 [chūtái] 'come forth'

52: 内蒙古 [Nèi Ménggǔ] 'Inner Mongolia'

53: 新疆 [Xīnjiāng] 'Xinjiang (Hsin Kiang)'

53: 喀什 [Kāshén] '(place name)'

53: 伊犁 [Yīlí] '(place name)'

54: 西藏 [Xīzàng] 'Tibet'

54: 云南 [Yúnnán] 'Yunnan'

54: 德宏 [Déhóng] '(place name)'

55: 西双版纳 [Xīshuāngbǎnnà] '(place name)'

55: 吉林 [Jílín] 'Jilin'

58: 地域 [dìyù] 'region, district'

GRAMMAR EXERCISES

1. 用适当的词语填空，再把下列的句子翻译成英文:
   以后、X 由Y V、了、及、和、地、由place、的
   一) "双向开放"这个构想＿＿国家民委副主任向大会作了披露。
   二) 设计人员认真＿＿研制出了一套卫星装置。
   三) 发展少数民族经济新构想得到＿＿高级领导人的赞赏。
   四) 解放军队的苏冰＿＿湖南的张秋萍超过两项亚洲记录。
   五) 中国男篮＿＿曼谷飞回到北京。
   六) 少数民族地区的产业结构变化＿＿，精神面貌也将会改变。

2. 用所给的词语改写下列的句子:
   一) 过去，位于中国西部的少数民族受到较大的压力。(了)
   二) 这个构想意在促进少数民族精神面貌的改变。(尽可能地)
   三) 我国将实行新构想，对发达国家开放，也对邻国开放。
       (一是..., 二是...)
   四) 机械行业的两个大污染源是含油废水、煤烟尘。 (和)

3. Match the Chinese grammatical pattern with its English counterpart:
   一) X 以 Y V O   一) 'Do verb1 in order to do verb2'
   二) S 把 O V   二) 'Marker for noun modification'
   三) S 被 V   三) 'Subject was verbed'
   四) X 使 Y V O   四) 'Because of X, (also, then) Y'
   五) V1 以 V2   五) 'X is more Vp than Y'
   六) 除了 X 以外, 都 Y   六) 'Subject verbs the object'
   七) 由于 X, 也 Y   七) 'Subject verbs the object by means of Y'
   八) V1, 却 V2   八) 'Contrary to what V1 leads
                               you to expect, it's actually V2'
   九) 的 Noun   九) 'Except for X, Y'
   十) X 比 Y Vp   十) 'X causes Y to verb the object'

SIGHT READINGS

#1 DEVELOPING MINORITY CADRE AND LEADERS

1   培养少数民族干部
2   造就一批领袖人物

3   本报北京 2月 20日讯　记者袁建达报道："培养成千
4   上万的少数民族干部和他们当中的领袖人物，是推进民族
5   团结进步事业的根本大计，我们要以极大的紧迫感和责任
6   感做好培养少数民族干部的工作。"这番话是中共中央书
7   记处书记阎明复在全国民委主任会议上强调的。
8   他透露，中央统战部和国家民委设想用一年左右时间，
9   在 55个少数民族中掌握一批党内外优秀的中青年干部和代
10   表人物名单，有计划地培养、推荐和提拔任用。
11   阎明复要求大家对分裂势力的破坏活动保持高度警惕，
12   并进行坚决斗争。在事关国家统一的重大问题上，不能有
13   任何含糊。
14   在会上，阎明复还就民族工作部门如何治理经济环境、
15   整顿经济秩序和全面深化改革问题谈了意见。
16   在谈到各有关部门 都要真正从民族地区的实际出发，
17   加快民族地区的发展时，阎明复强调，民族地区应加强智
18   力投资和智力开发，办好民族教育，培养各方面专门人才。

VOCABULARY

1: 培养　[péiyǎng] 'develop, train'
2: 造就　[zàojiù] 'bring up, train'
3: 成千上万　[chéngqiān shàngwàn] 'thousands upon thousands'
5: 团结　[tuánjié] 'solidarity'

5: 紧迫感 [jǐnpògǎn] 'sense of urgency'

7: 书记处 [shūjìchù] 'secretariat'

7: 阎明复 [Yán Míngfù] '(name of a person)'

7: 强调 [qiángdiào] 'emphasize'

8: 设想 [shèxiǎng] 'conceive of'

9: 掌握 [zhǎngwò] 'have in hand'

10: 推荐 [tuījiàn] 'recommend'

10: 提拔 [tíbā] 'promote'

11: 分裂 [fēnliè] 'divide, break up'

11: 保持 [bǎochí] 'maintain, uphold'

11: 警惕 [jǐngtì] 'vigilance'

12: 斗争 [dòuzhēng] 'struggle'

12: 国家统一 [guójiā tǒngyī] 'national unity'

13: 含糊 [hánhu] 'ambiguity'

14: 就 X [jiù] X 'concerning X'

14: 如何 [rúhé] 'how'

15: 整顿 [zhěngdùn] 'reorganize'

15: 秩序 [zhìxù] 'order'

17: 智力 [zhìlì] 'intelligence'

QUESTIONS

A. What fundamental reason is given for wanting more minority cadre?

B. Where was this speech delivered?

C. What qualities is the party looking for in candidates from the 55 national minorities?

D. What does Secretary Yan warn about in the third paragraph?

E. What three things does Secretary Yan urge minority areas do to train talented people?

F. What overall attitude towards China's minorities is conveyed in this article?

#2 PLANNED CHILDBIRTH IN URUMQI

1 　　　　　　乌鲁木齐新春
2 　　　　　　少数民族群众
3 　　　　　　搞好计划生育

4 　　　新华社乌鲁木齐 2 月 8 日电　　（记者瓦哈甫·阿扎买
5 提）新春佳节期间乌鲁木齐市各级计划生育工作人员冒着
6 严寒，走街串户慰问少数民族的计划生育光荣户。
7 　　　自去年 7 月 1 日起，乌鲁木齐市的维吾尔、哈萨克、
8 回、阿尔克孜、蒙古、乌孜别克等民族，实行自治区少数
9 民族计划生育暂行规定。在短短的半年内，涌现出了一批
10 计划生育先进单位和个人，全市少数民族中，自愿终身只
11 生育两个孩子的夫妻，领取《计划生育光荣证》的已超过
12 5000 对。在少数民族聚居的天山区，1988年全区少数民族
13 青年晚婚率达 88.98%，节育率达到 81.41%。

VOCABULARY

1: 乌鲁木齐 [Wūlǔmùqí] 'Urümqi'

3: 计划生育 [jìhuà shengyù] 'planned childbirth'

5: 新春佳节 [xīnchūn jiājié] 'Festival of 10-20 days after Lunar New Years'

6: 严寒 [yánhán] 'bitter cold'

6: 走街串户 [zǒujiē chuànhù] 'go from house to house'

6: 慰问 [wèiwèn] 'convey sympathy and solicitude for'

6: 光荣户 [guāngrónghù] 'glorious households'

8: 自治区 [zìzhìqū] 'autonomous region'

9: 暂行规定 [zànxíng guīdìng] 'temporary regulations'

10: 终身 [zhōngshēn] 'lifelong'

11: 领取 [lǐngqǔ] 'receive'

12: 对 [duì] 'couple, husband and wife'

13: 节育率 [jiéyùlǜ] 'birth control ratio'

QUESTIONS

A. What is happening in the first paragraph?

B. How many minority groups are mentioned in Urümqi?

C. How long has this planned childbirth campaign been going on?

D. How many children should minority couples have?

E. What do the percentages in the last line refer to?

F. What feeling about planned childbirth is given in the first paragraph?

G. What images does the writer use to portray that atmosphere?

Some Headlines About Minorities

继续加强少数民族地区政府法制工作

少數民族地區形成初級保健網

西藏上层爱国人士拥护戒严

称赞国务院决策代表西藏人民根本利益

多吉才讓在自治區專員市長會議上説

西藏現行方針政策不會改變

西藏召開「人大」會議

否定任何形式的獨立

達賴的「一國兩制」也遭到抨擊

达赖喇嘛实际上在分裂中国

李先念会见苏贝蒂议长时指出

达赖想借外国力量分裂祖国不可能得逞

拉萨骚乱与人权问题不相干

外交部发言人指出

少數民族地區經濟有新發展

五个自治区去年工农业总产值比上年增一成

西藏自治区又发布三个政府令

第4号 戒严区执勤人员严守纪律

第5号 敦促骚乱分子投案自首

第6号 要求外国人凭证出入

閻明復在全國民委主任會上強調

加強民族團結至關重要

不允許外國進行干涉

西藏問題是中國內政

姚依林會見挪威議長時重申

Reading Chinese Newspapers:
Tactics and Skills

Lesson Seven: China-U.S. Relations

國際・體育　人民日報（海外版）

吳學謙說中美友好相處有利世界和平

希望中美關係今後有更大發展

新華社華盛頓三月七日電（記者施魯佳）正在美國訪問的中國國務委員兼外交部長吳學謙今天在這裏說，中美兩個大國友好相處，互利合作，符合兩國人民的根本利益，也有利於世界和平與穩定，中國方面期望，兩國關係在第二個十年裏，將會得到更大的發展。

吳學謙外長是在美國國務卿舒爾茨今天中午爲他舉行的歡迎宴會上講這番話的。

吳學謙說："今年是中美兩國建交的第十個年頭，回顧過去，展望未來，我對兩國關係的進展懷有信心。建交以來，中美關係取得顯著的進展。高級領導人的互訪，經濟合作關係，兩國人民之間的來往，以及其他領域的交流與合作不斷增加和擴大。實踐證明，地處太平洋兩岸的中美兩個大國友好相處，互利合作，符合兩國人民的根本利益，也有利於世界和平與穩定。我們一貫認爲，國家關係的親疏好壞，不取決於社會制度和意識形態的異同。如果雙方嚴格遵循互相尊重主權和領土完整、互不干涉內政的基本原則，在平等互利的基礎上加強往來與合作，那末，我們之間在各個領域發展友好關係是完全可能的。"

吳學謙認爲，總的說來，近十年中美兩國關係的發展是順利的，但也出現過起伏和波折；兩國關係既蘊藏着巨大的發展潛力，也存在着障礙和困難。

吳學謙告訴美國朋友，中國人民正在一心一意地爲建設具有中國特色的社會主義現代化國家而努力。正是從這一點出發，我們希望有一個長期的國際和平環境。

他強調，"我們一貫堅持、並將繼續堅持獨立自主的和平外交政策。我們反對侵略擴張政策，反對強權政治，反對干涉別國內政的言行，主張通過和平談判解決國際爭端。"

吳學謙表示，中國願意在平等互利的基礎上，繼續擴大同世界各國的經濟技術合作和貿易往來。

吳學謙說："今年，中美關係將走完邦交正常化第一個十年的旅程。我們期望，兩國關係在第二個十年裏，將會得到更大的發展。"

吳學謙說："我相信，我的這次訪問將是成功的。因爲我們雙方都抱有發展中美關係的願望。通過開誠布公的會談和會晤，將加深我們之間的瞭解，這是增進友誼和合作的基礎。我期待，我們在這個基礎上，推動中美關係更加健康、穩定地向前發展。"

舒爾茨也在宴會上發表了講話。他在談到台灣問題時重申，美國關於只有一個中國的政策是"堅定不移的"。他說，台灣的前途應由海峽兩岸的中國人，而不是由美國來決定。

舒爾茨還說，在解決世界上的地區性爭端的努力中，中美兩國都可以發揮自己的作用。他認爲，兩國在這些問題上保持對話，"對於維持世界和平和安全是至關重要的"。他說，"美中之間健康而牢固的關係是和平的保障。"

們雙方都抱有發展願望。通過開誠布會晤，將加深我們這是增進友誼和合我期待，我們在這推動中美關係更加地向前發展。"

舒爾茨也在宴講話。他說，過去中兩國的經濟關係有了令人注目的發與此同時，兩國也題上存在分歧。他不在於是否出現分雙方如何對待這些"只要我們在指導幾個公報所包含的上對待這些問題，我們的關係將會繼和得到加強。"

舒爾茨在談到重申，美國關於只的政策是"堅定不移台灣的前途應由海國人，而不是由美

舒爾茨還說，上的地區性爭端的美兩國都可以發用。他認爲，兩國上保持對話，"對於平和安全是至關重說，"美中之間健康係是和平的保障。"

新華社華盛頓三月七日電　中國國務委員兼外交部長吳學謙今天上午在美國國務院同舒爾茨國務卿舉行了第一輪會談。

陪同吳外長參加會談的一位中國官員對新華社記者說，會談是在誠摯友好的氣氛中進行的，雙方就阿富汗、柬埔寨等共同關心的重大國際問題交換了意見。雙方一致認爲外國軍隊從它們佔領的別國領土上撤走是公正合理地解決地區性衝突的關鍵。

(reproduction of original text)

STRUCTURE NOTES (Line numbers here refer to the original text.)

Many newspapers, including the foreign edition of the 人民日報, are printed in full form characters, so you need to be able to work with this style of characters in addition to the simplified form presented in previous lessons if you want to be able to read any and all Chinese language materials. In addition to this lesson, the main texts of Lessons 8, 9 and 12 as well as several sight reading texts are presented in full form characters. A simplified character version of this main text is presented after the grammar notes for your reference.

7:    **,**   these two commas separate the subjects (友好相處 and 互利合作) from their first verb (符合). The second verb is marked by 也.

6-8: <u>Unmarked conditional</u> Chinese often uses juxtapositioning of phrases and clauses rather than an overt marker such as 如果 to indicate that a second situation depends on occurrence of a first. This first portion of Minister Wu's comments can be understood as "<u>(When/if)</u> China and the US get along well and cooperate for mutual benefit, this meets the fundamental interests of the peoples of the two countries, and it also..." See 10:16-17 for further comments on unmarked conditionals.

9: Verb <u>於</u> [yú] X = 'Verb act is applied in the area of X' When suffixed to the verb, <u>於</u> indicates the origin, time, direction, or place of the verb action. <u>於</u> is thus helpful in locating the core verb of a sentence or comma unit. Note that verb <u>於</u> is used in writing but not in speech. See also l. 26, 28-29, and the sentences at 5:34 and 6:31. Two examples of this usage are:

   a. "雙向開放" 政策將實施<u>於</u>西部的少數民族地區。
   b. 使更多女幹部走上各級部門領導崗位有利<u>於</u>我國的社會主義建設。

9:    **,**   This comma would be a period in English. Several examples of Chinese comma usages that differ from English have been examined so far. While further examples will not be discussed in the remaining lessons, it will always be important for you to keep in mind how Chinese use commas.

11: 將 Verb Notice the 將 before the verb here and in l. 49, 59, 64, and 67. What tone does the repeated use of 將 verb give to this article? See 5:2.

12-14: 在 Place 上 Location phrases can be very simple, or they can be lengthy with involved modification structures as is the case here where the Place (歡迎宴會) is modified by a S(舒爾茨) T(中午) 為 X(他) V(舉行) structure. The parameters of a location phrase can usually be determined by finding the head-marker 在, though 在 can be omitted when the location phrase is the first element of a sentence, and by looking for an end-marker such as 上, 下, 中, 外, etc. Though the end-marker is also sometimes omitted, either 在 or the end-marker must be used to indicate a location phrase. Remember, when Place comes before the subject for emphasis, it must be end-marked with a comma as it is in l. 79. See also l. 61 and 69 wherein a location phrase in its normal position after the subject is emphasized by being separated from the verb by a comma. Since location phrases tend to come before the verb and object in Chinese but after them in English, work at developing the skill to notice them but hold them in mind until you have translated the verb and object. Examples are:

a. 在今天的錦標賽中，南京隊以總分 850分居各路健兒之首。
b. 由於大氣污染嚴重，沈阳市在十六個制高點上設立了一些煙塵瞭望哨。

18: X 以來 = 'From X right up to the present' X may be either a specific point in time or an event. This structure is often headed by 自,從, or 自從. The variant form 下來 never has 自, 從 or 自從 at the head. Consider its use in the modification structure at 2:4.

a. 自從三月份以來，我一直都沒看電影。好忙啊！
b. 十多年以來，中美人民的友好往來有增無已。

30-35: 如果 X, 那麼 Y = 'If X, (then) Y' When you see 如果 (or synonyms such as 要是, 假如, 若是, etc.) head a comma unit, expect at least one following comma unit marked by 那麼, 也, 就 or 還. See further comments at 5:25. Examples are:

    a. 如果我錢多點兒，我明年就到中國去旅游。

    b. 假如男女社會地位平等，那麼我們國家就會更順利地發展。

35:   S 是 V 的 This is a more assertive way of saying S V. This pattern allows a point to be made in a more assertive manner, as it does here and in l. 37, 64 and 83. The key to distinguishing this from S 是 T P V O 的 (l. 12-14 and 2:15) is that only a verb comes between the 是 and the 的 in this pattern. See 4:10 for comments on how 是 is used in l. 15 and 68. Examples of the S 是 V 的 structure using vocabulary from previous lessons are:

    a. 我國這次 "長征三號" 火箭發射的成果是非常有意義的。

    b. 王教授提出的問題是不容易回答的。

39-41: 既 [jì] X, 也 Y = 'X is a given, and also Y' The conjunction 既 marks the core verb of the first comma unit in this structure which emphasizes the thematic inter-connectedness of two clauses. The second comma unit will be marked by 又, 也, 且 or a synonym. Two examples are:

    a. 中國婦女既佔人大代表的 21%，也佔人大常委的 9%。

    b. 市政府採取的措施既來得晚，且沒甚麼大的用處。

43-45:   Notice the use the literary pattern X 為 [wèi] Y 而 Verb = 'X(中國人民) verbs(努力) for Y(...國家)' in this sentence. See 3:43 for comments on the less formal pattern X 為 Y Verb phrase.

43:   Subject 正在 Verb = 'Subject is verbing' Variants are S 正 V (l. 45) and S 在 V (l. 73). Using 正 and/or 在 intensifies the progressive aspect of the verb action. 正 focuses on the time element and 在 focuses on the verb action (see the use of 在 at 6:35). They are useful in locating the core verb of a comma unit; though, as always, be thorough and look for a following 的 to determine if the verb structure modifies a noun and is thus not the core verb, as is the case in l. 4 above. Two examples of this pattern are:

    a. 上海環保局正在建立廢水監督管理隊伍。

b. 目前，中美友誼協會<u>正在</u>促進兩國之間的友好往來。

43: <u>地</u> What is the function of <u>地</u> here and in l. 70-71? See 6:36.

55: <u>，</u>   Notice the use of a comma here and in l. 69 and 79 to focus emphasis on the <u>Place</u> which the speaker considers to be the crucial element of the situation. Notice also the similar use of a comma to emphasize the <u>Time</u> element in l. 58 and 61.

76-77: <u>由</u> Is <u>由</u> used for 'from' or 'by' here? See 6:11, 41.

1　吳學謙説中美友好相處有利世界和平
2　　希望中美關係今後有更大發展

3　　　　新華社華盛頓三月七日電
4　（記者施魯佳）正在美國訪問
5　的中國國務委員兼外交部長吳
6　學謙今天在這裡説，中美兩個
7　大國友好相處，互利合作，符
8　合兩國人民的根本利益，也有
9　利於世界和平與穩定，中國方
10　面期望：兩國關係在第二個十
11　年裡，將會得到更大的發展。
12　　　吳學謙外長是在美國國務
13　卿舒爾茨今天中午爲他舉行的
14　歡迎宴會上講這番話的。
15　　　吳學謙説，"今年是中美
16　兩國建交的第十個年頭，回顧
17　過去，展望未來，我對兩國關
18　係的進展懷有信心。建交以來，
19　中美關係取得顯著的進展。

VOCABULARY

1:　吳學謙 [Wú Xuéqiān] '(name of a person)'

1:　相處 [xiāngchǔ] 'getting along with' WG>30: 互相 [hùxiāng] 'mutual'

1:　有利 [yǒulì] 'beneficial to' WG>7: 互利 [hùlì] 'mutually beneficial';
　　　　WG>8: 利益 [lìyì] 'interests'; WG>38: 順利 [shùnlì] 'smooth'

1:　和平 [hépíng] 'peace' WG:>32 平等 [píngděng] 'equality'

2: 發展 [fāzhǎn] 'development, growth' WG>17:展望 [zhǎnwàng]
      'look forward to'; WG>18:進展 [jìnzhǎn] 'progress'

3: 華盛頓 [Huáshèngdùn] 'Washington, D.C.'

5: 國務委員 [guówù wěiyuán] 'member of the State Council'

5: 兼 [jiān] 'hold two positions concurrently'

5: 外交部 [wàijiāobù] 'Ministry of Foreign Affairs' WG>16:建交 [jiànjiāo]
      'establish diplomatic relations'; WG>22: 交流 [jiāoliú] 'exchange';
      WG>59: 邦交 [bāngjiāo] 'relations between nations'

7: 互利 [hùlì] '?' 利 WG:1, 互 WG:20

7: 合作 [hézuò] 'co-operation'; WG>7:符合 [fúhé] 'coincide with'

8: 利益 [lìyì] '?' 利 WG:1

9: V 於 X [Verb yú X] 'verb act applies in the area of X' (SN)

9: 穩定 [wěndìng] 'stability'

10: 期望 [qīwàng] 'hope, expect' 望 WG:17; WG>46:長期 [chángqī] 'long
      term'; WG>69: 期待 [qīdài] 'look forward to'

12: 在 X 上 [zài X shàng] "location phrase markers" (SN)

12: 國務卿 [guówùqīng] 'Secretary of State'

13: 舒爾茨 [Shūěrcí] '(name of a person)'

14: 宴會 [yànhuì] 'banquet' WG>67:會晤 [huìwù] 'meeting'

14: 番 [fān] '(measure word for occurrences)'

16: 建交 [jiànjiāo] '?' 交 WG:5, 建 WG:43

16: 回顧 [huígù] 'review'

17: 展望 [zhǎnwàng] '?' 展 WG:2; 望 WG:10

17: 未來 [wèilái] 'future'

18: 進展 [jìnzhǎn] '?' 展 WG:2

18: 懷有 [huáiyǒu] 'have' WG>44:具有 [jùyǒu] 'possess' WG>65:抱有
      [bàoyǒu] 'embrace'

18: X 以來 X [yǐlái] 'From X to the present' (SN)

19: 顯著 [xiǎnzhù] 'striking'

20　高級領導人的互訪，經濟合作
21　關係，兩國人民之間的來往，
22　以及其他領域的交流與合作不
23　斷增加和擴大。實踐證明，地
24　處太平洋兩岸的中美兩個大國
25　友好相處，互利合作，符合兩
26　國人民的根本利益，也有利於
27　世界和平與穩定。我們一貫認
28　為國家關係的親疏好壞，不取
29　決於社會制度和意識形態的異
30　同。如果雙方嚴格遵循互相尊
31　重主權和領土完整、互不干涉
32　內政的基本原則，在平等互利
33　的基礎上加強往來與合作，那
34　末，我們之間在各個領域發展
35　友好關係是完全可能的。"

VOCABULARY

20: 領導人 [lǐngdǎorén] 'leaders' WG>22:領域 [lǐngyù] 'areas';
　　WG>31:領土 [lǐngtǔ] 'territory'

20: 互訪 [hùfǎng] 'exchange visits' WG>7:互利 [hùlì] 'mutually beneficial';
　　WG>30: 互相 [hùxiāng] 'mutual'

21: 之間 [zhījiān] 'between'

22: 領域 [lǐngyù] '?' 領 WG:20

22: 交流 [jiāoliú] '?' 交 WG:5

22: 不斷 [búduàn] 'without stopping'

23: 擴大 [kuòdà] 'enlarge'; WG>50; 擴張 [kuòzhāng] 'expansionist'

23: 實踐 [shíjiàn] 'practical experience'

23: 證明 [zhèngmíng] 'prove, verify'

23: 地處 [dìchǔ] 'be located at'

24: 太平洋 [Tàipíngyáng] 'Pacific Ocean'

24: 兩岸 [liǎng'àn] 'both shores'

27: 一貫 [yīguàn] 'consistently'

28: 親疏 [qīnshū] 'closeness'

28: 取決 [qǔjué] 'hinge upon'

29: 制度 [zhìdù] 'system'

29: 形態 [xíngtài] 'shape, form'

29: 異同 [yìtóng] 'differences and similarities'

30: 如果 X,那末 Y [rúguǒ X, nàmè Y] 'If X, then Y' (SN)

30: 嚴格 [yángé] 'strict'

30: 遵循 [zūnxún] 'adhere to'

30: 互相 [hùxiāng] '?' 相 WG:1, 互 WG:20

30: 尊重 [zūnzhòng] 'respect'

31: 主權 [zhǔquán] 'sovereignty' WG>51:強權 [qiángquán] 'power'

31: 領土 [lǐngtǔ] '?' 領 WG:20

31: 干涉 [gānshè] 'interfere with'

32: 內政 [nèizhèng] 'domestic politics' WG>50:政策 [zhèngcè] 'policy'; 51:政治 [zhèngzhì] 'politics'

32: 平等 [píngděng] '?' 平 WG:1

33: 那末 [nàme] 'then, in that case' (same as 那麼)

35: S 是 V 的 [S shì V de] "Stronger S V statement" (SN)

36　　　吳學謙認爲，總的説來，
37　近十年中美兩國關係的發展是
38　順利的，但也出現過起伏和波
39　折；兩國關係既蘊藏着巨大的
40　發展潛力，也存在着障礙和困
41　難。
42　　　吳學謙告訴美國朋友，中
43　國人民正在一心一意地爲建設
44　具有中國特色的社會主義現代
45　化國家而努力。正是從這一點
46　出發，我們希望有一個長期的
47　國際和平環境。
48　　　他強調："我們一貫堅持、
49　並將繼續堅持獨立自主的和平
50　外交政策。我們反對侵略擴張
51　政策，反對強權政治，反對干
52　涉別國內政的言行，主張通過
53　和平談判解決國際爭端。"
54　　　吳學謙表示，中國願意在
55　平等互利的基礎上，繼續擴大
56　同世界各國的經濟技術合作和
57　貿易往來。

VOCABULARY

36: 總的説來 [zǒngde shuōlái] 'in summary' (the synonym 總的來説
　　is more common.)

38: 順利 [shùnlì] '?' 利 WG:1

38: 起伏 [qǐfú] 'rise and fall'

38: 波折 [bōzhé] 'twists and turns'

39: 既 X,也 Y [jì X, yě Y] 'Given X, also Y' (SN)

39: 蘊藏 [yùncáng] 'contain'

39: 巨大 [jùdà] 'huge'

40: 潛力 [qiánlì] 'potential' WG>45:努力 [nǔlì] 'work hard'

40: 障礙 [zhàng'ài] 'obstacle'

43: 正在 V [zhèngzài] Verb "verbing" (SN)

43: 建設 [jiànshè] 'build, establish' WG>16:建交 [jiànjiāo]
        'establish diplomatic relations'

44: 具有 [jùyǒu] '?' 有 WG:18

44: 現代化 [xiàndàihuà] 'modernized' WG>59:正常化 [zhèngchánghuà]
        'normalization'

45: 努力 [nǔlì] '?' 力 WG:40

46: 出發 [chūfā] 'set forth from' WG>72:發表 [fābiǎo] 'issue, put forth';
        WG>80:發揮 [fāhuī] 'bring into play'

46: 長期 [chángqī] '?' 期 WG:10

48: 堅持 [jiānchí] 'insist on' WG>75:堅定 [jiāndìng] 'steadfast'; 持 WG:82

49: 獨立 [dúlì] 'independent'

49: 自主 [zìzhǔ] 'self-determination'

50: 政策 [zhèngcè] '?' 政 WG:32

50: 反對 [fǎnduì] 'oppose'

50: 侵略 [qīnlüè] 'aggression'

50: 擴張 [kuòzhāng] '?' 擴 WG:23

51: 強權 [qiángquán] '?' 權 WG:31

51: 政治 [zhèngzhì] '?' 政 WG:32

52: 言行 [yánxíng] 'words and actions'

52: 通過 [tōngguò] 'by means of' (in other contexts could mean 'approve, ratify')

53: 談判 [tánpàn] 'negotiation'

53: 爭端 [zhēngduān] 'dispute, conflict'

56: 技術 [jìshù] 'technology'

58 　　吳學謙說，"今年，中美
59 關係將走完邦交正常化第一個
60 十年的旅程。我們期望，兩國
61 關係在第二個十年裡，將會得
62 到更大的發展。"

63 　　吳學謙說："我相信，我
64 的這次訪問將是成功的。因爲
65 我們雙方都抱有發展中美關係
66 的願望。通過開誠布公的會談
67 和會晤，將加深我們之間的瞭
68 解，這是增進友誼和合作的基
69 礎。我期待，我們在這個基礎
70 上，推動中美關係更加健康、
71 穩定地向前發展。"

72 　　舒爾茨也在宴會上發表了
73 講話。他在談到台灣問題时重
74 申，美國關於只有一個中國的
75 政策是"堅定不移的"。他說，
76 台灣的前途應由海峽兩岸的中
77 國人，而不是由美國來決定。

78 　　舒爾茨還說，在解決世界
79 上的地區性爭端的努力中，中
80 美兩國都可以發揮自己的作用。
81 他認爲，兩國在這些問題上保
82 持對話，"對於維持世界和平
83 和安全是至關重要的"。他說:
84 "美中之間健康而牢固的關係
85 是和平的保障。"

VOCABULARY

59: 邦交 [bāngjiāo] '?' 交 WG:5

59: 正常化 [zhèngchánghuà] '?' 化 WG:44

60: 旅程 [lǔchéng] 'route'

65: 抱有 [bàoyǒu] '?' 有 WG:18

66: 開誠布公 [kāi chéng bù gōng] 'sincere and frank'

67: 會晤 [huìwù] '?' 會 WG:14

67: 加深 [jiāshēn] 'deepen' WG>70:更加 [gèngjiā] 'even more'

68: 友誼 [yǒuyì] 'friendship'

69: 期待 [qīdài] '?' 期 WG:10

70: 推動 [tuīdòng] 'push forward'

70: 更加 [gèngjiā] '?' 加 WG:67

70: 健康 [jiànkāng] 'health'

72: 發表 [fābiǎo] '?' 發 WG:46

73: 台灣 [Táiwān] 'Taiwan'

74: 重申 [chóngshēn] 'reaffirm'

75: 堅定 [jiāndìng] '?' 堅 WG:48

75: 不移 [bùyí] 'unchanging, unbudging'

76: 前途 [qiántú] 'future'

76: 海峽 [hǎixiá] '(ocean) straits'

80: 發揮 [fāhuī] '?' 發 WG:46

80: 作用 [zuòyòng] 'function, role'

81: 保持 [bǎochí] 'maintain' 持 WG:48; WG>82:維持 [wéichí] 'maintain (social structures)'; 保 WG:85

82: 維持 [wéichí] '?' 持 WG:81

83: 至關 [zhìguān] 'most crucial'

84: 牢固 [láogù] 'firm, steadfast'

85: 保障 [bǎozhàng] 'guarantee'; WG>81:保持 [bǎochí] 'maintain (conditions and abstract situations)'

Simplied Character Version of the Main Text

1　　　吴学谦说中美友好相处有利世界和平
2　　　　希望中美关系今后有更大发展

3　　　　　新华社华盛顿三月七日电
4　（记者施鲁佳）正在美国访问
5　的中国国务委员兼外交部长吴
6　学谦今天在这里说，中美两个
7　大国友好相处，互利合作，符
8　合两国人民的根本利益，也有
9　利于世界和平与稳定，中国方
10　面期望：两国关系在第二个十
11　年里，将会得到更大的发展。
12　　　吴学谦外长是在美国国务
13　卿舒尔茨今天中午为他举行的
14　欢迎宴会上讲这番话的。
15　　　吴学谦说，"今年是中美
16　两国建交的第十个年头，回顾
17　过去，展望未来，我对两国关
18　系的进展怀有信心。建交以来，
19　中美关系取得显著的进展。
20　高级领导人的互访，经济合作
21　关系，两国人民之间的来往，
22　以及其他领域的交流与合作不
23　断增加和扩大。实践证明，地
24　处太平洋两岸的中美两个大国
25　友好相处，互利合作，符合两
26　国人民的根本利益，也有利于
27　世界和平与稳定。我们一贯认
28　为国家关系的亲疏好坏，不取
29　决于社会制度和意识形态的异
30　同。如果双方严格遵循互相尊

31　重主权和领土完整、互不干涉
32　内政的基本原则，在平等互利
33　的基础上加强往来与合作，那
34　末，我们之间在各个领域发展
35　友好关系是完全可能的。"
36　　　吴学谦认为，总的说来，
37　近十年中美两国关系的发展是
38　顺利的，但也出现过起伏和波
39　折；两国关系既蕴藏着巨大的
40　发展潜力，也存在着障碍和困
41　难。
42　　　吴学谦告诉美国朋友，中
43　国人民正在一心一意地为建设
44　具有中国特色的社会主义现代
45　化国家而努力。正是从这一点
46　出发，我们希望有一个长期的
47　国际和平环境。
48　　　他强调："我们一贯坚持、
49　并将继续坚持独立自主的和平
50　外交政策。我们反对侵略扩张
51　政策，反对强权政治，反对干
52　涉别国内政的言行，主张通过
53　和平谈判解决国际争端。"
54　　　吴学谦表示，中国愿意在
55　平等互利的基础上，继续扩大
56　同世界各国的经济技术合作和
57　贸易往来。

58 吴学谦说，"今年，中美
59 关系将走完邦交正常化第一个
60 十年的旅程。我们期望，两国
61 关系在第二个十年里，将会得
62 到更大的发展。"

63 吴学谦说："我相信，我
64 的这次访问将是成功的。因为
65 我们双方都抱有发展中美关系
66 的愿望。通过开诚布公的会谈
67 和会晤，将加深我们之间的了
68 解，这是增进友谊和合作的基
69 础。我期待，我们在这个基础
70 上，推动中美关系更加健康、
71 稳定地向前发展。"

72 舒尔茨也在宴会上发表了
73 讲话。他在谈到台湾问题时重
74 申，美国关于只有一个中国的
75 政策是"坚定不移的"。他说，
76 台湾的前途应由海峡两岸的中
77 国人，而不是由美国来决定。

78 舒尔茨还说，在解决世界
79 上的地区性争端的努力中，中
80 美两国都可以发挥自己的作用。
81 他认为，两国在这些问题上保
82 持对话，"对于维持世界和平
83 和安全是至关重要的"。他说：
84 "美中之间健康而牢固的关系
85 是和平的保障。"

GRAMMAR EXERCISES

1. 選擇適當的詞語填空，並把下列的句子翻成英語:

   一) 中國願意_____平等互利的基礎上擴大同世界各國的貿易往來。
        (把、在、於)
   二) 高級領導人的互訪將會有利_____中美關係的進一步進展。
        (於、兼、和)
   三) 如果中美兩國友好相處，_____有利於世界和平。
        (由、就、既)
   四) 中國國務委員_____外交部長吳學謙目前在美國訪問。
        (兼、和、同)
   五) 吳學謙説，中國人民願意一心一意_____推動中美友好關係。
        (得、的、地)

2. 選擇下列詞語填空，並把句子翻成英語: 上、於、如果、在、既、
      以來、是…的

   一) 吳部長認為，兩國關係的好壞不該取決_____社會制度的異同。
   二) 美國國務卿強調，美國_____有"一個中國政策"，台灣問題也
      就不應該由美國方面來決定。
   三) 舒爾茨説，_____美中關係健康而牢固，世界和平就更會有保障。
   四) 他是在美國國務卿為他舉行的歡迎宴會_____講這番話的。
   五) 他説，_____雙方遵循不干涉內政的基礎上，兩國關係一定會
      有進展。
   六) 他在宴會上説，"美中建交_____，美國的政策是「只有一個
      中國」。"

3. 語法練習:用適當的詞語完成句子之後，就把句子翻成英文:
　　將verb、 正在verb、的noun、X使Y verb、X為Y verb、由X verb
　　or 除了X以外,...

一) 吳學謙告訴美國朋友:中國人民正在＿＿＿建設社會主義而
　　努力。
二) 雙方的開誠布公的會談將要＿＿＿我們兩國之間的瞭解加深。
三) 吳部長說：中國方面期望兩國關係＿＿．要有很大的進展。
四) ＿＿＿蘊藏着發展潛力以外，兩國關係也存在着障礙和困難。
五) 台灣的前途應＿＿＿住在海峽兩岸的中國人來決定。
六) 兩國人民的來往＿＿＿兩國之間的關係向前發展。

Some Headlines on US-China Relations

李鵬总理和布什总统举行会谈
就中美关系和国际问题交换意见

外 交 部 发 言 人 说
中国奉行独立自主和平外交政策
批准南太平洋无核区条约二、三号议定书体现上述立场

万里离京出访加拿大美国
姚依林彭冲及加美两国驻华使节前往机场送行

SIGHT READINGS

#1 FORMS OF CHINA-U.S. COOPERATION CAN BE FLEXIBLE AND VARIED

1   李鵬會見尤特時説
2   中美合作方式可以靈活多樣

3   據新華社北京2月3日電 國務院代總理李鵬今天下午
4 在中南海紫光閣會見了美國貿易代表克萊頓・尤特一行。
5   應客人的要求，李鵬着重介紹了中國的改革。他説，
6 "中國的改革已經有了大的方向和藍圖，我們要在改革的
7 大方向的指引下一邊做、一邊補充和完善，不斷前進。"
8   李鵬説，最近有些外國朋友誤認爲中共13大後，中國
9 的改革步子放慢了。其實不然，最近我們除進一步完善企
10 業承包責任制外還正在研究一系列的改革措施。
11   在回答客人們提出的美國能幫助中國做些什麼時，李
12 鵬説，美國擁有發達的技術和先進的企業管理經驗，美國
13 可以向中國傳授企業管理經驗和轉讓技術。這樣做不會給
14 美國構成危害。他説，中國可以爲美國提供大量加工部件
15 和產品，合作方式可以靈活多樣。
16   尤特説，美國和美國人民對中國和中國人民懷有友好
17 的情意，這是美中關係的重要方面。美國願意向中國介紹
18 先進管理經驗。

VOCABULARY

1: 李鵬 [Lǐ Péng] '(name of a person)'
1: 尤特 [Yóutè] '(name of a foreigner; see line 4)'
2: 方式 [fāngshì] 'pattern, style'
2: 靈活 [línghuó] 'flexible'
3: 代總理 [dàizǒnglǐ] 'Acting Prime Minister'
4: 中南海 [Zhōngnánhǎi] 'Zhongnanhai Park (Beijing)'

4: 紫光閣 [Zǐguānggé] 'Purple Rays Pavilion'

4: 克萊頓・尤特 [Kèláidùn Yóutè] '(personal name)'

5: 應要求 [yìng yāoqiú] 'respond to a request'

5: 着重 [zhuózhòng] 'emphasize'

6: 藍圖 [lántú] 'blue print'

7: 指引 [zhǐyǐn] 'direction'

7: 補充 [bǔchōng] 'supplement'

7: 不斷 [búduàn] 'without stopping'

8: 誤 [wù] 'mistakenly'

8: 十三大 [Shísān Dà] '(abbr. for 十三屆人民代表大會) 13th National People's Congress'

9: 其實不然 [qíshí bùrán] 'reality is to the contrary'

10: 承包 [chéngbāo] 'contract'

10: 責任制 [zérènzhì] 'responsibility system'

10: 系列 [xìliè] 'series'

12: 擁有 [yǒngyǒu] 'possess'

12: 先進 [xiānjìn] 'advanced'

13: 傳授 [chuánshòu] 'pass on'

13: 轉讓 [zhuǎnràng] 'transfer'

14: 構成 [gòuchéng] 'constitute'

14: 危害 [wēihài] 'harm'

14: 提供 [tígōng] 'supply, provide'

14: 部件 [bùjiàn] 'components'

17: 情意 [qíngyì] 'sentiment'

QUESTIONS

A. What did Li Peng say about reforms in paragraph #2?

B. Why did Li Peng say 其實不然 in the third paragraph?

C. What two items does Li especially hope to get from the US?

D. What impressions are given in l. 5, 11 and 16-18?

E. What did the American say about American feelings for China?

#2 WE PROTEST U.S. INTERFERENCE IN OUR TIBETAN AFFAIRS

1 　　　　　　朱啓禎約見美駐華大使洛德
2 　　　　就美國會粗暴干涉我西藏事務
3 　　　　向美政府表示強烈不滿和抗議

4 　　　新華社北京十二月十一日電　外交部副部長朱啓禎十
5 二月十日約見美國駐華大使洛德，就美國國會參、眾兩院
6 聯席會議十二月三日通過所謂"中華人民共和國在西藏侵
7 犯人權"的修正案，向美國政府表示強烈不滿和抗議。
8 　　　朱啓禎指出，"修正案"打着維護西藏人權的幌子，
9 歪曲事實真象，對中國政府和中國人民進行誣蔑和誹謗，
10 粗暴干涉中國內政。
11 　　　他説,西藏自古以來就是中國領土不可分割的一部分，
12 藏族人民是中華民族大家庭的一個成員，任何有關西藏的
13 問題完全是中國的內部事物，外國無權干涉。
14 　　　他強調説，互相尊重主權和領土完整，互不干涉內政
15 是中美雙方一致同意的指導兩國關係的根本原則。只有切
16 實做到互不干涉內政，中美關係才能順利發展。他説，中
17 國政府強烈要求美國政府採取措施制止這一干涉中國內政
18 的事件進一步發展，並防止此類損害中美關係的事情再次
19 發生。

VOCABULARY

1: 朱啓禎 [Zhū Qǐzhēn] '(name of a person)'

1: 約見 [yuējiàn] 'see (officially)'

1: 駐　[zhù] 'be stationed at'

1: 大使 [dàshǐ] 'ambassador'

1: 洛德 [Luòdé] '(name of a foreigner)'

2: 美國會 [Měi Guóhuì] 'US Congress'

2: 粗暴 [cūbào] 'crudely'

2: 西藏 [Xīzàng] 'Tibet'

3: 抗議 [kàngyì] 'protest'

5: 參 [cān] '(abbr. for 參議院) US Senate'

5: 眾 [zhòng] '(abbr. for 眾議院) US House of Representatives.'

6: 聯席 [liánxí] 'joint'

6: 侵犯 [qīnfàn] 'violate'

7: 修正案 [xiūzhèng'àn] 'admendment'

8: 打···幌子 [dǎ...huǎngzi] 'under the pretense of ...'

9: 歪曲 [wāiqǔ] 'twist'

9: 誣蔑 [wūmiè] 'smear'

9: 誹謗 [fěibàng] 'slander'

11: 分割 [fēn'gé] 'cut apart'

12: 成員 [chéngyuán] 'member'

13: 無權 [wúquán] 'have no rights'

14: 完整 [wánzhěng] 'integrity'

15: 一致 [yīzhì] 'consistently, uniformly'

15: 指導 [zhǐdǎo] 'guide'

16: 切實 [qièshí] 'earnestly'

17: 制止 [zhìzhǐ] 'curb, stop'

18: 防止 [fángzhǐ] 'prevent'

18: 損害 [sǔnhài] 'damage'

QUESTIONS

A. What form does the Chinese protest take in the first paragraph?

B. What specific action is protested in the first paragraph?

C. What problems do the Chinese see with the Congressional admendment?

D. What Chinese attitudes towards Tibet are mentioned in paragraph 3?

E. What specific words, especially verbs, give an impression of China's attitude towards this matter?

(See Lesson 12.3, page 218 for a related story)

海峽兩岸

Reading Chinese Newspapers:
Tactics and Skills

Lesson Eight: Relations with Taiwan

人 民 日 報（海外版）

1987年12月1日 星期二 第五版

嚴厲抨擊台少數人搞台獨行為

《瞭望》週刊發表署名文章

新華社北京電 十一月二十八日出版的《瞭望》週刊發表署名文章，嚴厲抨擊台灣少數人主張"台獨"。文章指出，搞"台獨"背離全國人民意願，無異飲鴆止渴。

文章說，自去年夏季以來，類似台獨的"自決"論調，開始逐步升級。去年九月底，民進黨一成立就將"自決"論加以改綱化，把所謂"住民自決"的主張列入該黨黨綱。在去年十二月底和今年十月底，民進黨常委謝長廷利用兩次"台獨黨綱大辯論"的機會，公開系統地"暢論自決獨立"。不久前，有的民進黨籍"立委"在"立法院"的施政總質詢中，公然鼓吹"承認台灣獨立已經成立於中國之外的一個"新而獨立的國家"。最近，更有人公開打着主張台獨的標語遊行。民進黨內有相當一部分人甚至要將台獨主張政綱化，提出把"人民有主張台灣獨立"的自由 列入該黨的"黨綱行動綱領；此一意見雖然通到台決，但還是要進了該黨第二次代表大會通過的決議。

文章指出，種種迹象表明，台灣確有少數人頭腦發脹，將台獨言行逐步升級，把鼓吹"台灣獨立"作為個人權力和利益的手段。他們企圖利用台灣民眾渴望民主，希望台灣有個光明前途的情緒，鑽台灣社會所謂"轉型期"的空檔，把"台灣獨立"的主張強加於台灣民眾。

文章認為，台灣同胞曾長期遭帝國主義的殖民統治，當怕了"二等公民"，懷有真正做國家主人的強烈願望，又由於不少台胞不滿於台灣的政治現狀，對祖國大陸感到隔膜，在國外對台灣前途感到彷徨，在國外勢力及少數煽惑之下，有些人產生了編與煽惑之下，有些人產生了政治幻想，有"台灣獨立"的思想傾向。"我們要嚴格地將這部分台胞與極少數主張台獨的野心分子區別開來，同時也要將某些一時的言詞或情緒渲泄，與那些系統地或一貫地主張台獨的言行加以區分。

文章說，台灣當局一方面在反對台獨，另一方面又在助長台獨，或者說是以"治標養本"的辦法對待台獨，比如，台灣當局雖然一再強調"中國只有一個，台灣是中國的一部分"，堅決反對"兩個中國"及"一中一台"；但在實際行動上又鼓吹海峽兩岸是"兩個政治實體"，台灣要有獨立的主權和國際人格，主張把台灣返回國國際化，要求國際社會把台灣視做"一個"國家"，搞什麼"革新保台"，以種種借口維持兩岸之間的分裂現狀，並企圖使這種分裂狀態他固化，長期化。這些做法與台胞份子的所謂"台灣與中國分離可以避免中共併吞的攻擊"等叫器，實在難分左右。

文章指出，要真正解決台獨問題，治本的辦法，或者說金底抽薪的辦法，就是全面開放兩岸間的正常往來，實現"三通"，並進而促進祖國的和平統一。至於島內台獨絕狀態的一時高漲，那不過是少數人對於兩岸開始突破隔絕狀態的一種異常反應。隨着兩岸"三通"的實現及和平統一事業的逐漸發展，所謂"台獨意識"也必將逐漸式微以致消亡。

台灣一週動態

（十一月二十二至二十八日）

由地區"居住五年減縮爲兩年，以適應形勢發展的需要。

△據台灣《中國時報》二十四日報道，台北市議員林文郎二十三日呼籲成立台灣海峽事務協調會，以因應開放親友探親後所衍生的民、主委。

補在開放探親後的第一個月受理案件可超過逾一萬五千件。

△據台灣《中央日報》二十六日報道，國民黨中常會二十五日通過由馬頓方出任國民黨台灣省委會主委。

我將在港舉辦技術

本報香港十一月二十九日貿易部主辦的"中國技術出口？月四日至十三日在香港展覽中？這次交易會曲內地員有技？

香港臨官四

物業市道仍然穩定 高價成交

反映了香港地

STRUCTURE NOTES (Line numbers here refer to the original text.)

1:   《...》 What does this set of punctuation markers signify? See 3:7.

2: In this headline 台少數人 is used both as the object of the verb 抨擊 and as the subject of 搞.

4:   " " are used to mark that the words they enclose are used for a special meaning, see 6:6. Here they imply that linking 台 'Taiwan' and 獨 'independence' is not usual, and thus suggest that it is not right. Similarly in l. 6, the use of " " indicates that 自 'self' and 決 'determination' do not properly belong together in this context. What is implied by placing 國家 in " " in l. 39?

7: 一 Verb 1, 就 Verb 2 = 'As soon as/whenever verb 1, then verb 2' This structure is used to indicate the sequential nature of a set of verb acts. .Whenever you see 一 before a verb, expect this pattern. Look for 就 (or a synonym) to mark the core verb of the second comma unit.   Examples are:
  a. 中美政府一建交，兩國之間的友好往來就增多了。
  b. 廣州市一建立了廢水排放管理局，飲水污染率就下降了。

7-9: 將 Object/把 Object This text has an unusual number and variety of 將/把 Object structures, see 2:28 and 5:32 for comments on 把 and 將. These two lines have an alternation of 將 O and 把 O, as do lines 17-18. There are simple 將 O structures in l. 14, 30 and 31-32; see the comparable use of 把 O in l. 38. Compare these with the more complicated 把 O usages in l. 14 and 20. Note the 把 O1 Verb 為 O2 in l. 18 and 39. What is the use of 將 in l. 50?

9: 和 Be careful to distinguish the use of 和 to link two time phrases here from its use as the vocabulary item 和平 in l. 44. See comments at 6:9.

10: ...地 [dě] Verb What is the function of 地 here? see 6:37.

12: 為 [wéi] When in the second tone, 為 has usages different from its fourth tone use in the patterns X 為 Y Verb phrase (3:34) and 為了 X Vp (3:43) and in vocabulary such as 認為 (l. 22). One use of [wéi] is in written texts as a synonym of 是 'to be' (X 是 Y 4:10), as it is in this line: "...台灣為已經獨立於中國之外的一個'新而獨立的國家'" "Taiwan is a 'new and independent nation' that is independent from China." 為 can also be translated as 'considered to be, act as.' This value is frequently seen in the pattern 以 X 為 Y = 'take X to be Y'. [wéi] is also used for this meaning as a verb suffix, verb 為 X = 'verb it to be X'; e.g., 作為 l. 18 and 視為 in l. 39. This usage frequently occurs in the pattern S 把 O1 Verb 為 O2 'subject verbs O1 so that it is O2', see l. 18 and 39. [wéi] also has an infrequent use as a passive marker in X 為 Y (所) V = 'X was verbed by Y.' See this use in the sentences at 10:SR2.7 and 11:2.

　　a. "雙向開放" 為我國發展少數民族地區的新政策。
　　b. 煤煙污染為一個嚴重社會問題。

12: Verb 於 What is the function of 於 here? See 7:9.

13: Verb 1 着 [zhě], verb 2 = 'Do verb 2 while doing verb 1' This structure indicates two concurrent verb actions. Note that English usually structures this with Verb 2 placed before Verb 1. 着 is also used to mark that a single verb act is in the process of happening; in this usage it is sometimes found in conjunction with the 正在 Verb pattern (7:43). Except when it is part of a word such as 着重 [zhuózhòng] or 着急 [zháojí], a verb always precedes 着, which makes it a very handy marker for finding core verbs. For example:

　　a. 中國婦女遭受着各種歧視仍要為繁衍後代盡社會責任。
　　b. 少數民族地區靠着中央實施邊境經濟發展戰略。

15: ; marks a break in grammatical structures, though there is a continuity in the theme of the sentence. Remember this function of ; and you will always have one more tool to help you find the basic boundaries between grammatical structures.

15-16: 雖然 X, 但(是) Y = 'Even though X, Y' If you remember that 雖然 marks the first clause and 但是 (or a synonym such as 可是 or 不過) generally marks the second clause, you will be able to see the relationship of the comma units in which they appear, even when in lengthy sentences such as lines 35-40 below. In 雖然 X, X will be a factual situation; in 即使 [jíshǐ] X, 'even though X,' X is a hypothetical situation. See 5:25 for comments on translating tandem clauses such as these. 儘管 [jǐnguǎn] X, 但 Y 9:8 is a literary synonym of 雖然.

17: 種種 = 'All types of, all kinds of' Duplicated measures (and some nouns) mean 'all of, each one of the measure/noun'. Examples are:

   a. 屆屆全運會規模都很大，有各種比賽。
   b. 最近人人天天都贊賞中國航天工業的巨大成果。

22: 曾 [céng] Verb = 'Verb (did happen)' Writers use 曾(經) to mark that the verb act did indeed occur (much) earlier, but has ceased. The verb is often followed by 過 or 了. 曾(經) is best translated in the English past tense or sometimes as 'used to V.' Compare this with 已經 [yǐjīng] Verb which marks a verb situation completed in the very recent past, one which might be continuing. Since 曾 is placed directly at the head of the verb phrase, it is very useful in locating the core verb of comma units and sentences. Examples are:

   a. 中國男籃隊曾經擊敗老對手菲律賓隊。
   b. 中國外交部長和美國國務卿曾商談到美國的「只有一個中國」
     政策。

23: 又 Verb What function and connotative value does 又 have here and in line 37? See 2:2.

34: 一方面 X, 一方面 Y What meaning does this pattern convey? See 4:35.

35: 以 X, Verb Object What is 以 used for here and in l. 41 below? See 2:14.

39: <u>(X), 讓 [ràng] Y Verb Object</u> = '(X) causes/allows Y to verb the object' 讓 often conveys an element of desire for <u>Y</u> to do the verb. Compare this with the more neutral <u>X 使</u> [shǐ] Y V O in l. 41 and 4:26. Examples are:

    a. 全國婦聯主席講這番話的目的是<u>讓</u>人人都認識到姐妹們付出的代價。

    b. 國際政治現狀<u>讓</u>美中的合作取得顯著的進展。

41: <u>並</u> Clause   What specific function does 並 have at the head of a comma unit? See 4:22. How does this compare with its use before a negative adverb such as <u>不</u> or <u>沒</u>? See 2:35.

1　　　　　　　《瞭望》週刊發表署名文章
2　　　　嚴厲抨擊台少數人搞台獨行為

3　　　　新華社北京電　十一月二十八日出版的《瞭望》週刊發表
4　署名文章，嚴厲抨擊台灣少數人主張"台獨"。文章指出，搞
5　"台獨"背離全國人民意願，"無異飲鴆止渴"。
6　　　　文章說，自去年夏季以來，類似台獨的"自決"論調，開
7　始逐步升級。去年九月底，民進黨一成立就將"自決"論加以
8　政綱化，把所謂"住民自決"的主張列入該黨黨綱。在去年十
9　二月底和今年十月底，民進黨常委謝長廷利用兩次"台灣前途
10　大辯論"的機會，公開系統地"暢論自決獨立"。不久前，

VOCABULARY

1: 瞭望 [Liàowàng] 'Lookout (Magazine)' WG>20: 渴望 [kěwàng] 'thirst for'

1: 週刊 [zhōukān] 'weekly publication'

1: 署名文章 [shǔmíng wénzhāng] 'signed article'

2: 嚴厲 [yánlì] 'severe, strict' WG>28: 嚴格 [yángé] 'rigorous'

2: 抨擊 [pēngjī] 'attack (in writing)' WG>41: 攻擊 [gōngjī] 'attack'

2: 台　[Tái] '(abbr. for 台灣) Taiwan' WG>2: 台獨 [táidú] '(abbr. for
　　　台灣獨立運動) Taiwan Independence Movement'

2: 搞　[gǎo] 'engage in, mess around at'

5: 背離 [bèilí] 'deviate from' WG>41: 分離 [fēnlí] 'separate'

5: 人民 [rénmín] 'the people' WG>5: 民進黨 [Mínjìndǎng] (abbr. for 民主
　　　進步黨) 'Democratic Progressive Party' ('DPP'); WG>8: 住民
　　　[zhùmín] 'inhabitants'; WG>20: 民眾 [mínzhòng] 'populace'; WG>20:
　　　民主 [mínzhǔ] 'democracy'; WG>23:殖民 [zhímín] 'colonists'; WG>24:
　　　公民 [gōngmín] 'citizens'

5: 無異 [wúyì] 'not different from' WG>47: 異常 [yìcháng] 'abnormal'

5: 飲鴆止渴 [yǐn zhèn zhǐ kě] 'seek relief regardless of the consequences'
      (lit: "drink poisoned wine to stop thirst")

6: 夏季 [xiàjì] 'summer'

6: 類似 [lèisì] 'analogous, similar'

6: 自決 [zìjué] 'self determination' WG>15:自由 [zìyóu] 'freedom'

6: 論調 [lùndiào] '(invalid) argument' WG>10:大辯論 [dàbiànlùn] 'debate'

7: 逐步 [zhúbù] 'step by step' WG>49:逐漸 [zhújiàn] 'little by little'

7: 升級 [shēngjí] 'escalate'

7: 底   [X dǐ] 'at the end of X'

7: 民進黨 [Mínjìndǎng] '?' 民 WG:5, 黨 WG:8

7: 一 V [yī Verb] 'as soon as/whenever V1, then V2' (SN)

8: 政綱 [zhènggāng] 'political program' WG>11:施政 [shīzhèng]
      'administration'; WG>8:黨綱 [dǎnggāng] 'party platform'; WG>15:
      綱領 [gānglǐng] 'guiding principles'

8: 化   [huà] '-ize' 政綱化 [zhènggānghuà] 'transform into a political platform';
      WG>39:國際化 [guójìhuà] 'internationalize';WG>42:固定化 [gùdìng
      huà] 'regularize'; WG>42:長期化 [chángqīhuà] 'make long-term'

8: 住民 [zhùmín] '?' 民 WG:5

8: 列入 [lièrù] 'put on a list'

9: 常委 [chángwěi] 'member of standing committee'

9: 謝長廷 [Xiè Chángtíng] '(name of a person)'

9: 利用 [lìyòng] 'utilize, take advantage of'; WG>18: 利益 [lìyì] 'benefit'

10: 大辯論 [dàbiànlùn] '?' 論 WG:6

10: 公開 [gōngkāi] 'publicly' WG>11:公然 [gōngrán] 'publicly';WG>44:和平
      共存 [hépíng gòngcún] 'peaceful co-existence'; WG>23公民
      [gōngmín] 'citizens'

10: 系統 [xìtǒng] 'systematically' WG>23: 統治 [tǒngzhì] 'govern'

10: 暢   [chàng] 'without hesitation'

10: 獨立 [dúlì] 'independence' 台 WG:2; WG>11:立委 [lìwěi] '(abbr. for 立法
      委員) legislator'; WG>11:立法院 [Lìfǎyuàn] 'Legislative Branch (of
      ROC government)'; WG>31: 立場 [lìchǎng] 'stand, views'

11 有的民進黨黨籍"立委"在"立法院"的施政總質詢中，公然
12 鼓吹"承認台灣為已經獨立於中國之外的一個'新而獨立的國
13 家'"。最近，更有人公開打着主張台獨的標語遊行。民進黨
14 內有相當一部分人甚至要將台獨主張政綱化，提出把"人民有
15 主張台灣獨立的自由"列入該黨的"黨綱行動綱領"；此一意
16 見雖然遭到否決，但還是寫進了該黨第二次代表大會通過的決
17 議。

18 　　文章指出，種種跡象表明，台灣確有少數人頭腦發脹，將
19 台獨言行逐步升級，把鼓吹"台灣獨立"作為個人權力和利益
20 的手段。他們企圖利用台灣民眾渴望民主，希望台灣有個光明
21 前途的情緒，鑽台灣社會所謂"轉型期"的空檔，把"台灣獨
22 立"的主張強加於台灣民眾。

VOCABULARY

11: X 籍 [X-jí] 'have membership in X'

11: 立委 [lìwěi] '?' 立 WG:10

11: 立法院 [Lìfǎyuàn] '?' 立 WG:10

11: 施政 [shīzhèng] '?' 政 WG:8

11: 質詢 [zhìxún] 'hearings'

11: 公然 [gōngrán] '?' 公 WG:10, 仍 WG:38

12: 鼓吹 [gǔchuī] 'preach, advocate'

12: 承認 [chéngrèn] 'admit, recognize'

12: 為 [wéi] 'to be' (SN)

13: V1 着,V2 [Verb 1 zhě, Verb 2] 'Do verb 2 while doing verb 1'

13: 標語 [biāoyǔ] 'slogan' WG>33: 治標 [zhìbiāo] 'eliminate outward signs'

13: 遊行 [yóuxíng] 'parade, march'

14: 甚至 [shènzhì] 'even so far as'

15: 自由 [zìyóu] '?' 自 WG:6

15: 綱領 [gānglǐng] '?' 綱 WG:8

15: 遭到 [zāodào] 'suffer, encounter' WG>23:遭受 [zāoshòu] 'be subjected to'

16: 否決 [fǒujué] 'veto' WG>16:決議 [juéyì] 'resolution'; WG>34: 堅決 [jiānjué] 'resolutely'; WG>44:解決 [jiějué] 'resolve'

16: 決議 [juéyì] '?' 決 WG:16

18: M M   Measure Measure "each one of the measure" (SN)

18: 跡象 [jīxiàng] 'signs, indications'

18: 表明 [biǎomíng] 'manifest clearly' WG>20:光明 [guāngmíng] 'brilliant'

18: 確   [què] 'truly'

18: 頭腦 [tóunǎo] 'brains, head'

18: 發脹 [fāzhàng] 'swell, bloat' WG>48:發展 [fāzhǎn] 'develop'

19: 權力 [quánlì] 'power, right' WG>28:勢力 [shìlì] 'influence'

19: 利益 [lìyì] '?' 利 WG:9

20: 手段 [shǒuduàn] 'tactic, ploy'

20: 企圖 [qìtú] 'seek to, plot'

20: 民眾 [mínzhòng] '?' 民 WG:5

20: 渴望 [kěwàng] '?' 望 WG:1

20: 民主 [mínzhǔ] '?' 民 WG:5

20: 光明 [guāngmíng] '?' 明 WG:18

21: 情緒 [qíngxù] 'sentiment'

21: 鑽   [zuān] 'burrow into'

21: 轉型 [zhuǎn xíng] 'transitional'

21: 空檔 [kòngdàng] 'empty spot'

22: 強加於 [qiángjiāyú] 'impose upon' WG>24:強烈 [qiángliè] 'intense'

23　　　文章認爲，台灣同胞曾長期遭受帝國主義的殖民統治，當
24　怕了"二等公民"，懷有真正做國家主人的強烈願望；又由於
25　不少台胞不滿於台灣的政治現狀，對祖國大陸又缺乏瞭解，對
26　台灣前途感到徬徨，在國外勢力及少數別有用心分子的欺騙與
27　煽惑之下，有些人產生了政治幻想，有"台灣獨立"的思想傾
28　向。"我們要嚴格地將這部分台胞與極少數頑固主張台獨的野
29　心分子區別開來；同時也要將某些一時的言詞或情緒宣洩與那
30　些系統地或一貫地主張台獨的言行加以區分。"
31　　　　文章同時還批評了台灣當局對待台獨的立場。文章説，台
32　灣當局一方面在反對台獨，另一方面又在助長台獨；或者説是
33　以"治標養本"的辦法對待台獨。比如，台灣當局雖然一再強
34　調"中國只有一個，台灣是中國的一部分"，堅決反對"兩個
35　中國"及"一中一台"；但在實際行動上又鼓吹 海峽兩岸是

VOCABULARY

23: 同胞 [tóngbāo] 'compatriots' WG>25: 台胞 [Táibāo] 'Taiwan compatriots'

23: 曾 V [céng Verb] "verb act did happen" (SN)

23: 遭受 [zāoshòu] '?' 遭 WG:16

23: 帝國主義 [dìguó zhǔyì] 'imperialism'

23: 殖民 [zhímín] '?' 民 WG:5

23: 統治 [tǒngzhì] '?' 統 WG:10

24: 二等 [èrděng] 'second class'

24: 公民 [gōngmín] '?' 民 WG:5, 公 WG:10

24: 強烈 [qiángliè] '?' 強 WG:22

25: 台胞 [táibāo] '?' 胞 WG:23

25: 不滿 [bùmǎn] 'dissatisfied'

25: 現狀 [xiànzhuàng] 'present condition' WG>40: 狀態 [zhuàngtài] 'condition'

25: 大陸 [dàlù] 'Mainland China'

25: 缺乏 [quēfá] 'lack'

26: 感到 [gǎndào] 'feel (emotionally)'

26: 徬徨 [pánghuáng] 'hesitation'

26: 勢力 [shìlì] '?' 力 WG:19

26: 別有用心 [biéyǒu yòngxīn] 'have ulterior motives'

26: 欺騙 [qīpiàn] 'deceit'

27: 煽惑 [shānhuò] 'agitation'

27: 幻想 [huànxiǎng] 'illusion'

28: 傾向 [qīngxiàng] 'inclination'

28: 嚴格 [yángé] '?' 嚴 WG:2, 格 WG:36

28: 頑固 [wángù] 'stubborn' 固 WG:40

28: 野心 [yěxīn] 'wild ambition'

29: 區別 [qūbié] 'distinguish' WG>30: 區分 [qūfēn] 'differences'

29: 同時 [tóngshí] 'simultaneously' WG>29: 一時 [yīshí] 'momentary'

29: 某　　[mǒu] 'a certain person, unnamed someone'

29: 一時 [yīshí] '?' 時 WG:29, 一 WG:30

29: 渲洩 [xuānxiè] 'outbursts'

30: 一貫 [yīguàn] 'consistently' WG>29: 一時 [yīshí] 'momentary';
　　　　WG>35: 一再 [yīzài] 'time and time again'

30: 區分 [qūfēn] '?' 區 WG:29

31: 批評 [pīpíng] 'criticize'

31: 對待 [duìdài] 'handle, treat' WG>32: 反對 [fǎnduì] 'oppose'

31: 当局 [dāngjú] 'authorities'

31: 立場 [lìchǎng] '?' 立 WG:10

32: 反對 [fǎnduì] '?' 對 WG:31, 反 WG:47

32: 助長 [zhùzhǎng] 'abet, foster'

33: 治標 [zhìbiāo] '?' 標 WG:13

33: 養本 [yǎngběn] 'nurture the roots'

33: 一再 [yīzài] '?' 一 WG:30

34: 堅決 [jiānjué] '?' 決 WG:16

35: 實際 [shíjì] 'real, actual' WG>36: 實體 [shítǐ] 'entity'; 際 WG:39;
　　　　WG>45: 實現 [shíxiàn] 'achieve, realize'

35: 海峽 [hǎixiá] '(ocean) straits'

36　　"兩個政治實體"，台灣要有獨立的主權和國際人格，主張把
37　台灣問題國際化，要求國際社會把台灣視爲一個"國家"，讓
38　台灣重返國際社會，等等。特別是台灣當局迄今仍然僵持"三
39　不"，搞什麼"革新保台"，以種種借口維持兩岸之間的分裂
40　現狀，並企圖使這種分裂狀態固定化、長期化。這些作法與台
41　獨分子的所謂"台灣與中國分離可以避免中共的攻擊，可以重
42　返國際社會，也可以與中共談判和平共存"等叫囂，實在難分
43　左右。

44　　　文章指出，要真正解決台獨問題，治本的辦法，或者說釜
45　底抽薪的辦法,就是全面開放兩岸間的正常往來,實現"三通"，
46　並進而促進祖國的和平統一。 至於島內台獨言論之一時高漲，
47　那不過是少數人對於兩岸開始突破隔絕狀態的一種異常反應。
48　隨着兩岸"三通"的實現及和平統一事業的逐漸發展，所謂
49　"台獨意識"也必將逐漸式微以致湮沒。

VOCABULARY

36: 實體 [shítǐ] '?' 實 WG:35

36: 人格 [rén'gé] 'status' 格 WG:28

37: 國際化 [guójìhuà] '?' 化 WG:8, 際 WG:35

37: 讓 Y Vp [ràng Y Verb phrase] 'allow Y to verb phrase' (SN)

38: 重返 [chóngfǎn] 'return'

38: 等等 [děngděng] 'et cetera'

38: 迄今 [qìjīn] 'up to the present'

38: 仍然 [réngrán] 'still' 然 WG:11

38: 僵持 [jiāngchí] 'stubbornly maintain' WG>39: 維持 [wéichí] 'maintain'

39: 三不 [sānbù] 'Three Nevers' (ROC policy of 不接觸 'No Contacts',
　　　　不談判 'No Discussions', 不妥協 'No Compromise' with the PRC)

39: 革新保台 [géxīn bǎoTái] 'renew and protect Taiwan'

39: 借口 [jièkǒu] 'excuse'

39: 維持 [wéichí] '?' 持 WG:38

39: 分裂 [fēnliè] 'split apart' WG>41: 分離 [fēnlí] 'separate'

40: 狀態 [zhuàngtài] '?' 壯 WG:25

40: 固定化 [gùdìnghuà] '?' 化 WG:8, 固 WG:28

40: 長期化 [chángqīhuà] '?' 化 WG:8

41: 分離 [fēnlí] '?' 離 WG:5, 分 :39

41: 避免 [bìmiǎn] 'avoid'

41: 攻擊 [gōngjī] '?' 擊 WG:2

42: 談判 [tánpàn] 'negotiate'

42: 和平共存 [hépíng gòngcún] 'peaceful co-existence'

42: 叫囂 [jiàoxiāo] 'clamorings'

44: 解決 [jiějué] '?' 決 WG:16

44: 釜底抽薪 [fǔdǐ chōuxīn] 'take drastic measures' (lit: "take firewood
         from beneath the cauldron")

45: 正常 [zhèngcháng] 'normal' 常 WG:47

45: 實現 [shíxiàn] '?' 實 WG:35

45: 三通 [sāntōng] 'Three Openings' (Policy of 通郵 'Mail', 通航 'Travel',
         and 通商 'Commerce' contacts between Taiwan and the Mainland.)

46: 島內 [dǎo nèi] 'on the island (of Taiwan)'

46: 高漲 [gāozhàng] 'upsurge'

47: 不過是 [búguòshì] 'is nothing more than'

47: 突破 [tūpò] 'break through'

47: 隔絕 [géjué] 'completely cut off'

47: 異常 [yìcháng] '?' 異 WG:5

47: 反應 [fǎnyìng] 'reaction' 反 WG:32

48: 逐漸 [zhújiàn] '?' 逐 WG:7

48: 發展 [fāzhǎn] '?' 發 WG:18

49: 式微 [shìwēi] 'decline'

49: 以致 [yǐzhì] 'with the result that'

49: 湮沒 [yānmò] 'fall into oblivion'

Simplified Character Version of the Main Text

1   《了望》周刊发表署名文章
2   严厉抨击台少数人搞台独行为

3   新华社北京电　十一月二十八日出版的《了望》周刊发表
4   署名文章，严厉抨击台湾少数人主张"台独"。文章指出，搞
5   "台独"背离全国人民意愿，"无异饮鸩止渴"。
6   文章说，自去年夏季以来，类似台独的"自决"论调，开
7   始逐步升级。去年九月底，民进党一成立就将"自决"论加以
8   政纲化，把所谓"住民自决"的主张列入该党党纲。在去年十
9   二月底和今年十月底，民进党常委谢长廷利用两次"台湾前途
10 大辩论"的机会，公开系统地"畅论自决独立"。不久前，
11 有的民进党党籍"立委"在"立法院"的施政总质询中，公然
12 鼓吹"承认台湾为已经独立于中国之外的一个'新而独立的国
13 家'"。最近，更有人公开打着主张台独的标语游行。民进党
14 内有相当一部分人甚至要将台独主张政纲化，提出把"人民有
15 主张台湾独立的自由"列入该党的"党纲行动纲领"；此一意
16 见虽然遭到否决，但还是写进了该党第二次代表大会通过的决
17 议。
18   文章指出，种种迹象表明，台湾确有少数人头脑发胀，将
19 台独言行逐步升级，把鼓吹"台湾独立"作为个人权力和利益
20 的手段。他们企图利用台湾民众渴望民主，希望台湾有个光明
21 前途的情绪，钻台湾社会所谓"转型期"的空档，把"台湾独
22 立"的主张强加于台湾民众。
23   文章认为，台湾同胞曾长期遭受帝国主义的殖民统治，当
24 怕了"二等公民"，怀有真正做国家主人的强烈愿望；又由于
25 不少台胞不满于台湾的政治现状，对祖国大陆又缺乏了解，对
26 台湾前途感到彷徨，在国外势力及少数别有用心分子的欺骗与

27 煽惑之下，有些人产生了政治幻想，有"台湾独立"的思想倾
28 向。"我们要严格地将这部分台胞与极少数顽固主张台独的野
29 心分子区别开来；同时也要将某些一时的言词或情绪宣泄与那
30 些系统地或一贯地主张台独的言行加以区分。"
31 文章同时还批评了台湾当局对待台独的立场。文章说，台
32 湾当局一方面在反对台独，另一方面又在助长台独；或者说是
33 以"治标养本"的办法对待台独。比如，台湾当局虽然一再强
34 调"中国只有一个，台湾是中国的一部分"，坚决反对"两个
35 中国"及"一中一台"；但在实际行动上又鼓吹 海峡两岸是
36 "两个政治实体"，台湾要有独立的主权和国际人格，主张把
37 台湾问题国际化，要求国际社会把台湾视为一个"国家"，让
38 台湾重返国际社会，等等。特别是台湾当局迄今仍然僵持"三
39 不"，搞什么"革新保台"，以种种借口维持两岸之间的分裂
40 现状，并企图使这种分裂状态固定化、长期化。这些作法与台
41 独分子的所谓"台湾与中国分离可以避免中共的攻击，可以重
42 返国际社会，也可以与中共谈判和平共存"等叫器，实在难分
43 左右。
44 文章指出，要真正解决台独问题，治本的办法，或者说釜
45 底抽薪的办法,就是全面开放两岸间的正常往来,实现"三通"。
46 并进而促进祖国的和平统一。至于岛内台独言论之一时高涨，
47 那不过是少数人 对于两岸开始突破隔绝状态的一种异常反应。
48 随着两岸"三通"的实现及和平统一事业的逐渐发展，所谓
49 "台独意识"也必将逐渐式微以致湮没。

N.B. Note the use of two 成語 'set phrases, idioms' in this piece. Usually four characters long, 成語 are used for much more than just their surface meanings:飲鴆止渴 (l. 5) is literally 'sip/poison wine/ stop/ thirst', but conveys the idea of 'temporary relief which will lead to future disasters', a comment about where 台獨 will inevitably lead. 釜底抽薪 (l. 45) 'cauldron/bottom/take out/ firewood' is used to say 'Take drastic measures to deal with a problem' and gives a metaphoric statement about the incendiary possibilities of the situation. A well chosen 成語 can summarize and categorize a situation with breath taking brevity and clarity while simultaneously adding color and depth to the writing; and, since many of the 成語 derive from historical situations, they also appeal to the innate love the Chinese have for their past. There are 成語 dictionaries several hundred pages long, which gives you an idea of how many 成語 exist. Keep track of them as you come across them and learn to use them appropriately in your speech and writings.

GRAMMAR EXERCISES

1. 選詞、填空、翻譯:

一) 中國政府主張堅決反對台獨＿＿＿主張海峽兩岸實現"三通"政策。 (使、為、並)

二) 台灣當局＿＿＿反對台獨，但是他們在另一方面助長台獨。
　　　　(雖然、為、一Verb)

三) 中國政府、中國人民反對＿＿＿台獨行為。
　　　　(種種、以X Verb、却)

四) 台灣人民＿＿＿長期遭受過帝國主義的壓迫。(為、曾、以)

五) 文章＿＿＿指出台獨分子的企圖，＿＿＿批評台灣當局的立場。
　　　　(一方面、只要、雖然)

六) 台獨分子想＿＿＿台灣成為一個"新而獨立的國家"。
　　　　(使、被、把)

七) 台灣民眾渴望民主＿＿＿希望台灣有個光明前途。 (曾、並、讓)

八) "革新保台"＿＿＿台灣政府的口號。(為、將、正在)

2. 把下列詞語或標點符號分別填入各句後翻譯成英語:　並、以、着、
雖然、却、一 verb、"…"、種種

一)　＿＿＿有些人有台獨思想傾向，但是我國人民都會把自己的言行
　　與台獨分子的主張加以區分。
二)　台獨分子＿＿＿種種借口反對台灣的政治現狀。
三)　文章指出，搞＿＿＿台獨＿＿＿行為背離着全國人民的意願。
四)　台灣當局反對所謂"兩個中國"，＿＿＿鼓吹海峽兩岸是"兩個
　　　政治實體"。
五)　台灣同胞懷有＿＿＿海峽兩岸統一的強烈願望。
六)　不少台胞對祖國缺乏瞭解，＿＿＿對台灣前途感到徬徨。
七)　去年九月底，民進黨＿＿＿成立，就把"自決"論加以政綱化。

3. 請用指定的詞語改寫下列的句子:

一)　"台獨"、"住民自決"是民進黨黨綱的兩個條文。 (和)
二)　台灣少數人頭腦發脹，他們的台獨言行也升級。
　　　　(一 verb 1，就 verb 2)
三)　台灣當局考慮怎麼把台灣問題國際化。(着)
四)　文章説明台獨的論調，批評台獨分子的立場。
　　　　(一方面 X，一方面 Y)
五)　中央領導想「三通」是一個特別有效的政策。
　　　　(把 O1 verb 為 O2)

SIGHT READINGS

#1 TAIWAN WILL SET UP A "CHINA UNIFICATION ALLIANCE"

1 台将成立"中国统一联盟"

2 由台湾夏潮联谊会和中华杂志社等团体筹组的"中华
3 统一联盟"，最近举行第二次筹备会，会上通过组织章程，
4 决定把各个赞成统一的团体及个人组织起来,并于今年 4 月
5 5 日举行成立大会。据台湾《中国时报》报道，"中国
6 统一联盟"自今年一月份筹组以来，所包括的单位与个人
7 除夏潮联谊会和中华杂志社外，还有"政治受难人互助联
8 谊会"，"中国民主促进联盟"，"世界中华全球统一大
9 同盟"，台湾民、青两党部分人士，以及台大教授张晓春、
10 东吴大学教授曾祥铎等人。该联盟这次召开的筹备会，在
11 通过组织章程的同时，还决定待联盟正式成立后，将探讨
12 台海两岸学术交流、人员互访、通商贸易等问题，并举行
13 民众大会，宣传该联盟的统一思想。

VOCABULARY

1: 联盟 [liánméng] 'alliance'

2: 夏潮联谊会 [Xiàcháo liányìhuì] 'Xiachao Friendship Club'

2: 中华杂志社 [Zhōnghuá zázhìshè] 'China Magazine (Publishing House)'

2: 筹组 [chóuzǔ] 'planned, organized'

3: 章程 [zhāngchéng] 'regulations'

4: 赞成 [zànchéng] 'approve'

4: 团体 [tuántǐ] 'groups'

8: 全球 [quánqiú] 'Worldwide'

9: 同盟 [tóngméng] 'League'

9: 台大 [Táidà] '(abbr. for 台湾大学) National Taiwan Univ.'

9: 张晓春 [Zhāng Xiǎochūn] '(name of a person)'

10: 东吴大学 [Dōngwú dàxué] 'Soochow University'

10: 曾祥铎 [Zēng Xiángduó] '(name of a person)'

11: 待 [dài] 'wait until'

11: 正式 [zhèngshì] 'formally'

11: 探讨 [tàntǎo] 'inquire about'

12: 学术交流 [xuéshù jiāoliú] 'scholarly exchange'

12: 通商 [tōngshāng] 'have trade relations'

13: 宣传 [xuānchuán] 'make known'

QUESTIONS

A. What second meeting was recently held?

B. What two decisions were made at the second meeting?

C. What is the source of information for this article?

D. When did the Alliance start?

E. What will happen on April 5 of this year?

F. How broadly based is the Alliance?

G. What three areas of interchange does the Alliance hope to promote?

#2 TAIWAN LAW INSTITUTE ESTABLISHED IN BEIJING

1 　　　台灣法律研究所在京成立

2 　　本報北京三月九日訊 由北京部分法學專家和學者
3 　自願組成的台灣法律研究所最近成立。
4 　隨着近年來大陸與台灣經濟、文化和社會交往的擴大，
5 　以及探親人數的增加，一系列法律問題應運而生，幾乎涉
6 　及從民法到刑法等所有法律範疇。這個所將通過研究，向
7 　有關當局提出預防和解決兩岸間法律問題所帶來衝突的措
8 　施。
9 　　這個研究所目前將以台灣的民法與商法為研究重點，
10 　出版刊物，召集學術研討會。

VOCABULARY

1: 法律 [fǎlǜ] 'law'

2: 專家 [zhuānjiā] 'experts'

5: 探親 [tànqīn] 'visit relatives'

5: 應運而生 [yìngyùn ér shēng] 'emerge in response to the times'

5: 幾乎 [jīhū] 'almost'

5: 涉及 [shèjí] 'involves'

6: 範疇 [fànchóu] 'category'

7: 預防 [yùfáng] 'guard against'

7: 衝突 [chōngtū] 'conflict'

10: 出版 [chūbǎn] 'publish'

10: 刊物 [kānwù] 'publications'

10: 召集 [zhāojí] 'convene (meetings)'

QUESTIONS

A. When was this news reported?

B. What parties established this Institute?

C. What four recent factors have prompted increased legal problems in this area?

D. What sort of measures will the Institute suggest?

E. What will the research focus of the Institute be?

F. What two types of activities will the Institute engage in?

Reading Chinese Newspapers:
Tactics and Skills

Lesson Nine: Chinese Law

最高檢察院檢察長劉復之說

中國檢察機關將堅持秉公執法

為建設廉潔政府發揮監督作用

中國新一任最高檢察長劉復之，對通過檢察機關的法律監督，建設廉潔政府持樂觀態度。他在接受記者採訪時說，儘管相當一部分法紀案件涉及國家工作人員及一些領導幹部，常使中國檢察官們感到棘手，但檢察機關仍將秉公執法，對犯罪行為決不手軟。

在解釋對處理這類案件之所以有信心的原因時，劉復之檢察長強調指出，關鍵在於準確。他說，由於貪污、受賄犯罪行為多發生在國家機關內部，查處時將比其它案件難度更大。一些人可以通過關係網、保護層進行說情或施加壓力。但是，只要掌握充分的證據，正確運用法律，那麼，就可以克服來自不同方面的阻力。他說，為了在建設廉潔政府中發揮監督作用，檢察機關對凡是證據確鑿的貪污、受賄和其他違法案件，不管牽涉到什麼人，不管涉嫌人有什麼背景，都將依法予以嚴處。

劉復之認為，在新形勢下，這種法律監督應該注意兩個問題。一是在繼續加強對刑事案件的檢察監督同時，加強對重大民事案件包括重大經濟糾紛案件的監督。一些重要的涉外經濟糾紛案件，應列入檢察機關的日常業務中；二是除對公安機關辦理的刑事案件進行監督外，對自行受理和偵查的刑事案件，檢察機關內也應建立自我制約的機制，否則，也容易出現新的錯案。他表示，將在自己的任期內，致力完善和改進檢察機關的監督職能和程序，在法律規定的範圍內擴大和加強這種職能。

這位曾長期從事政法工作的最高檢察官告訴記者，面對改革的深化和開放的擴大，檢察工作將面臨諸多新的課題。因此，檢察機關在打擊經濟犯罪活動中將持更加慎重的態度。談到一些涉及科技人員和工程技術人員業餘兼職的問題時，他說，只要是國家政策允許的合法收入，就應予以法律保護，就不屬於貪污和受賄。近年來這種案件增加很快，檢察機關由於缺乏經驗，在處理這類案件中有時難免造成差錯。他表示，對這類案件的錯案，一經發現，將堅決予以糾正。

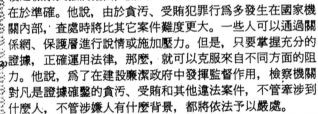

本報記者 張志業

專訪

上五

本報訊道，上海經濟皖滬五省一市制後，第一季遍持續增長，任制具有強大

今年開始外貿承包，層月創匯額、經濟調動了各省市活力，今年第去年同期大幅百分之二十一長百分之十點

河洛

本報鄭州傑、中央人民團報道，四月時許，在河南的小會議室裏廳局的主要負設洛陽經濟技的論證意見上內蓋了十五個長程維高簽發文件。這樣，要一兩個月才幾個小時就拍

去年年底政府決定，利用資源豐富、交充足等優勢，兩個經濟技術引國內外的資一條我國中部

(reproduction of original text)

STRUCTURE NOTES (Line numbers here refer to the original text.)

4-7: Notice the relatively complex location phrase (對 X, Y) in this sentence, which has the structure S (劉復之) 對 X (...監督), Y (V 建設 O ...政府) V (持) O (...態度).

7: 在 Verb What information is conveyed by placing the 在 structure before the verb phrase as it is here and in l. 14 and 25. See 7:43.

8-13: 儘管 [jǐnguǎn] X, 但 Y = 'Even though X, (however) Y' The first clause of this tandem structure will be head-marked by 儘管, a formal prose synonym of 雖然 suīrán 8:15. X will be a factual situation. The second clause will usually be marked by 但 or a synonym such as 但是, 仍然, 却, 然而, or 可是. These two sets of markers are useful in determining the parameters of the total structure and its internal sub-divisions.

This main text is interesting for its large number of tandem clause structures, some of which we are seeing in this textbook for the first time. See comments on translating tandem clauses in 5:25.

    a. 文章指出，儘管兩岸住民大多數人反對台獨，但是還有少數人鼓吹 "台獨"。

    b. 武漢的工業建設儘管大大地發展了，然而該市的污染率却下降了。

10: 些 is used here and in l. 18, 26 and 36. What tone does the repeated use of 些 give to this article? See 5:6.

13: 決 Negative = 'Definitely negative' 決, sometimes written 絕, is placed before negative adverbs to intensify their negative value, but 決 carries no particular connotation other than emphasis. Compare this with the synonymous 並 [bìng] Negative which conveys a sense of correcting the record by emphasizing the negative; see 2:35.

    a. 全國婦女聯合會主席強調，中國婦女決不願意繼續受社會的輕視和歧視。

b. 研制出全新的衛星器件<u>絕</u>不是一天完得成的。

15:   <u>S 之所以</u> Verb phrase = 'That by means of which the subject verbs the object', or more simply, 'Why/how the subject verbs the object'. This structure comes from the Neo-classical style of writing and is not used in speaking.

19-21: <u>只要</u> X, <u>就</u> Y = 'If (only) X, then Y' The first clause indicates one condition which is necessary for the second situation to occur. The main focus of this structure is on clause two. <u>Y</u> will usually be marked with <u>就</u> or a synonym, which makes it easier to determine where <u>X</u> ends and <u>Y</u> starts. Note that in line 37-38, two situations will result if the conditions set in the <u>只要</u> clause are met. Compare this with <u>只有</u> X, <u>才</u> Y in 10:23 which marks <u>X</u> as the only condition which allows <u>Y</u> to happen. Examples are:

a. <u>只要</u>有領導階層的互訪，中美兩國的關係<u>就</u>會有更大的發展。

b. <u>只要</u>明天的發射成功，我國的 "長征三號" 運載火箭<u>就</u>會投入國際市場，為國際用戶服務。

22-23: <u>不管</u> X，<u>將</u> Y = 'Regardless of X, (it will be) Y' This pattern is used to say that the situation mentioned in the second clause will not change, no matter the conditions identified in the first clause. <u>不论</u> búlùn and <u>无论</u> wúlùn are synonyms used in formal prose. An indefinite question word such as <u>什麼</u>, <u>誰</u>, <u>多麼</u>, etc. must be part of the first clause. <u>將</u> in this clause reinforces the idea that the second condition will occur, see 5:2. Other adverbs are also used to mark <u>Y</u>. Two examples of this pattern are:

a. <u>不管</u>企業發展多麼重要，我們都應該先治理環境污染。

b. 少數民族地區<u>不管</u>從前遇到過多大壓力，通過 "雙向開放" <u>將</u>要變為經濟發達地區。

24-29: <u>一是</u> What do you expect to follow when you see <u>一是</u>? See 6:7.

27-29: <u>除</u> X <u>外</u>, <u>也</u> Y Should this shumianyu variant of the <u>除了</u> X <u>以外</u>, pattern be understood as "Besides X,..." or as "Except for X,..."? See 5:15.

33: 曾 Verb   What value does 曾(經) have before a verb? Should it be translated as "already"? See 8:22.

38-39: 由於   What sentence structure do you expect when you see 由於? Did you find it here? How about in l. 17-18 above? See 5:25.

40:   一 Verb   Do not confuse this 一 Verb structure with the adverb 已經. What does 一 Verb 1, 將 Verb 2 mean? See 8:7.

1　　　　　最高檢察院檢察長劉復之説
2　　　　中國檢察機關將堅持秉公執法
3　　　　為建設廉潔政府發揮監督作用

4　　　中國新一任最高檢察長劉復之，對通過檢察機關的法律
5　監督，建設廉潔政府持樂觀態度。他在接受記者採訪時説，
6　儘管相當一部分法紀案件涉及國家工作人員及一些領導幹部，
7　常使中國檢察官們感到棘手，但檢察機關仍將秉公執法，對
8　犯罪行為決不手軟。
9　　　在解釋對處理這類案件之所以有信心的原因時，劉復之
10　檢察長強調指出，關鍵在於準確。他説，由於貪污、受賄犯
11　罪行為多發生在國家機關內部，查處時將比其他案件難度更
12　大。一些人可以通過關係網、保護層進行説情或施加壓力。

VOCABULARY

1: 檢察院 [jiǎncháyuàn] 'Procuratorate'　("District Attorney's Office")

1: 劉復之 [Liú Fùzhī] '(name of a person)'

2: 機關 [jīguān] 'office, agency' WG>10:關鍵 [guānjiàn] 'key point'; WG>12:
　　　關係網 [guānxiwǎng] 'network of relationships'

2: 秉公 [bǐnggōng] 'impartial, just'

2: 執法 [zhífǎ] 'law enforcement' WG>4:法律 [fǎlǜ] 'law'; WG>6:法紀 [fǎjì]
　　　'law and order'; WG>16:違法 [wéifǎ] 'break the law'; WG>17:依法
　　　[yīfǎ] 'according to law'; WG>27:政法 [zhèngfǎ] 'politics and law'

3: 廉潔 [liánjié] 'honest'

3: 監督 [jiāndū] 'supervision'

4: S對 X,YVO "sentence structure"　(SN)

4: 一任 [yīrèn] 'allow, appoint' WG>24:任期 [rènqī] 'term of office'

4: 法律 [fǎlǜ] '?'　法 WG:2

5: 樂觀 [lèguān] 'optimistic'

5: 態度 [tàidu] 'attitude' WG>11:難度 [nándù] 'degree of difficulty'

6: 儘管 X,但 Y [jǐnguǎn X, dàn] Y 'Even though X, (however) Y' (SN)

6: 法紀 [fǎjì] '?' 法 WG:2

6: 涉及 [shèjí] 'involve, touch upon' WG>16:牽涉 [qiānshè] 'involve,
    drag in'; WG>16:涉嫌人 [shèxiánrén] 'suspect'; WG>20:涉外
    [shèwài] 'about foreign matters'

7: 棘手 [jíshǒu] 'thorn in the side' WG>8:手軟 [shǒuruǎn] 'irresolute,
    softhearted'

7: 仍 [réng] 'still, yet'

8: 決 Neg [jué] Negative 'definitely negative' (SN)

8: 手軟 [shǒuruǎn] '?' 手 WG:7

9: 解釋 [jiěshì] 'explain'

9: 信心 [xìnxīn] 'confidence'

10: 關鍵 [guānjiàn] '?' 關 WG:2

10: 準確 [zhǔnquè] 'accuracy, precision' WG>13:正確 [zhèngquè]
    'correctly'; WG>15:確鑿 [quèzuò] 'conclusive'

10: 貪污 [tānwū] 'corruption'

10: 受賄 [shòuhuì] 'accept bribes' ; WG>22:受理 [shòulǐ] 'accept and
    hear a case'

11: 查處 [cháchǔ] 'investigate and punish'; WG>22 偵查 [zhēnchá]
    'investigate (a crime)'

11: 難度 [nándù] '?' 度 WG:5, 難 WG:33

12: 關係網 [guānxiwǎng] '?' 關 WG:2

12: 保護層 [bǎohùcéng] 'layers of protection'

12: 說情 [shuōqíng] 'plead for mercy for someone'

12: 施加 [shījiā] 'exert'

12: 壓力 [yālì] 'pressure' WG>14:阻力 [zǔlì] 'obstructions'; WG>24: 致力
    [zhìlì] 'devote oneself to'

13 但是，只要掌握充分的證據，正確運用法律，那麼，就可以
14 克服來自不同方面的阻力。他説，爲了在建設廉潔政府中發
15 揮監督作用，檢察機關對凡是證據確鑿的貪污、受賄和其他
16 違法案件，不管牽涉到什麼人，不管涉嫌人有什麼背景，都
17 將依法予以嚴處。

18 　　劉復之認爲，在新形勢下，這種法律監督應該注意兩個
19 問題：一是在繼續加強對刑事案件的檢察監督同時，加強對
20 重大民事案件包括重大經濟糾紛案件的監督。一些重要的涉
21 外經濟糾紛案件，應列入檢察機關的日常業務中；二是除對
22 公安機關辦理的刑事案件進行監督外，對自行受理和偵查的
23 刑事案件，檢察機關內也應建立自我制約的機制，否則，也
24 容易出現新的錯案。他表示，將在自己的任期內，致力完善
25 和改進檢察機關的監督職能和程序，在法律規定的範圍內擴
26 大和加強這種職能。

VOCABULARY

13: 只要 X,就 Y [zhǐyào X, jiù Y]'If only X, then Y' (SN)

13: 掌握 [zhǎngwò] 'control'

13: 充分 [chōngfèn] 'abundant, ample'

13: 證據 [zhèngjù] 'proof, evidence'

13: 正確 [zhèngquè] '?' 確 WG:10

13: 運用 [yùnyòng] 'utilize'

14: 克服 [kèfú] 'overcome, defeat'

14: 阻力 [zǔlì] '?' 力 WG:12

15: 凡是 [fánshì] 'every, all, any'

15: 確鑿 [quèzuò] '?' 確 WG:10

16: 違法 [wéifǎ] '?' 法 WG:2

16: 不管 X,將 Y [bùguǎn] X, [jiāng] Y 'Regardless of X, it will be Y' (SN)

16: 牽涉 [qiānshè] '?' 涉 WG:6

16: 涉嫌人 [shèxiánrén] '?' 涉 WG:6

16: 背景 [bèijǐng] 'background'

17: 依法 [yīfǎ] '?' 法 WG:2

17: 予以 [yǔyǐ] 'give, supply'

18: 形勢 [xíngshì] 'situation'

18: 注意 [zhùyì] 'pay attention to'

19: 刑事 [xíngshì] 'criminal matters' WG>20:民事 [mínshì] 'civil (law)';
　　　WG>27:從事 [cóngshì] 'engage in, work at'

20: 民事 [mínshì] '?' 事 WG:19

20: 包括 [bāokuò] 'include'

20: 糾紛 [jiūfēn] 'disputes, issues'

20: 涉外 [shèwài] '?' 涉 WG:6

21: 列入 [lièrù] 'list among' WG>31:收入 [shōurù] 'income'

22: 辦理 [bànlǐ] 'handle, conduct'

22: 自行 [zìxíng] 'voluntarily' WG>23: 自我 [zìwǒ] 'self, oneself'

22: 受理 [shòulǐ] '?' 受 WG:10

22: 偵查 [zhēnchá] '?' 查 WG:11

23: 自我 [zìwǒ] '?' 自 WG:22

23: 制約 [zhìyuē] 'regulatory' WG>23:機制 [jīzhì] 'mechanism'

23: 否則 [fǒuzé] 'otherwise'

24: 錯案 [cuò'àn] 'misjudged cases' WG>33:差錯 [chācuò] 'mistake'

24: 任期 [rènqī] '?' 任 WG:4

24: 致力 [zhìlì] '?' 力 WG:12

24: 完善 [wánshàn] 'perfect'

25: 職能 [zhínéng] 'function' WG>30:兼職 [jiānzhí] 'part-time job'

25: 程序 [chéngxù] 'procedure' WG>30:工程 [gōngchéng] 'engineering'

25: 範圍 [fànwéi] 'scope, sphere'

25: 擴大 [kuòdà] 'enlarge'

27　　　　這位曾長期從事政法工作的最高檢察官告訴記者，面對
28　改革的深化和開放的擴大，檢察工作將面臨諸多新的課題。
29　因此,檢察機關在打擊經濟犯罪活動中將持更加慎重的態度。
30　談到一些涉及科技人員和工程技術人員業餘兼職的問題時，
31　他說,只要是國家政策允許的合法收入，就應予以法律保護，
32　就不屬於貪污和受賄。近年來這種案件增加很快，檢察機關
33　由於缺乏經驗，在處理這類案件中有時難免造成差錯。他表
34　示，對這類案件的錯案，一經發現，將堅決予以糾正。

VOCABULARY

27: 從事 [cóngshì] '?' 事 WG:19

27: 政法 [zhèngfǎ] '?' 法 WG:2

27: 面對 [miànduì] 'faced with' WG>28: 面臨 [miànlín] 'be confronted with'

28: 深化 [shēnhuà] 'deepening'

28: 面臨 [miànlín] '?' 面 WG:27

28: 諸多 [zhùduō] 'a great deal of'

28: 課題 [kètí] 'task, question'

29: 活動 [huódòng] 'activities'

29: 慎重 [shènzhòng] 'prudent, careful'

30: 科技 [kējì] 'science and technology' WG>30: 技術 [jìshù] 'technology'

30: 工程 [gōngchéng] '?' 程 WG:25

30: 技術 [jìshù] '?' 技 WG:30

30: 業餘 [yèyú] 'sparetime, after hours'

30: 兼職 [jiānzhí] '?' 職 WG:25 (see Lesson 4 line 21)

31: 允許 [yúnxǔ] 'permitted, allowed'

31: 收入 [shōurù] '?' 入 WG:21

33: 缺乏 [quēfá] 'lack'

33: 難免 [nánmiǎn] 'hard to avoid' 難 WG:11

33: 差錯 [chācuò] '?' 錯 WG:24

34: 堅決 [jiānjué] 'resolutely'

GRAMMAR EXERCISES

1. There are two sentences in this text in which a comma separates the subject from the rest of the sentence and nine sentences in which a comma separates the verb from its object. How many of them can you find? What other comma usages do you see (e.g., <u>S P, V,</u> ... <u>時</u>,, listing commas)?

2. 請用下列的詞完成句子，然後把句子翻成英文：
　　除、不管、因此、儘管、一方面、就、只要

一) ＿＿＿改革深化，將要更加開放。
二) 由於國家政策允許業餘兼職這種收入，＿＿＿就不屬於犯法行為。
三) ＿＿＿一些涉嫌人通過什麼關係網，中國檢察機關都要查處案件。
四) ＿＿＿國家工作人員外，一部分法紀案件也涉及到領導幹部。
五) ＿＿＿諸多檢察員的經驗不夠，但是造成的差錯卻十分少。
六) 檢察長一發現有貪污、受賄違法案件，他＿＿＿＿要依法予以嚴處。

3. 請用下列的詞或標點符號填空，然後把句子翻成通順的英語：
　　但是、之所以、決、又、：、着、並、；

一) 儘管犯罪行為發生在國家機關內部，＿＿＿還得立案處理。
二) 檢查院目前有兩種問題必須注意＿＿＿一是查處經濟糾紛案件，二是建立制約的機制。
三) 我們對所有的違法案件＿＿＿不予以法律保護。
四) 劉復之指出，打擊犯罪活動＿＿＿有利於政府的改革是因為維護了人民的利益。

Simplified Character Version of the Main Text

1   最高检察院检察长刘复之说
2   中国检察机关将坚持秉公执法
3   为建设廉洁政府发挥监督作用

4   中国新一任最高检察长刘复之，对通过检察机关的法律
5   监督，建设廉洁政府持乐观态度。他在接受记者采访时说，
6   尽管相当一部分法纪案件涉及国家工作人员及一些领导干部，
7   常使中国检察官们感到棘手，但检察机关仍将秉公执法，对
8   犯罪行为决不手软。
9   在解释对处理这类案件之所以有信心的原因时，刘复之
10   检察长强调指出，关键在于准确。他说，由于贪污、受贿犯
11   罪行为多发生在国家机关内部，查处时将比其他案件难度更
12   大。一些人可以通过关系网、保护层进行说情或施加压力。
13   但是，只要掌握充分的证据，正确运用法律，那么，就可以
14   克服来自不同方面的阻力。他说，为了在建设廉洁政府中发
15   挥监督作用，检察机关对凡是证据确凿的贪污、受贿和其他
16   违法案件，不管牵涉到什么人，不管涉嫌人有什么背景，都
17   将依法予以严处。
18   刘复之认为，在新形势下，这种法律监督应该注意两个
19   问题：一是在继续加强对刑事案件的检察监督同时，加强对
20   重大民事案件包括重大经济纠纷案件的监督。一些重要的涉
21   外经济纠纷案件，应列入检察机关的日常业务中；二是除对
22   公安机关办理的刑事案件进行监督外，对自行受理和侦查的
23   刑事案件，检察机关内也应建立自我制约的机制，否则，也
24   容易出现新的错案。他表示，将在自己的任期内，致力完善
25   和改进检察机关的监督职能和程序，在法律规定的范围内扩
26   大和加强这种职能。
27   这位曾长期从事政法工作的最高检察官告诉记者，面对
28   改革的深化和开放的扩大，检察工作将面临诸多新的课题。
29   因此，检察机关在打击经济犯罪活动中将持更加慎重的态度。
30   谈到一些涉及科技人员和工程技术人员业余兼职的问题时，
31   他说，只要是国家政策允许的合法收入，就应予以法律保护，
32   就不属于贪污和受贿。近年来这种案件增加很快，检察机关
33   由于缺乏经验，在处理这类案件中有时难免造成错误。他表
34   示，对这类案件的错案，一经发现，将坚决予以纠正。

SIGHT READING

#1 Zhejiang Deals Severely with Crimes by Government Officials

1 　　　　浙江嚴辦國家公務員犯罪案.
2 　　今年頭三月查處經濟犯罪案一千八百多起

3 　　　中新社杭州五月二日電　　浙江省人民檢察院副檢察
4 長耿小平日前表示，他的一項重要的職責之一，就是領導
5 他的檢察官們去依法查處國家公務人員的經濟犯罪和瀆職
6 犯罪行為。　這位年輕的檢察長在接受採訪時坦率地承認，
7 當前浙江省的經濟犯罪現象是嚴重的，國家公務人員玩忽
8 職守等瀆職案件也時有發生。
9 　　　從去年一月到今年三月，浙江省檢察機關共立案查處
10 各類經濟犯罪案件一千八百五十七起，其中近四成是國家
11 機關、企事業單位內部人員作案。
12 　　　這些官銜大小不等的"領導幹部"的經濟犯罪行為，
13 主要是貪污、受賄。
14 　　　從去年一月到今年三月，浙江省檢察機關共查處國家
15 公務人員的玩忽職守犯罪案八十一起，其中被告中有中共
16 黨員二十九名，縣級領導幹部一名。

VOCABULARY

1: 浙江 [Zhèjiāng] 'Zhejiang Province'
1: 公務 [gōngwù] 'public duty'
2: 頭 X [tóu-X] 'first X'
2: 起　[qǐ] '(measure for criminal cases)'
4: 耿小平 [Gěng Xiǎopíng] '(name of a person)'
4: 職責 [zhízé] 'duties'
5: 瀆職 [dúzhí] 'dereliction of duty'

6: 坦率 [tǎnshuài] 'candidly'

7: 玩忽 [wánhū] 'neglect, trifle with'

8: 職守 [zhíshǒu] 'post, duty'

9: 立案 [lì'àn] 'put a case on file for investigation and prosecution'

10: 各類 [gèlèi] 'each category'

10: 四成 [sìchéng] '40%'

12: 官銜 [guānxián] 'official title'

12: 不等 [bùděng] 'varying in rank'

15: 被告 [bèigào] 'defendants'

16: 縣級 [xiànjí] 'county level'

QUESTIONS

A. What principal duty of the Assistant Chief Procuratorate is mentioned here?

B. What two concerns are discussed in the first paragraph?

C. What was the forum at which Gěng Xiǎopíng made these statements?

D. Over what time period did 1,857 criminal cases occur?

E. What principal kinds of crimes are discussed?

F. What 'shocking' news is revealed in the last paragraph?

#2 COACHING CLASS FOR LAW EXAM

1   律师资格考试
2   辅导班即将开办

3   为迎接今年全国律师资格统考，中国政法大学法律系
4 特邀请了具有丰富教学经验的教授和讲师 ，开办辅导班。
5 该辅导班将按照最近出版的《全国律师资格统一考试复习
6 大纲》开设课程。据主办单位介绍，学员报名不受学历和
7 单位限制，上课从四月中旬到六月份利用晚上和星期天进
8 行，地点就设在北京海淀区学院路中国政法大学校内。

VOCABULARY

1: 律师 [lǜshī] 'lawyer'

1: 资格 [zīgé] 'qualifications'

2: 辅导班 [fǔdǎobān] 'training classes'

3: 统考 [tǒngkǎo] '(abbr. for 统一考试) national exam'

3: 法律系 [fǎlǜxì] 'Law Department'

4: 丰富 [fēngfù] 'rich, plentiful'

4: 讲师 [jiǎngshī] 'lecturers'

6: 课程 [kèchéng] 'curriculum'

7: 中旬 [zhōngxún] 'middle of the month'

8: 海淀区 [Hǎidiànqū] '(place name in Beijing)'

QUESTIONS

A. What statement is made about those who will teach the classes?

B. What prompted the establishment of these law review classes?

C. What two considerations are specifically waived for prospective students?

D. About how many weeks will the review classes last?

E. Where will the classes be held?

#3 LEGAL NOTICES

A.

1   阅忠堂： 你妻周还爱已向本庭起诉，提出与你离婚。

2   限你自公告之日起三个月内来本庭应诉，逾期则依法判决。

3   山西省五台县茹村人民法庭   1989 年 1 月 5 日

---

4   黄玉明：   你夫丛星已向本院起诉，提出与你离婚。

5   限你自公告之日起三个月内来本院应诉，逾期则依法判决。

6   辽宁省岫岩满族自治县人民法院 1989 年 1 月 5 日

VOCABULARY

1: 起诉 [qǐsù] 'bring a legal suit'

1: 离婚 [líhūn] 'divorce'

2: 应诉 [yìngsù] 'respond to the suit'

2: 逾期 [yúqī] 'exceed time limit'

2: 判决 [pànjué] 'court decision'

QUESTIONS

A. What basic difference is there between the two announcements?

B. What similarities are there between the two?

C. What is interesting about the name of the person suing for a divorce in the top announcement?

B.

更正　　本报 1988 年 11 月 8 日法院公告栏中，王新杰诉刘振茂的法庭地址应为山东省莱州市驿道人民法庭特此更正。

VOCABULARY & QUESTION

1: 更正 [gēngzhèng] 'correction'

A. What error is being corrected here?

C.

中华人民共和国主席令 第三号

《中华人民共和国全民所有制工业企业法》已由中华人民共和国第七届全国人民代表大会第一次会议于1988 年 4 月13 日通过，现予公布，自1988年8月1日起施行。

中华人民共和国主席 杨尚昆

1988 年 4 月13 日

QUESTIONS

A. What do 《》 signal?

B. What is being announced in this decree?

C. When does the decree take effect?

D. What official is issuing this decree?

Reading Chinese Newspapers:
Tactics and Skills

*Lesson Ten: Science and Economic
Development*

我们四校根据教育要为社会主义现代化建设服务的方针，愿在培养人才和科技方面与社会各界开展广泛合作，欢迎加强联系。

华中理工大学　华南理工大学　青岛海洋大学　大连理工大学

发挥科技优势为经济建设做出更大的贡献

——在全国科技工作会议上的讲话

（一九八八年三月十日）

李　鹏

这次全国科技工作会议是继一九八五年全国科技工作会议的又一次重要会议。它对贯彻落实党的十三大精神，加快和深化改革，推动科技与经济结合，实现国民经济的振兴，必将起到重要的促进作用。下面，就如何发挥科技优势为经济建设做出更大贡献，讲几点意见。

（一）科技进步的战略意义

党的十三大提出，把发展科学技术放在经济发展战略的首要位置。这是从社会主义现代化建设事业的全局出发，根据国际经济和科技发展的实际情况，做出的正确决策。我们现在正处在一个新技术迅速发展的时代，科学技术（包括现代化管理）的进步决定着生产力发展的水平和速度。在开放的竞争的国际环境中，离开了科技进步，我国社会生产力就不可能迅速发展，同发达国家的差距将会越来越大，我们就不可能自立于世界民族之林。我们是在经济比较贫穷、技术比较落后的基础上进行现代化建设的。我们国家人口多，底子薄，人均资源相对不足。目前，我国国民生产总值的单位能耗和原材料消耗都比发达国家高出许多，劳动生产率、固定资产增殖率、人均国民生产总值以及出口总额占国民生产总值的份额等，与发达国家相比，差距就更大了。只有依靠科学技术进步，才能大幅度地提高经济效益，增加生产，比较迅速地改变贫穷落后的面貌。我们确实面临这样一种严峻的挑战形势，全国人民，首先是全体科技工作者，要充分认识科技进步在实现我国四个现代化艰巨任务中所占据的战略地位，增强紧迫感。

加速我国科技进步既是十分紧迫的，也是完全可能的。党的十一届三中全会以来，我们坚持四项基本原则坚持改革开放，国民经济持续稳定地发展，取得了世界瞩目的成就，积累了宝贵的经验，扩大了国际科技交流，引进了一批先进技术和管理经验，为进一步推动科技进步打下了良好的基础。加速科技进步，我们还有自己的优势。

（下转第二版）

（一九八八年三月十日）

10周年

……了可贵的经验，在

……11期共407名少年……15岁，最小的11岁。……毕业，其中考取国内……年班40名学生，已……8名被免试推荐为……有3名获得了科技……宋若奖学金。

……给曾经视察过他们……他们的学业情况。

……著名数学家谷超……力超常少年，是我……一条新途径，也是我……紫阳总书记的来信……的殷切期望。我们……继续把少年班办……

……会提出宪法修正案草案

（3月12日通过）

……允许私营经济在法……围内存在和发展。……社会主义公有制经……国家保护私营经济……利和利益，对私营

占、买卖或者以其他形式非法转让土地。土地的使用权可以依照法律的规定转让。"

STRUCTURE NOTES   (Line numbers here refer to the original text.)

This article is printed in a right-to-left format with individual lines presented vertically. This traditional style of printing is frequently used for headlines, but it is found in only about 10% of the texts of articles appearing in mainland editions of newspapers and perhaps 25% of the articles in the overseas version of the 人民日报. Newspaper texts printed in Taiwan use the vertical format exclusively; see lesson 12. Starting from the top of the first sentence to the right in the top row in the article, read down to the end of the line. When finished with the first column, move to the top of next column to the left and read down it. When finished with the first row of sentences, go down to the top of the right-most sentence of the continuation row and repeat the process. Mainland vertical texts are presented in one physically contiguous area; compare this with the format of Taiwan newspapers discussed in Lesson Twelve.

1: What is the grammatical structure of this headline? See 3:34.

5-6: 是   After noting the important fact that 是 appears in this sentence, your next job is to decide if it is a S 是 T P V O 的, S 是 V 的, O 是 S V 的 or some other pattern. How is 是 used in 11-12, 17-18, 26, and 29? See 2:15, 4:10, 6:7, and 7:35.

6: 又 Verb   What does 又 Verb mean, and what does its use here say about the position of science and technology in China? See 2:2.

8-9: 就 X Verb phrase   In addition to the basic function of 就 to mark sequences of verb actions you learned very early in your study of Chinese, 就 is also used in written texts to introduce the object or scope of a verb action. In this usage, 就 can be translated as 'concerning, regarding, about X', etc. As is the case with 对 X phrases (see 4:12), 就 X phrases should be translated after the verb and object in English. The X object or scope can range from a simple noun to a complex verb phrase, as it is here: "Below, (I) will discuss several ideas concerning (就) how to bring scientific and technological superiority into play to make greater contributions for (为) economic development." Whenever you see 就, be careful to determine whether it marks the scope of the sentence or whether the main verb of a sentence follows it. Examples of this new usage of 就 are:

> a. 政府就少数民族地区的经济劣势提出了新的发展计划。
> b. 美国国务卿就台湾问题指出："美国的只有一个中国的政策是'坚定不移的'"。

13: <u>正</u> Verb What does 正 bring to a verb? See 7:43. Notice its earlier use in this sentence in the vocabulary item 正确 [zhèngquè].

15: <u>Verb 着</u>[zhě] What does the use of 着 after the verb rather than a marker such as 了 or 过 say about the impact of science and technology in the world? See 8:13.

15-16: <u>在</u> What does this 在 mark, and how can you determine the end of the 在 structure here and in 17-18 and 27? Why is there a comma after the 在 structure here? See 7:12. How can you distinguish between this 在 and the 在 which marks on going verb action? See 7:43.

16-17: The two clauses in this conditional structure starting with 离开了 and ending with 发展 should be understood as "When/if clause 1, then clause 2." Chinese 'unmarked' conditional structures often have no overt markers (e.g.要是, 假如 etc.) in the first clause, but they are usually discernible as such by the juxtapositioning of the two clauses and the use of markers such as 就 or 还 before the core verb in the second clause. 21-23 (劳动生产率 to 更大了) is another conditional structure, as is the last sentence in the article. It is sometimes difficult to decide if you are looking at an 'unmarked' conditional structure or simply two clauses; see 26-29 which can be understood either way. Examples are:

> a. 省政府把指导思想转变一下，当地经济就振兴起来。
> b. 市环保部门明年兴建大型污水处理厂，后年饮水污染率就会下降。

17: 越[yuè] X 越 Y = 'The more X it is, the more Y it is' A wide range of grammatical constructions can appear in the X and Y positions, though a simple 来 very often appears as X for the meaning 'It is getting to be more and more Y.' When you see one 越 marker, expect another one somewhere later in the sentence. Sometimes there can be three or more 越 markers as happens in lines 1-2 of Sight Reading #2 in Lesson 10. Examples are:

a. 中国最高检察长强调，涉嫌人越通过保护层进行说情，检察官越感到棘手。

b. 胡副市长告诉记者，海城市越来越注重培养乡土人才。

20-21: 比 tells you to expect a comparison structure. See 5:22. Comparisons are usually structured as X 比 Y Verb phrase, though notice the formal prose comparative structure X, 与 Y 相比 = 'comparing X and Y' in lines 22-23.

24-25: 只有 X, 才 Y = 'Only if X, then Y' This pattern stresses and emphasizes that X is the only condition which will permit the second clause action to happen. The focus is on clause 1. Compare this with the 只要 X, 就 Y structure in 9:19 in which X is just one of the conditions necessary for Y to happen. When you see 只有, expect 才 to mark the second clause. Examples are:

a. 只有男女比例正常，所有的男光棍才有娶上妻子的希望。

b. 只有中美互相尊重主权、互不干涉内政，两国关系才会有更大的发展。

25: ...地 Verb Why is 地 so useful in finding the core verb of sentences and comma units? See line 32 and 6:37.

28: 所 Verb What is the function of 所 here? See 5:19.

30-31: <u>Time 以来</u> What does this structure mean? See 7:18.

35: <u>下轉</u>[zhuǎn] X 版[bǎn] = 'Continued on p. X' This idiomatic structure is used to direct the reader to the subsequent page on which an article is continued.

1 发挥科技优势为经济建设作出更大的贡献
2 —— 在全国科技工作会议上的讲话
3 李鹏

4 　　这次全国科技工作会议是继一九八五年全国科技工作会议
5 之后，科技界的又一次重要会议。它对贯彻落实党的十三大精
6 神，加快和深化改革，推动科技与经济结合，实现国民经济的
7 技术进步，必将起到重要的促进作用。下面，就如何发挥科技
8 优势为经济建设作出更大的贡献，讲几点意见。

9 　　　　　　　　(一) 科技进步的战略意义
10 　　党的十三大提出，把发展科学技术放在经济发展战略的首
11 要位置。这是从社会主义现代化建设事业的全局出发，根据国
12 际经济和科技发展的实际情况，做出的正确决策。我们现在正
13 处在一个新技术迅速发展的时代，科学技术（包括现代化管理）
14 的进步决定着生产力发展的水平和速度。在开放的竞争的国际
15 环境中，离开了科技进步，我国社会生产力就不可能迅速发
16 展，同发达国家的差距将会越来越大，我们就不可能自立于世
17 界民族之林。我们是在经济比较贫穷、技术比较落后的基础上
18 进行现代化建设的。我们国家人口多，底子薄，人均资源相对
19 不足。目前，我国国民生产总值的单位能耗和原材料消耗都比

VOCABULARY

1: 科技 [kējì] 'science and technology'

1: 优势 [yōushì] 'superiority'

1: 贡献 [gòngxiàn] 'contribution'

3: 李鹏 [Lǐ Péng] '(name of a person)'

4: 继 [jì] 'continues'

5: X 界　X [jiè] 'world of X, in X circles'

5: 贯彻 [guànchè] 'carry out'

5: 十三大 [Shísān dà] '(abbr. for 十三届全国人民代表大会) 13th
   National People's Conference'

5: 精神 [jīngshén] 'spirit, feeling'

7: 促进 [cùjìn] 'promotional'

7: 就 X [jiù] X 'concerning X' (SN)

9: 战略 [zhànlüè] 'strategic' WG>25:挑战 [tiǎozhàn] 'challenge to battle'

11: 位置 [wèizhì] 'position'

12: 正确 [zhèngquè] 'accurate' WG>25:确实 [quèshí] 'really'

12: 决策 [juécè] 'policy decision'

13: 迅速 [xùnsù] 'rapidly' WG>14:速度 [sùdù] 'rate of speed'; WG>28:加速
   [jiāsù] 'speed up'

13: 包括 [bāokuò] 'include'

14: 速度 [sùdù] '?' 速WG:13

14: 竞争 [jìngzhēng] 'competition'

15: Clause 1, 就 Clause 2 "if clause 1, then clause 2" (SN)

16: 差距 [chājù] 'disparity'

16: 越X越Y [yuè X yuè Y] 'the more X it is, the more Y it is' (SN)

16: 自立 [zìlì] 'stand on one's own feet'

17: X 之林 X-[zhīlín] 'circles/groups of X'

17: 贫穷 [pínqióng] 'impoverished'

17: 落后 [luòhòu] 'backwards'

18: 底子 [dǐzi] 'base, floor'

18: 薄　　[bó] 'thin, meager'

18: 人均 [rénjūn] 'per capita'

18: 资源 [zīyuán] 'natural resources' WG>20:资产 [zīchǎn] 'assets'

19: 不足 [bùzú] 'insufficient'

19: 总值 [zǒngzhí] 'total value' WG>21:总额 [zǒng'é] 'total figure'

19: 能耗 [nénghào] 'power consumption' WG>19:消耗 [xiāohào]
   'consumption'

19: 原材料 [yuán cáiliào] 'original and processed materials' WG>29: 原则
   [yuánzé] 'principles'

20 发达国家高出许多，劳动生产率、固定资产增值率、人均国民
21 生产总值以及出口总额占国民生产总值的份额等，与发达国家
22 相比，差距就更大了。这就说明，我们的浪费很大，生产的潜
23 力也很大。只有依靠科学技术进步，包括先进的科学的管理，
24 我们才能大幅度地提高经济效益，增加生产，比较迅速地改变
25 贫穷落后的面貌。我们确实面临这样一种严峻的挑战形势，全
26 国人民，首先是全体科技工作者，要充分认识科技进步在实现
27 我国四个现代化艰巨任务中所占据的战略地位，增强紧迫感。

28　　加速我国科技进步既是十分紧迫的，也是完全可能的。党
29 的十一届三中全会以来，我们坚持四项基本原则坚持改革开放，
30 国民经济持续稳定地发展，取得了世界瞩目的成就，积累了宝
31 贵的经验，扩大了国际科技交流，引进了一批先进技术和管理
32 经验，为进一步推动科技进步打下了良好的基础。加速科技进
33 步，我们还有自己的优势。　　　　　　　　　　（下转第二版）

VOCABULARY

20: 劳动 [laódòng] '(physical) labor'

20: 固定 [gùdìng] 'fixed, regular' WG>30:稳定 [wěndìng] 'stable'

20: 资产 [zīchǎn] '?' 资 WG:18

20: 增值率 [zēngzhílǜ] 'rate of increase'

21: 总额 [zǒng'é] '?' 总 WG:19, 额 WG:21

21: 占 [zhàn] 'constitute' WG>27:占据 [zhànjù] 'occupy'

21: 份额 [fèn'é] 'share, portion' 额 WG:21

22: 浪费 [làngfèi] 'waste'

23: 只有X,才Y [zhǐyǒu X, cái Y] 'only if X, then Y' (SN)

23: 依靠 [yīkào] 'rely on'

23: 先进 [xiānjìn] 'advanced' WG>31:引进 [yǐnjìn] 'attract'

24: 效益 [xiàoyì] 'efficiency'

25: 面貌 [miànmào] 'appearance' WG>25:面临 [miànlín] 'be faced with'

25: 确实 [quèshí] '?' 确 WG:12

25: 严峻 [yánjùn] 'rigorous, grim'

25: 挑战 [tiǎozhàn] '?' 战 WG:9

27: 任务 [rènwù] 'duty'

27: 占据 [zhànjù] '?' 占 WG:21

27: 紧迫感 [jǐnpògǎn] 'feeling of urgency'

28: 加速 [jiāsù] '?' 速 WG:13

29: 三中 [sānzhōng] 'third plenum'

29: 原则 [yuánzé] '?' 原 WG:19

30: 持续 [chíxù] 'continue'

30: 稳定 [wěndìng] '?' 定 WG:20

30: 瞩目 [zhǔmù] 'focus on'

30: 积累 [jīlěi] 'amass, accumulate'

30: 宝贵 [bǎoguì] 'precious'

31: 经验 [jīngyàn] 'experience'

31: 交流 [jiāoliú] 'exchange'

31: 引进 [yǐnjìn] '?' 进 WG:23

GRAMMAR EXERCISES

1. 请用各句后所列的词语填空，然后翻成英语：
   一) 中国____发挥科技优势，经济基础越稳定。 (越、为、就)
   二) 六届全运会快结束____，举重比赛还没完。 (着、时、吧)
   三) ____这次运载火箭发射成功，我国通信能力才比得上发达国家。
        (只要、只有、如果)
   四) 国家民委副主席____少数民族经济发展战略特别举行了一次记
        者招待会。 (由、就、又)
   五) 公民____承认的是科技进步的紧迫性。 (只、所、也)
   六) ____我国经济建设，我们应该加速科学技术进步。
        (把、为、由)

2. 请把下列的复合句翻成英语：
   一) 世界妇女得到社会的理解和同情，就被解放了。
   二) 辽宁选手打破213公斤的举重全国记录，就能居各路健儿之首。
   三) 民进党把台独主张政纲化，一定会引起两岸人民的反对。
   四) 李鹏指出，我们大幅度地提高经济效益，就会改变贫穷落后的
        面貌。

3. 请用指定的词语改写下列的句子：
   一) 按检察院统计，近几年来贪污、受贿犯罪行为比以前多。 (越来
        越 Y)
   二) 乡镇办学思想的转变涉及到我国经济建设的速度。 (只有X，才Y)
   三) 孙教授谈起通信卫星时说："这次发射成功对中央电视台转播节目
        的需要十分重要"。 (就 X verb)
   四) 如果环保局的服务小组帮助单位进行技术改造，本省的污染治理
        率将达到98%以上。 (two conditional clauses)

SIGHT READINGS

#1 GUIZHOU SETS UP SCI-TECH DEVELOPMENT FUNDS

1   鼓励基层科技人员为脱贫效力
2   贵州设县级科技发展基金

3   新华社贵阳电　　（记者龙文彬）　为充分发挥基层科技人
4 员在开发县级经济中的作用，贵州省设立县级科技发展基金，
5 先后扶持27个边远的少数民族县和科技基础薄弱的县开展科
6 研工作，收到了"养鸡下蛋"的效果。
7   贵州省70%以上的县财政长期靠国家补贴，近几年实行财
8 政包干后，一些贫困的少数民族地区遇到了科技发展与经费
9 短缺的尖锐矛盾，挫伤了基层科技人员的积极性。针对这种
10 情况，贵州省科委从1986年开始，坚持每年从科技三项费用
11 中挤出一部分资金，采取省、地、县三级匹配的办法，分期
12 分批设立县级科技发展基金。 3年来，使被扶持的27个县科
13 技发展基金达280万元。各县科委对这项基金实行有偿使用，
14 本着"计划指导、同行评议、择优支持"的原则，资助基层
15 科技人员结合当地自然资源、经济发展特点开展科技开发和
16 部分应用基础研究工作。
17   县级科技发展基金建立起来后，推动了基层科研工作的
18 开展，加速了当地的经济开发。

VOCABULARY

1: 鼓励 [gǔlì] 'encourage'
1: 基层 [jīcéng] 'grass roots level'
1: 脱贫 [tuōpín] 'escape poverty'
2: 县级 [xiànjí] 'county level'

2: 基金 [jījīn] 'funds'

5: 扶持 [fúchí] 'support'

5: 薄弱 [bóruò] 'weak'

6: 养鸡下蛋 [yǎngjī xiàdàn] 'raise chickens, get eggs'

7: 补贴 [bǔtiē] 'subsidies'

8: 包干 [bāogān] 'be responsible for a task until completion'

9: 尖锐 [jiānruì] 'sharp'

9: 矛盾 [máodùn] 'paradox'

9: 挫伤 [cuòshāng] 'discourage, dampen'

10: 挤出 [jǐchū] 'squeeze out'

11: 匹配 [pǐpèi] 'matching'

13: 有偿 [yǒucháng] 'compensatory'

14: 同行评议 [tóngháng píngyì] 'peer review'

14: 择优 [zéyōu] 'select the best'

15: 应用 [yìngyòng] 'applied'

QUESTIONS

A. What basic reason is given for setting up these funds?

B. In what type of areas is this policy being implemented?

C. Where has most of the revenues come from in the past?

D. When did this policy start, and where did the initial funding come from?

E. What three administrative levels receive allocations?

F. What three principles were followed in making funding decisions?

G. To what does 70% refer?

#2 KUNMING TECH INTENSIFIES APPLIED RESEARCH

1 　　　　　　　与大中型企业建立长期联系
2 　　　　　　　昆明工学院加强应用研究
3 　　本报讯 记者陈可报道：昆明工学院在扶持乡镇企业的同时，
4 积极与国营大中型企业合作，目前，已和全国 20 个省市的 124 家
5 大中型企业建立了长期联系。
6 　　近几年来，昆明工学院约有 90% 的教师、科技人员投入了应
7 用研究，在取得的 389 项科研成果中，已有 224 项为生产单位采
8 用。
9 　　他们打破行业、部门界限，先后与全国 20 个省市的 24 家大
10 企业、100 家中型企业建立了长期科技合作关系，并在人才培
11 养、毕业生分配等方面与一些企业达成了协议。

VOCABULARY

1: 大中型 [dà zhōng xíng] 'large and medium scale'

1: 企业 [qǐyè] 'enterprises'

1: 联系 [liánxì] 'relationships'

4: 国营 [guóyíng] 'state managed'

6: 投入 [tóurù] 'throw (oneself) into (some activity)'

9: 打破 [dǎpò] 'smash'

9: 界限 [jièxiàn] 'dividing line'

11: 毕业生 [bìyèshēng] 'graduates'

11: 分配 [fēnpèi] '(job) assignment'

11: 协议 [xiéyì] 'agreements'

QUESTIONS

A. According to the first paragraph, what is the geographical focus of this project?

B. What statistics are quoted to show how successful the faculty and staff of Kunming Tech have been on this project?

C. What boundaries does the article talk about smashing?

D. In what areas besides that of the fruit of applied research have agreements been made?

Identify the grammar of the following headlines and translate them into English:

学生面前难题多

专业选择出路有困惑   社会分配不公太刺激

中国人民大学研究生   刘华杰

人才"流外"的思索

改革使科技人员如鱼得水

瀋陽部分工程師富裕起來

安徽省最近一次抽样调查表明

中年科技人员不能很好发挥作用的占八成

对考试办法、专业范围等作出具体规定

国务院发布高等教育自学考试条例

单独拿出名额给中青年讲师竞争副教授

大连理工大学让人才公平竞争

三万女企业家大展风采

效率高了吸引力才大

我国劳动制度的重大改革

未获答复或不同意调出者，可自行离职到所要调往单位工作

新办法规定，工人提出调动工作书面申请三个月后仍

北京工人有了择业权

农村教育要为振兴当地经济服务

海城市积极培养地方乡土人才

目前，全市接受市、乡、村三级农民教育的人数已达30多万

沈阳成立人才流动争议仲裁机构

物价上涨远过收入成长

Reading Chinese Newspapers:
Tactics and Skills

Lesson Eleven: Anti-Smoking Campaign

1988年3月23日　星期三　第五版

人民日报

提倡戒烟　控制吸烟

控制吸烟是关系到人身健康的大事

吸烟危害人体健康，已为世界公认。但由于吸烟是个慢性过程，对健康的直接危害要经过一定时间才能显露出来，甚至要反映在子女身上。因而吸烟有害却难以为某些吸烟者，特别是青年人所接受，吸烟也就更增加了它潜在的危险性。当前，许多发达国家越来越多的人戒烟，一些跨国的烟草企业，不得不千方百计地向发展中国家拓宽烟叶与卷烟市场。由于我国人多，吸烟率高，种烟人数及烟制品产量都有不断增长的趋势，因此，我国面临戒烟和控制吸烟的问题就显得十分突出和艰巨。国务院领导同志提出，要不断地宣传吸烟的危害，以提高人们不吸烟的自觉性，在公共场所要禁止吸烟。

为了响应世界卫生组织确定的今年4月7日为"世界无烟日"的号召，中央爱国卫生运动委员会、卫生部联合发出了《关于围绕"世界无烟日"积极开展劝阻吸烟活动的通知》，对控制吸烟和禁止吸烟问题提出了具体要求。一些地区和单位还因地制宜地制订了一些规定，如河北定州市人民政府专门发出了《关于提倡戒烟和控制吸烟的公告》，规定了一些公共场所和有关人员严禁吸烟。

为了把控制吸烟这一有利于民族健康的大事做好，国家有必要采取有力的具体措施。一些发达国家已开始采取立法的手段。如美国纽约市已通过了一项法案，规定在一切公共场所吸烟均要受罚。由于种种原因，我国控制吸烟的活动困难重重。我认为，认识的不统一，宣传教育的不深入，以及缺乏必要的行政措施，是影响这一工作开展的主要原因。目前，我国约有2.5亿吸烟者，他们中一部分人已经吸烟几十年，毫无戒烟愿望，一部分人则处于欲戒又止，反反复复的状态，一部分人尤其是青少年，因吸烟时间不长，自觉危害不深，反而以为吸烟是一种消遣。根据这种状况，我认为，应采取"早、少、小"的三字措施来控制吸烟。

所谓"早"，即早采取措施，包括预防措施和除戒措施。青少年是禁烟的重点人群。调查表明，我国一些地区，10岁以下的少年儿童中已有吸烟者。如果动员社会力量，特别是动员孩子的家长和教师做好青少年的禁烟工作，就会有成效。教育部门应该规定"中小学生严禁吸烟"，并认真落实。

所谓"少"，即劝阻那些一时不能戒烟者尽量少吸，在不允许吸烟的场所不吸，劝说他们尽快戒烟。同时，我们也要求，我国生产的烟草制品中焦油及其它有害物质的含量，要大幅度减少，以减轻对人体的危害。

所谓"小"，即逐渐缩小吸烟的危害程度，把某些与吸烟有关的疾病加以防治，使之发病率逐年降低。

控制吸烟，不仅是吸烟者要遵守的社会公德，负有执行有关规定的责任；不吸烟者，也有宣传、劝阻与帮助吸烟者戒烟的责任。在这个问题上，人们应该表现出互相关心、互相帮助的好风气。这不仅将有效地保证控制吸烟工作广泛、深入、持久地开展下去，而且也标志着我国的文明程度达到了一个新的标准。

　　　　中央爱国卫生运动委员会办公室副主任　**韩长林**

吸烟为何屡禁不止

(reproduction of original text)

革除公共场所吸烟的

吸烟对人体健康的危害是很大的，尤其在乘坐火车、轮船时，车厢里、船舱里，人员多，通风不好，人们受烟害尤为严重。在车厢、船舱这种公共场所吸烟，是一种陋习，应刻不容缓地革除。我相信，这种做法一定会得到广大公民拥护。

据我所知，建国以来发生的车船火灾事故，许多是吸烟者扔烟头引起的，真正"自燃"或因为高温高压引起的车船火灾事故，没成效甚微；有的部门依旧你说你的，我干我的。这一对矛盾，有认识上的问题，也有实际上协调统一起来，禁止吸烟，只前，要使戒烟取得一点实效，停止进口香烟，其次在广泛宣

定，严禁在火车厉处罚。

会场

现在，只要会，一些吸烟者

STRUCTURE NOTES

The use of 已, 如, 则, 应, 反而, 因而, 无, and 为 give this letter to the editor a flavor of the Neo-classical prose style of writing.

Note the variety of punctuation markers in this piece; 。, 、, " ", 《 》, and ，. Use them to guide your reading.

2: 已 is an abbreviation of 已经 frequently used in the literary style of writing. See also lines 20, 21, and 32; line 25 has the full 已经.

2: 为 How is 为 used here and in line 4 after 难以? Does it have second or fourth tone? As part of the descriptive structure for 号召 in line 12, 为 has the same tone, but it is used for a very different meaning. See 8:12.

2-3: Verb 1, 才 Verb 2 = 'When the first verb action occurs, then and only then can the second verb action happen' 才 is a very useful guide to the position of a core verb. See its related usage in 10:25.

  a. 我学习了两年中文，才到中国去。
  b. 经济发展加速了，中国西部少数民族地区才能进入国际市场。

4: 却 Expect 却 to mark a change in direction of thought in the discourse. It is also useful to keep in mind that it is a marker of the second core verb in a tandem construction. See 4:8 for further comments.

6: 越 What structure do you expect when you see 越? See 10:17. While 越 X 越 Y comes right before a 的 here and so is part of a structure modifying a noun, it still conveys the same basic meaning of 'It is getting more and more Y'.

6: 不得[dé] 不 Verb = 'Have no choice but to verb' Two negatives make a positive.
  a. 到沈阳去以前我不得不念一两年中文。
  b. 广州饮水污染率一高，该市就不得不兴建一个污水处理厂。

9: Verb 得[dě] Verb phrase = 'Verb done in a particular manner' The verb phrase after the 得 generally translates into English as an adverb. Context makes it clear whether to read 得 as [dé], [děi] or [dě]. When a verb follows 得, it is read [děi] 'must verb'. When it is used in 不得不 (1. 6) or when a noun follows 得, it is read [dé] 'get the noun'. (When a noun follows 得到, it is [dédào] 'get the noun'; when a place name follows 得到, it is [děidào] 'must go to the place'.) When used as a verb complement in Verb 得 Verb 'able to verb' (see 3:12) or in Verb 得 Verb phrase 'manner of verbing' (this line) it is read [dě]. 得 is used for all three values in various vocabulary items: e.g., 获得 [huòdé] 'obtain', 记得 [jìdě] 'remember' and 必得 [bìděi] 'must'. Examples of 得 used to mark 'manner of verbing' are:

> a. 听说到天津来的那位留学生汉语说得非常好。
> b. 谈起妇女在生理上、精神上所付出的代价时，全国妇联主席讲得十分有说服力。

12: 为了 X, What do you look for to find the end of a 为了 adverbial phrase when it starts a sentence? See 3:44. The grammatical structure of this 为了 phrase is V(响应) O(号召). The 为了 X, phrase in 19 has the structure 把 O(大事) V(做好).

16: 如 X = 'For example/like X' 如 and its synonym 譬如 [pìrú] are used to introduce and mark clarifying examples.

22-24: The object of 认为 is structured as X 是 Y wherein X is clause 1, clause 2, 以及 clause 3 and Y is ...的 Y.

24: 亿 [yì] = '100,000,000' Multiply 2.5 times 100,000,000 to find out how many smokers there are in China.

25: Note that duration of time, that is the length of time involved in doing a verb action, goes after the verb and before the object.

> a. 我们已经学习了两三年中文了。
> b. 中美两国建交已经有十多年了。

26: 则 [zé] Verb 'However/but verb' 则 is used as an adverb in writings to indicate 'change' or 'comparison', among other things. Here it marks a change of focus from people who have absolutely no desire to quit smoking to some who want to stop but are having trouble doing so.

30: 即 [jí] = 'That is, i.e.' The clarification that 即 introduces may be as simple as a noun or as complex as the structures here and in 35-36 and 39-40. Be careful to distinguish between 即 and 既 [jì]; see 7:39.

38: 以 What is the function of 以 between the two verb phrases here and those in 10? See 4:38.

44-47: 不仅 X，也 Y is a literary synonym of 不但 X, 而且 Y. See 5:25 for comments on processing sentences with tandem structures. Note its use in line 41 without

也 in second clause.

45: Compare the use of 着 and 了 in this last comma unit. Why is 着 used after 标志 and 了 after 达到 rather than vice versa? What differing messages do their uses here convey about the anti-smoking campaign and the state of Chinese civilization?

1   控制吸烟是关系到人身健康的大事

2   吸烟危害人体健康，已为世界公认。但由于吸烟是个慢性
3   过程，对健康的直接危害要经过一定时间才能显露出来，甚至
4   要反映到子女身上。因而吸烟有害却难以为某些吸烟者，特别
5   是青年人所接受，吸烟也就更增加了它的潜在的危险性。当前，
6   许多发达国家越来越多的人戒烟，一些跨国的烟草企业，不得
7   不千方百计地向发展中国家拓宽烟叶与卷烟市场。由于我国人
8   多，吸烟率高，种烟人数及烟制品产量都有不断增长的趋势，
9   因此，我国面临戒烟和控制吸烟的问题就显得十分突出和艰巨。
10   国务院领导同志提出，要不断地宣传吸烟的危害，以提高人们
11   不吸烟的自觉性，在公共场所要禁止吸烟。

                          VOCABULARY

1: 控制 [kòngzhì] 'control' 制 WG:8,15
1: 吸烟 [xīyān] 'smoking' WG>6: 烟草 [yāncǎo] 'tobacco'; WG>7: 烟叶
        [yānyè] 'tobacco leaf'; WG>7: 卷烟 [juǎnyān] 'cigars and cigarettes';
        WG>8: 种烟 [zhòngyān] 'plant tobacco'; WG>8: 烟制品 [yānzhìpǐn]
        'tobacco products'
1: 人身 [rénshēn] 'human body' WG>31: 人群 [rénqún] 'crowd'
1: 健康 [jiànkāng] 'health'
2: 危害 [wēihài] 'harm, endanger' WG>4: 有害 [yǒuhài] 'harmful'; WG>5:
        危险 [wēixiǎn] 'danger'
2: 已   [yǐ] "abbreviation for 已经" (SN)
2: 慢性 [mànxìng] 'slow (in effect)'
3: 直接 [zhíjiē] 'direct'
3: 才V2 [cái] "then and only then verb 2"

3: 显露 [xiǎnlù] 'manifest itself'

4: 反映 [fǎnyìng] 'reflect' WG>26:反复 [fǎnfù] 'over and over'; WG>27:反而 [fǎn'ér] 'to the contrary'

4: 因而 [yīn'ér] 'thus, as a result' 而 WG:27

4: 有害 [yǒuhài] '?' 害 WG:2

4: 某些 [mǒuxiē] 'a certain number of'

5: 潜在 [qiánzài] 'latent'

5: 危险 [wēixiǎn] '?' 危 WG:2

6: 戒 X [jiè X] 'give up X, forego X' WG>30:除戒 [chújiè] 'swear off'

6: 跨国 [kuàguó] 'transnational'

6: 烟草 [yāncǎo] '?' 烟 WG:1

6: 不得不V [bùdébù verb] 'have no choice but to verb' (SN)

7: 千方百计 [qiānfāng bǎijì] 'by every possible means'

7: 发展中 [fāzhǎn zhōng] 'developing' WG>14:开展 [kāizhǎn] 'develop'

7: 拓宽 [tuòkuān] 'open up, broaden'

7: 烟叶 [yānyè] '?' 烟 WG:1

7: 卷烟 [juǎnyān] '?' 烟 WG:1

7: 市场 [shìchǎng] 'market' WG>11:场所 [chǎngsuǒ] 'arena'

8: 种烟 [zhòngyān] '?' 烟 WG:1

8: 烟制品 [yānzhìpǐn] '?' 烟 WG:1, 制 WG:15

8: 产量 [chǎnliàng] 'output, yield'

8: 不断 [búduàn] 'non-stop'

8: 趋势 [qūshì] 'trend'

9: 面临 [miànlín] 'be faced with'

9: V得 [Verb dě] "manner of verbing"

9: 艰巨 [jiānjù] 'formidable'

10: 宣传 [xuānchuán] 'give publicity to'

11: 场所 [chǎngsuǒ] '?' 场 WG:7

11: 禁止 [jìnzhǐ] 'prohibit, ban'

12　　　　为了响应世界卫生组织确定的今年4月7日为"世界无烟日"
13　的号召，中央爱国卫生运动委员会、卫生部联合发出了《关于
14　围绕"世界无烟日"积极开展劝阻吸烟活动的通知》，对控制
15　吸烟和禁止吸烟问题提出了具体要求。一些地区和单位还因地
16　制宜地制订了一些规定，如河北定州市人民政府专门发出了
17　《关于提倡戒烟和控制吸烟的公告》，规定了一些公共场所和
18　有关人员严禁吸烟。

19　　　　为了把控制吸烟这一有利于民族健康的大事做好，国家有
20　必要采取有力的具体措施。一些发达国家已开始采取立法的手
21　段。如美国纽约市已通过了一项法案，规定在一切公共场所吸
22　烟均要受罚。由于种种原因，我国控制吸烟的活动困难重重。
23　我认为，认识的不统一，宣传教育的不深入，以及缺乏必要的
24　行政措施，是影响这一工作开展的主要原因。目前，我国约有
25　2.5亿吸烟者，他们中一部分人已经吸烟几十年，毫无戒烟愿望；
26　一部分人则处于欲戒又止，反反复复的状态；一部分人尤其是
27　青少年，因吸烟时间不长，自觉危害不深，反而以为吸烟是一
28　种消遣。根据这种状况，我认为，应采取"早、少、小"的三
29　字措施来控制吸烟。

VOCABULARY

12: 响应 [xiǎngyìng] 'respond to'

12: 世界卫生组织 [Shìjiè wèishēng zǔzhī] 'World Health Organization'

12: 无　[wú] 'be without' WG>25: 毫无 [háowú] 'absolutely without'

13: 号召 [hàozhào] 'slogan'

13: 爱国 [àiguó] 'patriotic'

13: 运动 [yùndòng] 'movement' WG>32: 动员 [dòngyuán] 'mobilize'

13: 联合 [liánhé] 'jointly'

14: 围绕 [wéirǎo] 'center on'

14: 开展 [kāizhǎn] '?' 展 WG:7

14: 劝阻 [quànzǔ] 'dissuade from' WG>36:劝说 [quànshuō] 'persuade'

14: 通知 [tōngzhī] 'notice'

15: 具体 [jùtǐ] 'concrete, specific'

15: 因地制宜 [yīn dì zhì yí] 'suit measures to local conditions' 制 WG:1, 烟WG:8; WG>16:制订 [zhìdìng] 'formulate'

16: 规定 [guīdìng] 'rules, stipulations'

16: 如　[rú] 'for example' (SN)

17: 提倡 [tíchàng] 'advocate, promote'

20: 手段 [shǒuduàn] 'methods'

21: 一切 [yīqiè] 'every'

22: 受罚 [shòufá] 'be punished'

22: 重重 [chóngchóng] 'layer on layer'

23: 深入 [shēnrù] 'go deeply into'

24: 行政 [xíngzhèng] 'administration'

24: 影响 [yǐngxiǎng] 'influence'

24: 约　[yuē] 'approximately'

25: 亿　[yì] 'hundred million' (SN)

25: 毫无 [háowú] '?' 无 WG:12

26: 则V [zé] Verb 'however, verb' (SN)

26: 欲　[yù] 'desire'

26: 反复 [fǎnfù] '?' 反 WG:4

26: 状态 [zhuàngtài] 'state of affairs' WG>28:状况 [zhuàngkuàng] 'condition'

26: 青少年 [qīng shàonián] 'teenagers' WG>28:早少小 [zǎo shǎo xiǎo] (a slogan)'; 少 WG:38

27: 反而 [fǎn'ér] '?' 反 WG:4, 而 WG:4

28: 消遣 [xiāoqiǎn] 'pastime'

28: 状况 [zhuàngkuàng] '?' 状 WG:26

28: 早少小 '[zǎo shǎo xiǎo]' '?' 少 WG:26, 小 WG:39

30　　　所谓"早"，即早采取措施，包括预防措施和除戒措施。
31　青少年是禁烟的重点人群。调查表明，我国一些地区，10岁以
32　下的少年儿童中已有吸烟者。如果动员社会力量，特别是动员
33　孩子的家长和教师做好青少年的禁烟工作，就会有成效。教育
34　部门应该规定"中小学生严禁吸烟"，并认真落实。
35　　　所谓"少"，即劝阻那些一时不能戒烟者尽量少吸，在不
36　允许吸烟的场所不吸，劝说他们尽快戒烟。同时，我们也要求
37　我国生产的烟草制品中焦油及其它有害物质的含量，要大幅度
38　减少，以减轻对人体的危害。
39　　　所谓"小"，即逐渐缩小吸烟的危害程度，把某些与吸烟
40　有关的疾病加以防治，使之发病率逐年降低。
41　　　控制吸烟，不仅是吸烟者要遵守的社会公德，负有执行有
42　关规定的责任；不吸烟者，也有宣传、劝阻与帮助吸烟者戒烟
43　的责任。在这个问题上，人们应表现出互相关心、互相帮助的
44　好风气。这不仅将有效地保证控制吸烟工作广泛、深入、持久
45　地开展下去，而且也标志着我国的文明程度达到了一个新的标
46　准。
47　　　中央爱国卫生运动委员会办公室副主任　　韩长林

VOCABULARY

30: 所谓 [suǒwèi] 'so called'

30: 即　　[jí] 'i.e., that is' (SN)

30: 包括 [bāokuò] 'include'

30: 预防 [yùfáng] 'prevent' WG>40: 防治 [fángzhì] 'prevention and cure'

30: 除戒 [chújiè] '?' 戒 WG:6

31: 人群 [rénqún] '?' 人 WG:1

32: 儿童 [értóng] '(young) children'

32: 动员 [dòngyuán] '?' 动 WG:13

33: 家长 [jiāzhǎng] 'parents'

33: 成效 [chéngxiào] 'results' WG>44:有效 [yǒuxiào] 'effectively'

34: 认真 [rènzhēn] 'conscientiously'

34: 落实 [luòshí] 'implement, put into effect'

35: 尽量 [jìnliàng] 'as much as one can' WG>36:尽快 [jìnkuài] 'as soon as possible'; 量 WG:37

36: 允许 [yǔnxǔ] 'permit, allow'

36: 劝说 [quànshuō] '?' 劝 WG:14

36: 尽快 [jìnkuài] '?' 尽 WG:35

37: 焦油 [jiāoyóu] 'tar'

37: 物质 [wùzhì] 'substance'

37: 含量 [hánliàng] 'content' 量 WG:35

37: 幅度 [fúdù] 'extent' WG>39:程度 [chéngdù] 'degree'

38: 减少 [jiǎnshǎo] 'reduce' 少WG:27; WG>38:减轻 [jiǎnqīng] 'lighten'

39: 逐渐 [zhújiàn] 'gradually' WG>40:逐年 [zhúnián] 'year by year'

39: 缩小 [suōxiǎo] 'shrink' 小 WG:28

39: 程度 [chéngdù] '?' 度 WG:37

40: 疾病 [jíbìng] 'illness'

40: 防治 [fángzhì] '?' 防 WG:30

40: 逐年 [zhúnián] '?' 逐 WG:39

40: 降低 [jiàngdī] 'lower'

41: 遵守 [zūnshǒu] 'respect, observe'

41: 公德 [gōngdé] 'public morality'

41: 负 [fù] 'bear (responsibility)'

41: 执行 [zhíxíng] 'carry out'

44: 风气 [fēngqì] 'public attitude'

44: 不仅X,也Y [bùjǐn] X, [yě] Y 'not only X, also Y' (SN)

44: 有效 [yǒuxiào] '?' 效 WG:33

44: 保证 [bǎozhèng] 'guarantee'

44: 广泛 [guǎngfàn] 'extensively'

44: 持久 [chíjiǔ] 'enduringly'

45: 标志 [biāozhì] 'symbolize'

47: 韩长林 [Hán Chánglín] '(name of a person)'

GRAMMAR EXERCISES

1. 把下列的词语分别填入句中然后翻成英语: 才、由于、不得不、却、
   越...越、得、只要
   一) 世界公认控制烟制品产量问题显＿＿＿越来越重要。
   二) 只有戒烟运动深入人民的思想，戒烟者＿＿＿多。
   三) 尽管政府不断宣传吸烟的危害，而且一部分人＿＿＿毫无戒烟愿望。
   四) ＿＿＿烟叶含有焦油，吸烟就会危害人体健康。
   五) 调查表明十岁以下的儿童有吸烟者时，因此教育部＿＿＿严禁中小
       学生吸烟。
   六) 吸烟的危险性突出，政府＿＿＿通过一项控制吸烟的法案。

2. 选词填空并翻译:
   一) 不吸烟者＿＿＿有帮助吸烟者戒烟的责任。 (不、却、才)
   二) 因而一部分青少年以为吸烟是一种消遣，＿＿＿要继续吸烟。 (就、
       得、则)
   三) 目前我国戒烟的青少年＿＿＿来＿＿＿多。 (才、却、越)
   四) 大众要遵守社会公德＿＿＿不得不戒烟。 (就、则、以)
   五) 家长和教师必须把禁烟的工作做＿＿＿非常深入。 (得、为、成)
   六) 人们只有充分了解吸烟对人身有害＿＿＿有戒烟的愿望。 (则、越、
       才)

3. 改写下列的句子并翻成英文:
   一) 当地经济能够振兴以前，教委必须端正办学指导思想。 (verb 1，
       才verb2)
   二) 为了使通信卫星容量比以前增大，航天工业部的设计人员作了研
       究。 (三年)
   三) 为了打破省纪录，湖北体操选手当然作了很多练习。 (不得不)
   四) 中国外交部长同美国国务卿将要讨论一些重要的外交政策问题。
       (verb得认真)

SIGHT READINGS

#1 LETTER TO THE EDITOR: SMOKING HARMS EVERYBODY

1 吸烟害己害人
2 吸烟对人体有害无益，当前许多国家都劝导人们戒烟。近
3 年来，我国也开始宣传戒烟，但收效甚微。在国内纸烟销售量
4 有增无减的情况下，不少外国香烟又纷纷进入我国市场。如果
5 各国戒烟走在我国前面，我国进口的外国烟将越来越多，不但
6 经济上蒙受损失，还会使国人饱受烟害之苦。我认为，应该大
7 声疾呼戒烟！
8 　　　　　　　　　　郑州铁路分局调度所　　张振岭

VOCABULARY

2: 无益　[wúyì] 'without benefit'

2: 劝导　[quàndǎo] 'try to persuade'

3: 收效　[shōuxiào] 'results'

3: 甚　　[shèn] 'very'

3: 微　　[wēi] 'tiny, minute'

3: 销售量 [xiāoshòuliàng] 'sales capacity'

4: 纷纷　[fēnfēn] 'one after another'

6: 蒙受　[méngshòu] 'suffer'

6: 损失　[sǔnshī] 'losses, damages'

6: X 之苦 [X zhīkǔ] 'suffering because of X'

7: 疾呼　[jíhū] 'shout'

8: 郑州　[Zhèngzhōu] '(name of a city)'

8: 铁路　[tiělù] 'railroad'

8: 调度所 [diàodùsuǒ] 'dispatch office'

8: 张振岭 [Zhāng Zhènlǐng] '(name of a person)'

QUESTIONS

A. What two facts are established in the first sentence?

B. What two facts are quoted to demonstrate that anti-smoking efforts in China are not being successful?

C. Why does the writer think there may be more foreign cigarettes in China?

D. What will be the medical and non-medical harmful effects of more foreign cigarettes?

E. What does the writer suggest doing?

#2 SMOKING AND HEART DISEASE

1   吸烟与冠心病

2   吸烟者冠心病的发病率比不吸烟者高4倍左右。吸烟量越大，
3   持续的时间越长，开始吸烟的年龄越早，患冠心病的可能性也
4   越大。根据病理检查资料分析，各年龄组重度吸烟者的冠状动
5   脉病变较不吸烟者或少吸烟者严重。冠状动脉的病变程度与吸
6   烟量是平行的。
7   吸烟越来越成为一个社会问题。国家虽然每年可从烟草生
8   产中获得税利，但是每年成千上万因患肺癌、肺心病及冠心病
9   而需要治疗的人，却要国家为此支出巨大的医药费用。
10   (摘自《中老年保健》总第 4 期 柯元南文)

VOCABULARY

1: 冠心病 [guānxīnbìng] 'coronary disease'

2: 倍 [bèi] 'times'

3: 年龄 [niánlíng] '(years of) age'

3: 患 [huàn] 'contract an illness'

4: 病理 [bìnglǐ] 'pathology'

4: 资料 [zīliào] 'materials'

4: 重度 [zhòngdù] 'heavily'

4: 冠状动脉 [guānzhuàng dòngmài] 'coronary artery'

6: 平行 [píngxíng] 'parallel'

9: 税利 [shuìlì] 'tax revenues'

8: 肺癌 [fèi'ái] 'lung cancer'

9: 治疗 [zhìliáo] 'treatment'

9: 支出 [zhīchū] 'pay'

9: 医药 [yīyào] 'medical'

10: 摘 [zhāi] 'abridged'

10: 中老年保健 [Zhōnglǎonián bǎojiàn] '(name of a journal)'

10: 柯元南 [Kē Yuánnán] '(name of a person)'

QUESTIONS

A. How many more smokers than non-smokers have coronary problems?

B. What three factors in smoking cause a greater chance of coronary illness?

C. What two factors parallel each other?

D. What greater social problem is seen as a consequence of smoking?

E. What does the the name of the journal in which this article appears mean?

国 务 院 办 公 厅 通 知 各 地

立即关停计划外烟厂

会场上严禁吸烟

戒烟在我国为何收效甚微

吸 烟 为 何 屡 禁 不 止

革除公共场所吸烟的陋习

请　勿　吸　烟！

烟草专卖局申明严惩倒买倒卖

挪威立法禁止在公共场合吸烟

吸烟与戒烟

六城市劝阻吸烟效果调查表明

十五岁以上者「烟民」超过四成

今日台灣

Reading Chinese Newspapers:
Tactics and Skills

*Lesson Twelve: Selections from Taiwan
Newspapers*

中央日報　CENTRAL DAILY NEWS

(A) 大陸民航突然大幅加價
勢將大量流失內地遊客
已造成香港旅行業者雙重損失

【本報香港二十五日電】中共突然宣佈將大陸內地民航……

(B) 中共其担承財政因難重重
收入成長緩慢亦字逾年增加

(C) 甘肅慶陽地區暴雨成災
54人喪生數千人失居所

【本報香港二十五日電】……

(D) 深圳經濟詐欺案多
去年騙取金額龐大

【本報香港二十五日電】……

(E) 大陸菸酒高漲

(F) 溫州並龍舟賽 耗資逾千萬

(G) 大陸最後西雙版

TAIWAN NEWSPAPERS PAGE LAYOUT

As exemplified in the reproduction (on opposite page) of the top right 1/4 of a page from the Central Daily News, both page layout and line direction in newspapers from Taiwan are from right to left and top to bottom. Articles begin at the top right side of a page, so you should start reading from the top of the right-most line in an article. Read down to the end of the line and then go to the top of the next line to the left and read down it, and so on. The article of primary importance is generally placed at the top right of the page. This format differs greatly from the left to right page layout and predominantly horizontal line direction of Mainland papers.

Headlines are generally printed vertically, with the primary headline presented in larger typeface. As is the case in example articles A, C, D, E, F and G opposite , the right-most headline of each article should be read first. When headlines are presented horizontally, as in example B, they are to be read from right to left. This is opposite of how you read headlines in Mainland papers. Despite these differences in format, headlines in papers from Taiwan are similar to those from the Mainland in omitting grammatical markers and being concise. Headline information is presented in the body of the text in the manner we have repeatedly seen in Mainland papers.

A second obvious difference is that all Taiwan newspapers are always printed in the traditional full form characters. Less obvious but of importance to your work with these texts is a tendency to use more scholarly variant forms of characters; e.g., 纔 for 才 and 著 for 着, and to choose vocabulary for traditional literary values. Grammatical structures are fundamentally the same, though newspapers in Taiwan tend to employ a greater number of classical patterns. Punctuation usages are essentially the same in both.

Another major difference is in what might be called the physical cohesion of articles. All of a Mainland article tends to be placed together in a physically contiguous block, with occasional continuation on a different page, as we saw in Lesson Ten. Newspapers from Taiwan very often have articles that seem to meander off down the page. A simple example of this is article B which has a shorter second row of information placed directly under the right 1/4 of the beginning of the article. A third and fourth row are neatly placed directly under the second. An example of physically separate placement of the continuation of an article can be seen in D which has a final row of information placed away from it directly under the last row of article C. This type of layout is common, and it sometimes results in articles which seem to snake their way across and down the page. There are six rules which are helpful to keep in mind when reading articles of this type: 1) The continuation must start below and to the right of the end of the last line in the row you are reading. 2) There will be a physical divider of some sort between the continuation and other articles. In this example the divider is simply a blank space between articles. In other cases it may be some kind of printed line. 3) If the last line of the row is not end-marked with a period, question mark or exclamation mark, that is a firm indication that the article continues, somewhere. If a period is in the last space in the last line in a row, look around--there may be more to the piece. 4) The individual characters which represent words of two or more syllables can be separated by the end of one row and the start of another. For example, in article B the 改 of 改革 ends row 2 and 革 starts row 3, the 改 of 改進 ends row 3 and 進 starts row 4. When faced with this situation, look at the first character of the first line of a following row for a likely match. 5) Grammatical structures can be divided between the end of one row and the start of another as happens with 為 X V O in rows 1 and 2 of article B. The trick here is prediciting and then finding the rest of the structure. 6) Looking for vocabulary and themes presented earlier in the article can also help in finding the rest of the text. It is sometimes quite a challenge to find the end of an article, but using these rules helps.

The rest of this lesson will consist of articles from the 中央日報. The first one is on economics, an important topic we only lightly touched upon earlier. The rest of the readings will be on topics or variations on topics we worked with earlier, so although they are printed in the traditional, full form characters, you will already be familiar with much of the vocabulary. To help you read these texts more easily, some familiar words which are written with full form characters very different from their simplified character versions seen earlier are glossed next to the articles.

調查趙紫陽「反革命暴亂」

中共設專案小組　由保守派

據此間「南華早報」引述北京消息人士說，中共已經組成一個專案審查小組以調查前總書記趙紫陽涉及去年「反革命暴亂」的情形。

這個特別的任務編組是在去年底由中共「人民政治協商會議」副主席王任重領導成立的。

這個專案小組的成員包括彭真的一個兒子在內。彭真是中共前「全國人大」主席的馬列主義者。

這個小組將蒐集趙紫陽一夥在去年五、六月間的活動情形；蒐集的範圍包括他們曾經接觸過的人，以及他們發出的文件，以及他們與學生之間的關係。

據了解，關於王任重與彭真的這項任命，曾經過中共最高領導人鄧小平的批准。

不過，這個專案小組的結論，尤其是在如何處置趙紫陽的問題上所作的建議，都將由中共元老作最後的審查。

北京一位外交界人士指出，鄧小平任命出一位比較保守的人來領導這個調查小組，其部分原因是爲安撫黨內的保守派。

王任重與保守派元老彭真的密切關係，再加上彭真的兒子也是專案小組成員的事。

中共不與南韓建立官方關係

鄧小平曾提四原則　強調不爲利益所惑

香港／

此間「經濟日報」二十三日報導，去年十一月六日中共頭子鄧小平在與到訪的北韓首腦金日成會晤時，並未表示中共會與南韓建立政治關係；相反地，鄧小平提出了絕不與南韓發生官方關係的四條原則。

「經濟日報」引述一份中共內部文件說，鄧小平所提的四原則爲：一、絕不能使中共的行動違背朝鮮人民的國家統一；二、絕不在政治上承認南朝鮮，也不在政治上製造兩個朝鮮；三、絕不與南朝鮮進行官式往來；四、與南朝鮮的貿易局限於民間，基本的形式是間接的。

中共內部文件透露，鄧小平指出，中共以前是根據這些（原則）辦，以後也一定堅持這些原則。

報導說，鄧小平在與金日成的談話中還強調：「不管它（指南韓）有多大好處，我們都不會突破這些原則。」

「經濟日報」引述分析家認爲，鄧小平的講話概括了中共與南韓關係的全貌，界定了兩者的關係，也回答了外界對近年來兩者關係改善後引起的猜測。（中央社）

經濟改革造成物價紊亂

通貨膨脹、搶購及貪瀆現象續惡化

一路透社北平十八日電

中共經濟改革的主要鼓吹者今天表示，如果「政府」不減緩經濟成長以及變動物價制度，則通貨膨脹、搶購和物品短缺的情形也將更加嚴重。

隨著經濟的成長，這些物品短缺引起的通貨膨脹，將致民衆進行搶購。

隸屬中共「國務院」的「經濟技術社會發展研究中心」「總幹事」吳景連（譯音）指出，改革社會主義經濟的關鍵在於改革不合理的物價制度。

「如果不這樣，通貨膨脹、貨品短缺、搶購和官員貪瀆的現象將會惡化，而有發生社會秩序混亂之虞。」

北平「金融時報」本月十五日報導的廣泛搶購現象，是今年前五個月儲蓄華比去年同期下降的主因。

吳景連認爲，物價制度若不予改革，中國大陸的整體經濟改革計畫便無法成功。同也有人指出，改革中國大陸的工廠是關鍵所在，在改革物價制度之前必須先改革工廠。

中共「總理」李鵬前天在北平的零售價比去年同期上漲了百分之十四左右，這是一九四九年以來的最高漲幅。同一時期，工業生產增加百分之二十七．二。

吳某指出，「政府」必須從緊縮信用和控制貨幣問題，來減緩經濟成長。

他接受路透社訪問時說：「一件貨品如果稀少，它的價格應該高昂。但在中國大陸，情形卻相反。像煤、石油、原料和電力等極爲稀少的東西，價格反而最爲低廉。」

STRUCTURE NOTES

3: 路透 [Lùtòu] 'Reuter's' is an English news agency.

3: Beijing is referred to as 北平 in newspapers printed in Taiwan.

5: ， Commas are used in writings from Taiwan in the same way they are on the Mainland. Note that a comma separates the verb from its object here and in 13, 28, 34, 42, 46, and 49. Commas separate subjects from verbs in 25 and 43. See 19 and 32 where place and time structures are separated by commas.

5: 『 』 Chinese traditional parentheses are used here and in 8, 10-12, 27, 28, 34 and 41 for the same values as the Western style " " are used. See 6:6.

5-9: 如果 X, 則[zé] Y = 'If X, therefore Y' The use of 則 gives a more classical, literary flavor than using the colloquial 就. This tone is reinforced by the appearance of 但、若、却、而、極爲、反而 and 爲 in the piece.

19: 却 What function does 却 have? See 4:8.

29: 比 is the marker for the grammatical structure in this comma unit and for the grammar of the noun modification in 44. What structure do you expect when you see 比? See 5:22.

34: 某[mǒu] Referring to someone as 某 is a bit of a put down. It has the flavour of saying "whats'isface".

39-40 有 X 之虞[zhīyú] 'Have the anxiety resulting from X' is a structure which gives a literary feel to a text.

46: 若[ruò] = 'If' 若 gives a text more of a classical literary quality than the colloquial 要是 or 如果 can.

48: 便 Verb When directly before a verb, 便 is a literary synonym of 就.

48: 無[wú] is a more literary negative than 不 or 沒.

#1 MAINLAND ECONOMIC REFORMS CHAOTIC

1   經濟改革造成物價紊亂
2   通貨膨脹、搶購及貪瀆現象續惡化

3   (路透社北平十八日電)
4   中共物價改革的主要鼓吹者
5   今天表示，如果「政府」不
6   減緩經濟成長以及改變物價
7   制度，則通貨膨脹、搶購和
8   「官員」貪瀆的現象將會惡
9   化。
10   隸屬中共「國務院」的
11   「經濟技術社會發展研究中
12   心總幹事」吳景連(譯音) 指
13   出，改革社會主義經濟的關
14   鍵在於改革不合理的物價制
15   度。
16   他接受路透社訪問時說:
17   「一件貨品如果稀少，它的
18   價格應該高昂。但在中國大
19   陸，情形却相反。像煤、石
20   油、原料和電力等極爲稀少
21   的東西，價格 反而 最爲低
22   廉。」
23   隨著經濟的成長，這些
24   物品短缺的情形也更加嚴重。
25   物品短缺 引起的通貨膨脹，
26   導致民眾進行搶購。

VOCABULARY

1: 物價 [wùjià] 'prices' WG>18:價格 [jiàgé] 'prices';WG>29:零售價 [língshòujià] 'retail prices'

1: 紊亂 [wěnluàn] 'chaos' WG>40:混亂 [hùnluàn] 'confused'

2: 通貨膨脹 [tōnghuò péngzhàng] 'inflation' WG>17:貨品 [huòpǐn] 'products'; WG>35:貨幣 [huòbì] 'currency, money'

2: 搶購 [qiǎnggòu] 'panic buying'

2: 貪瀆 [tāndú] 'greed and malfeasance'

2: 惡化 [èhuà] 'worsen, deteriorate'

4: 鼓吹 [gǔchuī] 'advocate'

6: 減緩 [jiǎnhuǎn] 'retard, slow down'

10: 隸屬 [lìshǔ] 'subordinate to'

12: 總幹事 [zǒnggànshì] 'Director'

12: 譯音 [yìyīn] 'transliterated'

13: 關鍵 [guānjiàn] 'crux, key point'

17: 貨品 [huòpǐn] '?' 貨 WG:2

17: 稀少 [xīshǎo] 'rare, scarce'

18: 價格 [jiàgé] '?' 價 WG:1

18: 高昂 [gāo'áng] 'exorbitant'

19: 相反 [xiāngfǎn] 'reversed'

19: 煤   [méi] 'coal'

19: 石油 [shíyóu] 'petroleum'

20: 原料 [yuánliào] 'raw materials'

21: 低廉 [dīlián] 'cheap, low'

23: 著   [zhě] (variant way of writing 着)

24: 短缺 [duǎnquē] 'shortage'

25: 引起 [yǐnqǐ] 'give rise to, lead to'

26: 導致 [dǎozhì] 'result in'

27　　　　中共「總理」李鵬前天
28　在「國務院」表示，今年上
29　半年的零售價比去年同期上
30　漲百分之十四左右，是一九
31　四九年以來的最高漲幅。同
32　一時期，工業生產增加百分
33　之十七．二。
34　　　　吳某指出，「政府」必
35　須緊縮信用和控制貨幣問題，
36　來減緩經濟成長。
37　　　　「如果不這樣，通貨膨
38　脹、貨品短缺、搶購和官員
39　貪瀆的現象將會惡化，而有
40　發生社會秩序混亂之虞。」
41　　　　北平「金融時報」本月
42　十五日報道，物價上漲引起
43　的廣泛搶購現象，是今年前
44　五個月儲蓄率比去年同期下
45　降的主因。
46　　　　吳景連認爲，物價制度
47　若不予改革，中國大陸的整
48　體經濟改革計畫便無法成功。
49　也有人指出，改革中國大陸
50　的工廠是關鍵所在，在改革
51　物價制度之前必須先改革工
52　廠。

29: 零售價 [língshòujià] '?' 價 WG:1

29: 上漲 [shàngzhǎng] 'rise, go up' WG>31:漲幅 [zhǎngfú] 'rate of rise'

31: 漲幅 [zhǎngfú] '?' 漲 WG:29

35: 緊縮 [jǐnsuō] 'reduce, tighten'

35: 信用 [xìnyòng] 'credit'

35: 貨幣 [huòbì] '?' 貨 WG:2

40: 秩序 [zhìxù] 'order, stability'

40: 混亂 [hùnluàn] '?' 亂 WG:1

40: 之虞 [zhīyú] 'anxiety of'

41: 金融時報 [Jīnyóng shíbào] 'Banking Daily'

44: 儲蓄 [chǔxù] 'savings'

47: 不予 [bùyǔ] 'do not grant'

47: 整體 [zhěngtǐ] 'entire'

48: 計畫 [jìhuà] 'plan'

48: 無法 [wúfǎ] 'have no way to'

50: 工廠 [gōngchǎng] 'factory'

50: 所在 [suǒzài] 'location'

FURTHER READINGS FROM TAIWAN NEWSPAPERS

#2 ONE-CHILD POLICY A FAILURE (See Lesson Three)

1   中共坦承「一胎化」政策失敗
2   婦女平均仍育二至三個孩子

3   （法新社北平十五日電）中共
4   「官方」報紙今天在對一胎化政
5   策的失敗作罕見的承認中說，中
6   國婦女仍育有二至三個孩子，且
7   過去四年來，這個生育子女的平
8   均人數已經增加。
9   「光明日報」說，一九七八年
10 當中共採行控制人口政策時，每
11 個達生育年齡的婦女生育子女數
12 平均為二點七二，一九八二年此
13 平均數降低為二點五七，一九八
14 四年則為二點一九。
15 該報說，然而在一九八七年，
16 却回升為二點四九，這反映了由
17 於一九六零年代第一次嬰兒潮時
18 出生的女性，現已達生育年齡，
19 而造成這第二次的「嬰兒潮」。
20 西方分析家說，出生率不斷
21 增高顯示，迄今擁有全球最多人
22 口(十一億)的中共，其一胎化政
23 策已經失敗。
24 分析家說，該政策在大陸鄉
25 間廣受忽視，鄉下人寧願付罰款

26 而生第二或第三胎，尤其是當第
27 一胎是女兒時。
28
29 中共本月稍早曾宣布，它已
    放寬控制人口的政策，即允許大
30 多數省份的農民在頭胎生女兒的
31 情況下，可再生第二胎。
32 「農民日報」昨天舉例說明一
33 胎化政策已經失敗，它說，河北
34 省一名三十八歲的農民林良渚(譯
35 音)拒絕因生育一個以上子女而遭
36 結紮或罰款。
37 該報說，林氏夫婦可能被罰
38 款一萬一千七百六十元「人民幣」
39 (三千一百五十三美元)，相當於中
40 共工人平均工資十二年的收入。
41 在十六歲時生下頭胎，現則
42 育有九個孩子的林婦說，在中國，
43 女人沒生個兒子，就會被看成不
44 中用。
45 觀察家說，在鄉下販賣男嬰
46 的行為十分盛行。
47 西方外交人士說，中共不斷
48 增加的人口是其經濟發展的障礙，
49 他們說，此情況乃源自於毛澤東
50 認為人口成長是中共主要資產的
51 觀點。

VOCABULARY

1: 坦承 [tǎnchéng] 'frankly admit'

1: 一胎化 [yìtāihuà] 'one child policy'

1: 失敗 [shībài] 'be defeated'

2: 育 [yù] 'give birth to'

5: 罕見 [hǎnjiàn] 'rare'

8: 人數 [rénshù] 'number of people'

10: 採行 [cǎixíng] 'select and implement'

11: 達 [dá] 'reach, arrive at'

15: 然而 [rán'ér] 'however'

17: 嬰兒潮 [yīng'ércháo] 'baby boom'

21: 顯示 [xiǎnshì] 'show, demonstrate'

24: 鄉間 [xiāngjiān] 'countryside'

25: 忽視 [hūshì] 'ignore, neglect'

25: 寧願 [nìngyuàn] 'would rather'

25: 罰款 [fákuǎn] '(monetary) fines'

28: 宣布 [xuānbù] 'proclaim'

29: 放寬 [fàngkuān] 'relax, loosen'

30: 農民 [nóngmín] 'peasants'

35: 拒絕 [jùjué] 'refuse'

36: 結紮 [jiézá] 'tie (Fallopian tubes)'

40: 收入 [shōurù] 'income'

43: 不中用 [bùzhōngyòng] 'unfit for anything'

45: 觀察家 [guānchájiā] 'observers'

45: 販賣 [fànmài] 'peddling'

48: 障礙 [zhàng'ài] 'obstacle'

QUESTIONS

A. What exactly did the Chinese Communists admit in the first paragraph?

B. What would the information in the second and third paragraphs look like on a chart?

C. What happened in 1960, and what impact is it having now?

D. What type of people are most likely to disregard this policy, and what especially leads them to do so?

E. Do you see anything interesting about Ms. Lin?

F. What seems odd about lines 45-46? Do you believe what is said?

G. Who gets the blame for this situation?

#3 American Ambassador Concerned About Tibetan Human Rights
(See Lesson Seven)

1　　　　美駐中共「大使」

2　　　　關切西藏人權問題

3　　　〔美聯社北平十五日電〕

4　美國駐中共「大使」羅德今

5　天表示，他最近訪問西藏時

6　曾表達美國對當地人權的關

7　切，並要求西藏「政府」首

8　長取消對外國記者和其他旅

9　客的限制。

10　　　羅德指出，他告訴「西

11　藏自治區主席」多吉才讓説：

12　「如果他們希望西藏問題獲

13　得適當的報導，就應當讓記

14　者和任何其他人進入西藏。」

15　　　羅德在本月四至十日訪

16　問西藏省府拉薩和日喀則。

17　他是第一位訪問西藏的美國

18　駐中共「大使」。

19　　　自從去年秋季和今年三

20　月拉薩發生主張獨立和親中

21　共示威活動以來，西藏只允

22　許少數幾位經過挑選的外國

23　記者前往採訪。西藏也禁止

24　個別旅客前往游覽，只允許

25　觀光團入境。

VOCABULARY

1: 駐　[zhù] 'be stationed somewhere'

1: 大使 [dàshǐ] 'ambassador'

2: 關切 [guānqiè] 'be deeply concerned about'

4: 羅德 [Luódé] '(name of a person)'

7: 首長 [shǒuzhǎng] 'senior officials'

8: 取消 [qǔxiāo] 'abolish, rescind'

8: 旅客 [lǔkè] 'tourists'

11: 自治區 [zìzhìqū] 'autonomous region'

11: 多吉才讓 [Duōjícáiràng] '(name of a person)'

12: 獲得 [huòdé] 'get, obtain'

13: 適當 [shìdàng] 'appropriate'

13: 報導 [bàodǎo] 'news coverage'

13: 讓　[ràng] 'allow'

14: 任何 [rènhé] 'whatever'

16: 日喀則 [Rìkāzé] '(name of a place)'

19: 秋季 [qiūjì] 'autumn season'

20: 獨立 [dúlì] 'independence'

20: 親　[qīn] 'be in favor of, be on the side of'

21: 示威 [shìwēi] 'demonstrations'

21: 允許 [yúnxǔ] 'permit'

22: 挑選 [tiāoxuǎn] 'selection'

24: 游覽 [yóulǎn] 'go sight seeing'

24: 觀光團 [guānguāngtuán] 'tour groups'

25: 入境 [rùjìng] 'enter an area'

QUESTIONS

A. What two things did the US ambassador do while in Tibet?

B. What argument did he use in support of allowing Western journalists access
   to Tibet?

C. How many American ambassadors to China have previously gone to Tibet?

D. How long have journalists and individual travelers been kept out of Tibet?

E. What qualification must foreigners have now to go to Tibet?

#4 PEKING WILL NOT TOLERATE "TAIWAN INDEPENDENCE"
(See Lesson Eight)

1   北平絕不坐視「臺灣獨立」

2   【本報香港五日電】據
3 香港「南華早報」報導，假
4 如「民進黨」在臺灣取得政
5 權並搞臺獨，北平將使用武
6 力來完成其「統一」計劃。
7   報導說，這是中共「中
8 國社會科學院」副院長李慎
9 之和其他大陸學者日前會晤
10 臺灣「民進黨」助理和一羣
11 記者時所提出來的。
12   報導說，李慎之認爲，
13 臺灣若宣佈獨立，將破壞亞
14 洲的戰略均勢。
15   報導指出，李慎之強調，
16 美國絕不願看到大陸與臺灣
17 之間發生問題，因爲這只會

18 替蘇聯製造可乘之機。

19   報導說，大陸的學者也
20 指出，隨著台灣政治日趨多
21 元化，北平可能較不強調國
22 民黨在「統一」工作中的角
23 色。

24   報導說：「臺灣研究所」
25 陳姓所長指出，基於上述的
26 認知，北平保證將希望寄託
27 於國民黨當局，甚至更寄望
28 於「臺灣人民」，顯然具有
29 較大的意義。

30   報導說，陳某並強調，
31 北平將反對任何危害團結的
32 舉動。

VOCABULARY

1: 坐視 [zuòshì] 'sit idly by'

4: 政權 [zhèngquán] 'political power'

5: 臺獨 [Táidú] 'Taiwanese independence'

5: 武力 [wǔlì] 'military force'

8: 李慎之 [Lǐ Shènzhī] '(name of a person)'

9: 會晤 [huìwù] 'meet with'

10: 助理 [zhùlǐ] 'assistant'

13: 若 [ruò] 'if'

13: 宣佈 [xuānbù] 'announce, proclaim'

13: 破壞 [pòhuài] 'destroy'

13: 亞洲 [Yàzhōu] 'Asia'

14: 均勢 [jūnshì] 'balance of power'

18: X替 Y VO [X tì Y VO] 'X does verb to object for Y'

18: 可乘之機 [kě chéng zhī jī] 'a chance that can be exploited'

20: 日趨 [rìqū] 'day by day'

20: 多元化 [duōyuánhuà] 'pluralization'

21: 國民黨 [Guómíndǎng] 'Kuomintang (KMT) Party'

22: 角色 [juésè] 'role, part'

25: 陳姓 [Chén xìng] 'somebody named Chen'

25: 基於 [jīyú] 'based on'

26: 保證 [bǎozhèng] 'for sure, guaranteed'

26: 寄託 [jìtuō] 'entrust'

27: 寄望 [jìwàng] 'have expectations of'

31: 危害 [wēihài] 'harm, endanger'

31: 團結 [tuánjié] 'unity'

32: 舉動 [jǔdòng] 'movement, activity'

QUESTIONS

A. What does the first paragraph say will happen if the Minjin Party declares Taiwanese independence?

B. What is the title of the person who made this assertion?

C. Why was it specifically pointed out in the article?

D. What reason is given for the US not wanting problems between Taiwan and the Mainland?

E. What idea do lines 24-28 reinforce?

F. From what political perspective do you think this article was written?

#5 PRICE REFORMS LEAD TO LEGAL DISPUTES (See Lesson Nine)

1   物價改革未能掌握重點
2   經濟糾紛案件堆積如山

3   【本報香港三日電】 此間「文匯報」的一篇專論
4   指出，中共經濟改革必須抓住根本問題，全面地進行，
5   目前大陸各種經濟合同糾紛大量增加，就是沒有抓住
6   根本問題的表現。
7   報導說，大陸各級法院的經濟審判庭中，以經濟
8   合同糾紛為主，而且積案如山，甚至有的今年起訴案
9   子要到明年才輪到審理。這其中原因主要是案件太多，
10 而造成經濟糾紛多的根本原因，還是在於整個社會的
11 經濟活動未有置於法制軌道之下。

1: 未   [wèi] '(a negative marker)'
1: 掌握 [zhǎngwò] 'control'
2: 糾紛 [jiūfēn] 'disputes'
2: 堆積 [duījī] 'pile up'
3: 文匯報 [Wénhuì bào] 'The Wenhui Daily'
3: 專論 [zhuānlùn] 'special article'
5: 合同 [hétóng] 'contracts'
7: 審判庭 [shěnpàntíng] 'courtroom'
8: 起訴 [qǐsù] 'start a lawsuit'
9: 輪到 [lúndào] 'get to the point of'
9: 審理 [shěnlǐ] 'try, hear (a case)'
11: 法制 [fǎzhì] 'legal system'
11: 軌道 [guǐdào] 'track, path'

12 　　該文分析説，造成經濟合同糾紛的直接原因有：
13 一、簽約時不考慮有無履行合同的能力和條件；二、
14 簽約的一方擅自改變物品規則、價格或數量；三、由
15 於管理，技術或原材料供應等原因，造成合同履行不
16 當；四、「政府」指令性計劃指標，造成合同不能履
17 行；五、蓄意詐騙的行為。
18 　　專論中指出，「企業法」公布後，問題並沒有解
19 決，根本在於企業、上級主管乃至「政府」部門法律
20 意識淡薄，不把信守合同看作是企業生存的關鍵。加
21 以罰款或賠償攤在企業頭上，沒有人對此負責，更加
22 造成無人重視合同的履行。
23 　　由於這些問題，使外商不敢確信他所訂的貨物能
24 否如期交貨，這已成為他們和中共做生意最感頭痛的
25 事情。

13: 簽約 [qiānyuē] 'sign a contract'
13: 履行 [lǚxíng] 'fulfill'
14: 擅自 [shànzì] 'unilaterally'
14: 規則 [guīzé] 'specifications'
15: 供應 [gōngyìng] 'supply'
15: 不當 [búdàng] 'unsuitable'
16: 指令 [zhǐlìng] 'mandate, order'
17: 蓄意 [xùyì] 'premeditated'
17: 詐騙 [zhàpiàn] 'defraud, swindle'
18: 企業法 [Qǐyèfǎ] 'Commercial Code'
19: 主管 [zhǔguǎn] 'person in charge'
20: 淡薄 [dànbó] 'thin, hazy'
20: 信守 [xìnshǒu] 'abide by'
21: 賠償 [péicháng] 'compensation'
21: 攤在 [tānzài] 'spread out on'
23: 外商 [wàishāng] 'foreign business people'

23: 訂　[dìng] 'agree to buy'

24: 如期 [rúqī] 'on time'

24: 交貨 [jiāohuò] 'deliver products'

24: 頭痛 [tóutòng] 'headache'

QUESTIONS

A. What does the article say is the reason there are so many legal disputes about business arrangements on the Mainland?

B. How long does it take for a legal dispute to reach a decision?

C. Identify the principal reasons given for all the contactual disputes.

D. What does the article suggest in the next to the last paragraph is the underlying root cause of all this?

E. What basic problem has all this resulted in for foreign business people in China?

F. What understanding does this article convey about attitudes towards the law on the Mainland?

Reading Chinese Newspapers:
Tactics and Skills

*Lesson Thirteen: Newspaper Ads and
Announcements*

ANNOUNCEMENTS AND SCHEDULES

I. CLASSIFIED ADS

Chinese classified ads are written in a style of language which combines elements of classical prose and abbreviations reminiscent of the "4 rms rvr vu" or "tv 4 sale" format seen in American newspapers. A good example of this is the 'Lonely Hearts' ad from the 中央日報 below. In it classical prose usages are echoed by the classical negative adverbs 未, 無, and 非 and the vocabulary she uses to describe herself. The metered balance of classical prose is called to mind by the four character phrases in which she lists positive qualifications for a husband followed by three character phrases listing unacceptable habits. A quasi-classical structure announcing the need for nothing but good habits sums up her criteria for a spouse. Terseness is achieved by abbreviation; for example 大畢 for 大學畢業生 and 照 for 照片 'photograph.' The ad ends on a classical tone with another four character phrase starting with the classical negative 非 saying that the ad does not come from a "dating service".

    A. Lonely Hearts (1)

1   徵婚
2   女，未婚，大畢，秀美賢孝，
3   和善慧識健康，職祕書。誠
4   徵：男，適婚，博士或碩士
5   學歷，品學兼優，身心健康。
6   喜愛文藝。174 公分以上正
7   職。不抽菸、不酗酒、不打
8   牌、不賭博，無不良嗜好者。
9   請函照寄：臺灣省臺中市郵
10   政信箱 27 - 71 號張小姐轉交
11   ALICE 收。非介紹所

VOCABULARY

1: 徵 [zhēng] 'summon, request, ask for'

2: 秀 [xiù] 'beautiful'

2: 賢 [xián] 'capable, talented'

2: 孝 [xiào] 'filial'

3: 和 [hé] 'harmonious, affable'

3: 善 [shàn] 'good, virtuous'

3: 慧 [huì] 'intelligent, wise'

3: 識 [shí] 'knowledgeable, discerning'

3: 祕書 [mìshū] 'secretary'

4: 誠 [chéng] 'sincerely'

5: 適 [shì] 'suitable'

4: 碩士 [shuòshì] 'M.A. (degree)'

5: 品學 [pǐn xué] 'character and education'

5: 優 [yōu] 'superior'

6: 文藝 [wényì] 'literature and arts'

7: 抽菸 [chōuyān] 'smoke' (菸 = 煙 = 烟)

7: 酗酒 [xùjiǔ] 'excessive drinking'

8: 打牌 [dǎpái] 'play cards'

8: 賭博 [dǔbó] 'gamble'

8: 無 [wú] 'without'

8: 不良 [bùliáng] 'bad, undesirable'

8: 嗜好 [shìhào] 'habit, hobby'

9: 函照 [hán zhào] 'letter and photograph'

The next 'Seeking Marriage' classified from a Chengdu newspaper has much of the content of the one above, but the language is somewhat more colloquial. It is similarly organized with the writer describing her appearance and tastes followed by her criteria for a male companion: under 30, works in a national or collective enterprise, is sensitive, responsible, and unmarried. It ends with a mailing address. (This original text and some others below were poorly printed and do not reproduce well. However, you need to develop the ability to work with this type of material as well.)

Lonely Hearts (2)

1 　　　　女友，24 岁，未婚，高 1.63 米，
2 某县中学教师，现在蓉进修专科。爱
3 好广泛，体健貌美，人品好，重感情，
4 善于理解人。欲寻 30 岁以下，在全民
5 和集体企事业工作，特别是 在蓉部队
6 任干部职务的更佳、重感情，有责任
7 感的未婚男性为友。 来信 (并附照)
8 请寄解北大湾 56267 部队魏洪远。

VOCABULARY

2: 蓉　[Róng] '(another name for Chengdu)'
2: 进修 [jìnxiū] 'doing advanced studies'
2: 爱好 [àihào] 'interests, hobbies'
3: 貌　[mào] 'looks, appearance'
3: 重　[zhòng] 'put emphasis on'
4: 善于 [shànyú] 'good at'
4: 欲　[yù] 'desire'
4: 寻　[xún] 'seeking'
6: 更佳 [gèng jiā] 'better, desirable'
8: 魏洪远 [Wèi Hóngyuǎn] '(name of a person)'

The third piece is from a male in Chengdu who wants a female companion. After a minimal description of himself, he lists the qualifications he has in mind for her, including writing the essay "On Life".

Lonely Hearts (3)

1　　　　个体企业家，男，32 岁，
2　　1.67米，未婚。征：有才有智、
3　　有胆有识的女性为侣。意者请
4　　来信以"论人生"为题，寄成
5　　都晚报工交部小王收转。

VOCABULARY

1: 个体企业家 [gètǐ qǐyèjiā] 'independent entrepreneur'

3: 有才有智 [yǒucái yǒuzhì] 'talented and resourceful'

3: 有胆有识 [yǒudǎn yǒushì] 'courageous and knowledgeable'

3: 侣　[lǚ] 'companion'

4: 意者 [yìzhě] 'interested person'

5: 论人生 [Lùn rénshēng] 'On Life'

5: 收转 [shōuzhuǎn] 'receive and pass along'

B. FULL HEARTS (original newspaper ad is on the following page)

The 中央日報 often has parent's announcements of the marriages of their children in foreign countries. They follow a set pattern of telling whether the child is the older (長 [zhǎng]) or younger (次) followed by the name of the child, the date and place of the marriage ceremony, and the phrase (謹此)敬告 [(jǐncǐ) jìnggào] '(solemnly this) is respectfully announced.' The names of the parents (what two things are unusual about the parents' names in the middle announcement?) followed by the ritualistic phrase 敬啓 [jìngqǐ] 'informed with respect' end the announcement.

Notice the composition of the surrounding border of the announcement.

C. "EMPTY HEARTS"

Though mainly filled with physical description, the use of 于, 至, 未 and 与 give this notice of a missing boy a bit of the flavor of classical prose. What is poignant about the name of the contact person?

(4)

1   王鑫，男，14 岁，身高 1.60 米左右，北京市
2   二外附中学生，穿米黄色夹克上衣，草绿弹力尼
3   裤，蓝毛衣、绿毛裤、白球鞋、白袜子，于10 月
4   28日下午骑 4791070黑色凤凰自行车出走，至今未
5   归，有发现者请与北京市 340 信箱 81 分箱联系。
6   电话: 57.1731 转 285   联系人: 王子生

VOCABULARY

1: 王鑫 [Wáng Xīn] '(name of a person)'
2: 夹克 [jiákè] 'jacket'
2: 弹力尼裤 [tánlìní kù] 'stretch nylon pants'
4: 凤凰自行车 [Fènghuáng zìxíngchē] 'Phoenix Bicycle'
5: 未归 [wèiguī] 'has not returned'

D. HELP WANTED

The vocabulary involved here can vary greatly since potentially a large part of the whole range of jobs in a society could come up here. These ads are structured to tell of the type of job involved, conditions of employment, and the means of contact. As is usual for Chinese classifieds, brevity remains a hallmark and classical prose features continue to be used.

(5)

1 　　　　　　　　北京海关招聘启事

2 　　　经北京市人才交流中心批准，北京海关招聘干部
3 　20名。

4 　　　有在京正式户口，家住东城、西城、崇文、宣武、
5 　朝阳区；35岁以内，国家正式干部（男性）；身体健康，
6 　品学兼优，1.70米以上；中专以上文化，有英、日语
7 　基础，经考试择优录取。

8 　　　即日起报名，3日内止。持工作证，学历证书，
9 　户口簿，一寸免冠像片两张。交报名费3元，额满为
10 　止。

11 　　　报名地点：建国门内大街24号（北京海关招聘干部
12 　报名处）

13 　　　联系电话：5001462　　　联系人：田玉荣、胡景生

VOCABULARY

1: 海关 [Hǎiguān] 'Customs Office'

1: 招聘 [zhāopìn] 'invite applications for a job'

2: 批准 [pīzhǔn] 'authorization'

4: 户口 [hùkǒu] 'registered permanent residence'

4: 崇文、宣武、朝阳 [Chóngwén, Xuānwǔ, Cháoyáng] '(place names in Beijing)'

6: 中专 [zhōngzhuān] 'technical secondary school'

7: 择优 [zéyōu] 'select the best'

8: 即日 [jírì] 'this very day'

8: 报名 [bàomíng] 'sign up'

8: 持　[chí] 'carry, bring'

8: X 证 [X-zhèng] 'proof of X'

9: 额满 [émǎn] 'quota is filled'

1　　　　　國內繪圖員

2　　　　工程公司誠聘國內繪圖

3　　　　員居深圳或廣州有經驗

4　　　　優先有意詳履歷近照寄

5　　　　九龍觀塘 郵政信箱 694

6　　　27 號

VOCABULARY

1: 繪圖員 [huìtúyuán] 'draftsman'

3: 深圳 [Shēnzhèn] '(place name in Guangdong)'

4: 優先 [yōuxiān] 'preferred'

4: 履歷 [lǚlì] 'resume'

5: 九龍 [Jiǔlóng] 'Kowloon (Hong Kong)'

5: 觀塘 [Guāntáng] '(place name in Hong Kong)'

E. LOST AND FOUND

These two announcements from the Hong Kong paper 文匯報 are interesting not only for their content, but also for the side by side position of the two basic styles of Chinese newspaper layout (see the original on page 249).

(7)

1	遺失聲明	7	遺失聲明
2	茲遺失交通銀行旺角	8	本人陳志成之國內駕駛證
3	支行外幣定期存款單	9	廣東08港-0100574於8月1日
4	02753951979957　除向	10	在香港遺失現除報失外特
5	該行掛失外特此聲明	11	此聲明作廢
6	作廢　方燕啓	12	陳志成啓

VOCABULARY

1: 遺失 [yíshī] 'lost'

2: 茲 [zī] 'now; here'

2: 交通銀行 [Jiāotōng yínháng] 'Communications Bank'

3: 支行 [zhīháng] 'branch bank'

3: 外幣 [wàibì] 'foreign currency'

3: 存款單 [cúnkuǎndān] 'deposit slip'

5: 掛失 [guàshī] 'register a loss'

6: 作廢 [zuòfèi] 'null and void'

8: 駕駛證 [jiàshǐzhèng] 'drivers license'

10: 報失 [bàoshī] 'report a loss'

These two classifieds are from the 北京晚报.

(8)

声明

兹因不慎，将北京市公安局
签发的京居字第 H 0481 号《外国人
居留证》遗失，特此声明作废。

声明人: 莫拉克·巴巴拉

声·明·作·废

》中国康辉旅行社总社将巳字

第 9439501-9439700、9035551-9035600
号北京市统一银钱收据遗失。

　》北京市西城区晶晶服务部
将京西商 2095 号营业执照副本遗失。

F. HOUSING

Vocabulary in housing ads centers around facilities, location, cost, and how to make contact. Below are ads for a residence, a hotel and an office building.

(9)

1	租　　售
2	錦繡
3	850 全新超級豪華裝修
4	未住東南 0-719288 L 段
5	3 街口
6	恆運旅舍
7	銅鑼灣面對海景清靜冷氣
8	彩電獨立電話套房歡迎公
9	幹游客華僑台灣會親 60元
10	起 5-8921663 或 5-8921709

VOCABULARY

1: 錦繡 [jǐnxiù] '(place name)'
3: 豪華 [háohuá] 'luxurious'
3: 裝修 [zhuāngxiū] 'repaired'
4: 未住 [wèizhù] 'never before lived in'
4: 東南 [dōngnán] 'faces southeast'
6: 恆運旅舍 [Héngyùn lǚshè] 'Hengyun Hotel'
7: 銅鑼灣 [Tóngluó wān] '(place name in Hong Kong)'
7: 面對海景 [miànduì hǎijǐng] 'facing the seascape'
7: 冷氣 [lěngqì] 'air conditioning'
8: 彩電 [cǎidiàn] 'color television'
8: 套房 [tàofáng] 'suite of rooms'
8: 公幹 [gōnggàn] '(someone who is) on business'
9: 會親 [huìqīn] '(someone who is) meeting relatives'

(10)

1　　　　出租办公楼

2　　　办公楼近 3000 平方米，地处永内陶
3　然亭附近，交通方便，具备办公的一切
4　条件（租赁时间及租赁面积可商谈）。
5　　　联系人：晓红、晓军
6　　电　话：48.6061-310

VOCABULARY

1: 办公楼 [bàngōnglóu] 'office building'
2: 永内陶然亭 [Yǒngnèi Táorántíng] '(name of a place in Beijing)'
3: 具备 [jùbèi] 'completely equipped'
4: 租赁 [zūlìn] 'lease'
4: 面积 [miànji] 'area'

II. SCHOOL ANNOUNCEMENTS

There are many ads and announcements for educational opportunities in Chinese newspapers. They range from calls for Ph.D. students, to announcements for foreign language classes, to ads for classes to become a truck driver. The most prestigious universities as well as lesser known technical schools and evening schools regularly place announcements on the availability of new classes.

(11)

北 京 师 范 学 院

1988 年博士生招生

3	学科、专业	研究方向	指导教师
4	教育心理学	智力开发的心理学题	林传鼎教授
5	中国古代史	秦汉-隋唐五代社会	宁可教授
6		经济史	
7	世界近现代史	二次大战间的国际关系	齐世荣教授

8 报名日期: 1988年3月10日至4月10日，外地考生凭单位介
9 　　　　绍信可以函报。
10 报名地点: 北京师范学院研究生招生办公室(北京阜外花
11 　　　　园村)
12 考试日期: 1988年6月。
13 考试科目、招生人数、报考条件等详见招生简章
14 (简章备索)

VOCABULARY

1: 北京师范学院 [Běijīng shīfàn xuéyuàn] 'Beijing Teachers College'
3: 指导 [zhǐdǎo] 'supervising'
4: 教育心理学 [jiàoyù xīnlǐ xué] 'eductional psychology'
4: 智力 [zhìlì] 'intelligence'

7: 近现代史 [jìnxiàndàishǐ] 'modern and contemporary history'

7: 二次大战 [èrcì dàzhàn] 'World War II'

8: 凭　[píng] 'depend upon'

9: 函报 [hánbào] 'apply by mail'

13: 简章 [jiǎnzhāng] 'simple introduction'

14: 备索 [bèisuǒ] 'available'

(12)

1　　民办实用会计学校

2　　工商会计及原理、政经、珠算。
3　　七月参加电视中专考试，发国家
4　　承认证书。下午 5:30 在东大桥路
5　　11号楼居委会报名。

VOCABULARY

2: 会计 [kuàijì] 'accounting'

2: 珠算 [zhūsuàn] 'using an abacus'

3: 电视中专 [diànshì zhōngzhuān] 'televised technical middle school'

(13)

1   安贞汽车摩托车驾驶学校招生

2   我校现招收新学员，凡年满 18-45
3 周岁的公民持交通队核发的"北京市机
4 动车驾驶员登记表"到校报名即可。本
5 校教练车种类齐全有:大货车、小货车、
6 日产小客车。后三轮摩托车和增驾大客
7 车。每日备有大客车接送学员。报名地
8 点:安外安德里北街 (乘 58路汽车黄寺下
9 车往东)， 电话： 421.6371, 联系人：
10 金启明、张民杰、任中。

VOCABULARY

1: 安贞 [Ānzhēn] '(name of a school)'

1: 摩托车 [mótuōchē] 'motorized vechicle'

2: 凡   [fán] 'all'

3: 核发 [héfǎ] 'approved and issued'

4: 登记表 [dēngjìbiǎo] 'registration form'

4: 即可 [jíkě] 'that is acceptable'

5: 齐全 [qíquán] 'complete'

5: 货车 [huòchē] 'truck (for hauling things)'

7: 备有 [bèiyǒu] 'have available'

7: 接送 [jiēsòng] 'transport to and from'

8: 黄寺 [Huáng sì] '(name of a temple)'

III. PUBLIC SERVICE ANNOUNCEMENTS

There are various public service announcements in the papers. Note the the abbreviation of vocabulary items and the use of classical prose elements in the following announcement from the Beijing Transport Management Bureau which forbids bicycles with large baskets on the streets of the city.

(14)

1	北京市公安局交通管理局
2	通告
3	为了维护首都有一个良好的交通秩
4	序，保障交通安全，经市政府批准，从
5	本通告发布之日起，早六时至晚八时，
6	市区街道禁止骑自行车带大筐行驶。违
7	者，按交通违章处理。
8	特此通告
9	一九八八年三月十六日

VOCABULARY

2: 通告 [tōnggào] 'public notice'

3: 维护 [wéihù] 'safeguard'

4: 保障 [bǎozhàng] 'protect'

4: 批准 [pīzhǔn] 'approval'

5: 发布 [fābù] 'issue, release'

6: 禁止 [jìnzhǐ] 'prohibit'

6: 大筐 [dàkuāng] 'large basket'

6: 行驶 [xíngshǐ] 'operate a vechicle'

7: 违章 [wéizhāng] 'breaking rules and regulations'

In addition to notices placed by governmental agencies (see also Sight Reading 4C of Lesson Nine), companies also put notices in the paper, to get noticed. The language tends to be literary and of course the structures bring to mind classical grammar.

(15)   **(reproduction of original text)**

中国中山实业公司致意
时逢龙年伊始，我谨代表公司全体同仁，竭诚欢迎海内外各界朋友与本公司进行全面合作。
谢谢！

中国中山实业公司总经理　彭维思
1988年 2 月26日

VOCABULARY

1: 实业 [shíyè] 'industry and commerce'
1: 致意 [zhìyì] 'give one's regards'
2: 龙年 [lóngnián] 'Year of the Dragon'
2: 伊始 [yīshǐ] 'beginning'
2: 同仁 [tóngrén] 'colleague'
2: 竭诚 [jiéchéng] 'wholeheartedly'
5: 总经理 [Zǒngjīnglǐ] 'General Manager'

IV. ENTERTAINMENT SCHEDULES

Television schedules are straight forward. The programs on each
channel (频道 [píndào]) are listed in a 24 hour format. The genre name (e.g.,
series, plays about Taiwan, educational programs, sports and foreign productions) is
followed by the name of the specific program.

(16) 　　　　三月 17 日（星期四）电视节目
　　　　　　　　二频道
10:15　美术片：我们的朋友小海朱
16:10　电视连续剧：破产警告 3
20:00　世界各地：展望2000 年 (CBS) 提供
20:45　台湾故事片：汪洋中的一条船
22:05　电视连续剧：爱新觉罗。浩 4
22:50　迎春文艺节目展播：石油的旋律

Movie schedules state if the picture is in color, give type of screen ('broad'), and list
its name. If it is a foreign film the country of origin is given. A list of theaters and
showing times follows.

(17)
1　彩色宽银幕故事片　红　高　梁
2　　　西安电影制片厂摄制
3　崇文文化馆 19:55 明 8:00　10:15　12:30
4　　　　　14:45　17:00　19:15　21:30
5　崇文影剧院(地下) 20:40 明 8:45　11:00
6　　　　　13:15　15:30　17:45　20:00
7　首都影院　明 9:10　11:00　12:50　14:40

VOCABULARY

1: 彩色 [cǎisè] 'color'

1: 宽 [kuān] 'broad'

1: 银幕 [yínmù] '(silver) screen'

1: 红高梁 [Hóng gāoliáng] '(name of a movie)'

2: 制片厂 [zhìpiànchǎng] 'movie studio'

2: 摄制 [shèzhì] 'produce (movies)'

Announcements of stage and musical performances can simply give the names of the troupe, the piece, the leading performers and the time and theatre, or they can go into details such as the names of the writer, director, the costume and lighting designers, and the composer.

(18)

1   中华全国总工会歌舞团演出

2   大型民族古典舞剧　　三　　圣　　母

3   编导:黄伯寿、兰　衍、吴佩璋、蒋　玲

4   作曲:刘以健　　　指挥:刘　溪　　　舞美设计:薛殿杰

5   服装、造型设计：齐　静　灯光设计：刘弼源、曹乃介

6   主要演员:蔡芳、王颖、张琳、张庆洪、孙文举、李福、

7   孙立克、石雪烽、杨爱东、邵军、王跃康、蔡双林、杨红等

8   22、23、24、25、26、27日晚 7:15在天桥剧场

9   即日起办理团体票登记，20 日上午 9:00在本剧场售部分零票

10   电话 33.0513

VOCABULARY

1: 歌舞团 [gēwǔtuán] 'song and dance troupe'

2: 三圣母 [Sānshèngmǔ] '(name of a performance)'

3: 编导 [biāndǎo] 'writer and director'

4: 作曲 [zuòqǔ] 'composer'

4: 指挥 [zhǐhuī] 'conductor'

5: 服装 [fúzhuāng] 'costumes'

5: 灯光 [dēngguāng] 'lighting'

6: 演员 [yǎnyuán] 'actors'

V. ADVERTISEMENTS

There has been an explosion of commerical advertisements in the last several years. These ads come in all sizes and shapes, and their contents range all across the spectrum. They tend to be less classical in language than what we have seen so far, but they all share the need to define the product, list its appealing features, and state where it can be purchased. The following ad for woolen sweaters, the first of three representative ads included here, does that with a great economy of words. It is followed by an ad for a forklift factory and one for the Friendship Hotel in Beijing.

(19)

1	北京花市百货商场　　北京第二羊毛衫厂
2	北京第四羊毛衫厂　　北京第六羊毛衫厂
3	联合举办
4	春 季 羊 毛 衫 展 销
5	各种款式兔羊毛、羊仔毛、雪兰毛衫，计100个品种。
6	价格: 25 - 60 元
7	日期:即日起(售完为止) 地点: 花市百货商场北货场一楼

VOCABULARY

1: 百货商场 [bǎihuò shāngchǎng] 'shopping mall'

1: 羊毛衫 [yángmáoshān] 'wool sweater, cardigan'

4: 展销 [zhǎnxiāo] 'sales exhibition'

5: 款式 [kuǎnshì] 'pattern, style'

5: 兔羊毛 [tùyángmáo] 'angora wool'

5: 羊仔毛 [yángzǎımáo] 'lambs wool'

5: 雪兰毛 [xuělánmáo] '(type of wool)'

(20)

1   性能优良的锦州叉车   为您提供尽善尽美的服务
2   中国叉车公司锦州起重机械厂

---

3 我厂系机械部定点叉车生产厂   叉车连续四年被部评为"一等品"
4   主要产品：
       CPC - 2 吨柴油叉车   一九八四年机械部试验场同行业集中考核
6   CPQ - 2 吨汽油叉车   中可靠率、利用率分别为99.59%、97.63%。超
7   CPC-2.5 吨柴油叉车   过部优规定。根据用户要求可提供各种属具，
8   CPQ-2.5 吨汽油叉车   配备舒适的驾驶室、高、低门架、全视野叉车。

---

9 地址：辽宁省锦州室古塔区永安街249号   电话：8210   电报：2775

VOCABULARY

1: 叉车 [chāchē] 'forklift'
2: 起重机械 [qǐzhòng jīxiè] 'hoists, cranes, derricks'
3: 评为 [píngwéi] 'evaluated as'
5: 柴油 [cháiyóu] 'diesel'
5: 考核 [kǎohé] 'assessment'
7: 优规定 [yōuguīdìng] 'criteria for superior ranking'
7: 用户 [yònghù] 'customers'
7: 属具 [shǔjù] 'parts'
8: 配备 [pèibèi] 'equipment'
8: 驾驶室 [jiàshǐshì] 'driver's cab'

(21)   **(reproduction of original text)**

友誼旅遊飯店集團成員
北京友誼賓館

友誼賓館建於 1954 年，是中國最大的園林式賓館。建築古樸典雅，庭園優美，設備先進，設施齊全，是中外賓客理想的下榻之地，尤其適合長期居住和接待各種會議。

總經理: 張鈞孝
地址:　　北京白石橋路3號
電話:　　890621　890961
電掛:　　2222
電傳:　　222362　FHBJ CN
傳真:　　8314661

VOCABULARY

1: 友誼 [yǒuyì] 'friendship'

1: 集團 [jítuán] 'group'

2: 賓館 [bīnguǎn] 'hotel'

3: 建筑 [jiànzhù] 'architecture'

3: 古樸典雅 [gǔpǔ diǎnyǎ] 'simple yet elegant'

4: 設施 [shèshī] 'facilities'

4: 賓客 [bīnkè] 'guests'

4: 下榻 [xiàtà] 'stay (at a place on a trip)'

11: 傳真 [chuánzhēn] 'fax'

On the following pages we have reproduced most of the original ads and schedules used as texts for Lesson 13. Like classified ads in Western newspapers, Chinese ads are printed very small and are sometimes printed poorly, so reading such ads is a particular challenge for the Western student. We reproduce them here chiefly to give you an appreciation of ad formatting, layout and style. The ads reproduced here are in roughly the same order as they appear in Lesson 13. Some ads are individual cutouts while others appear beside other ads just as they did in the original newspaper.

① 徵婚

姐中好不上康士誠，女轉市者打正。學徽和，交郵。牌職喜歷：善未婚政請、。愛，男慈識，ALICE信函不不睹抽藝學適健大暈箱照27寄博芬。○兼婚康昱。｜：，、，優，，非71臺無不，博職秀介號灣不酗公身士祕美紹張省戾酒分心或書賢所小臺嗜、以健碩。李

② 女友，24岁，未婚，高1.63米，某县中学教师，现在蓉进修专科。爱好广泛，体健貌美，人品好，重感情善于理解人。欲寻30岁以下，在全民和集体企事业工作，特别是在蓉部队任干部职务的更佳、重感情，有责任感的未婚男性为友。来信（并附照）请寄解北大湾56267部队魏洪迎。

某女，29岁，高1.59米，高中毕业，本市区某省级企事业单位干部，品貌端正，体态匀称，性格内向但善理解人。觅36岁以下身高1.70米左右在本市工作而其它条件相宜的男子为友，诚者信照请寄锦城艺术宫罗佩收转，拒访。

菜女，离校助教，27岁，高1.6米，貌一般，身体健康，善良，活泼开朗，征大专以上学历，③ 男性。小天8路46号杨小科收转。拒访。

③ 个体企业家，男，32岁，1.67米，未婚。

征：有才有智、有胆有识的女性为侣。意者请来信以"论人生"为题，寄成都晚报工交部小王收转。

男，48岁，1.65米，市内某大学教师，体健开朗，正直善良，兴趣广泛，离异（有一女不在身边）觅44岁以下，开朗善良理解人，通情达理，品貌端生，高雅的女友为伴，有无婚史不限，须无小孩（条件优者，有一女孩也可），有意者信照

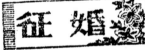

征婚

④ 王鑫，男，14岁，身高1.60米左右，北京市二外附中学生，穿米黄色夹克上衣，草绿色弹力尼裤，蓝毛衣、绿毛裤、白球鞋，白袜子，于10月28日下午骑4791070黑色凤凰自行车出走，至今未归，有发现者请与北京市340信箱81分箱联系。电话：57.1731转285　联系人：王子生。

Index: Structural Markers

This index is arranged by the total number of strokes in the first character of a pattern. The first number refers to the text and the second to the line where it occurs. Underlining marks discussion of the pattern, a lack of underlining indicates a point at which it is reviewed. Both full form and simplified forms are included in this index.

【一画】

一方面X, 一方面Y 4:35

一是X, 二是Y 6:7, 9:24

一Verb 1, 就Verb 2 8:7, 9:40

【二画】

又Verb 2:2, 8:23, 10:5

Verb 了 2:5, 6:11, 11:45

【三画】

之后 2:4

之时 3:7

之所以Verb 9:15

万 3:3

与 5:4, 6:9

及 6:9

Verb于 7:9, 8:12

才Verb 10:23, 11:2

下转 10:34

已 Verb 11:2

亿 11:24

【四画】

Verb bu Verb 3:12

不管 X, 将 Y 9:22

不得不 Verb 11:6

不仅 X, 也 Y 11:44

X为 Y Vp 3:34, 7:43

为了 Y Vp 3:43, 5:20, 8:12

Verb 为 3:40, 6:42

X为 Y 8:12, 11:2

X为 Y Vp 8:12

止 4:45

无 12:48, 13:1

【五画】

以后 2:4

以 X Vp 2:14, 8:35

Vp 1以 Vp 2 4:38, 11:38

以外 5:15

X以来 7:18, 10:30

以及 6:9

对 Place 4:12, 6:6, 9:4

比 5:22, 10:19, 12:29

由 X Vp 6:11, 7:76

由 Place 6:42

由于 X, 也 Y 5:25, 9:38

正 Verb 7:43, 10:12

X让 Y Vp 8:39

只要 x, 就 Y 9:19

只有 X, 才 Y 10:23

X来 13:1

【六画】

后 2:4

并 Negative 2:35

并 Y 4:22, 8:41

同 5:4, 6:9

向 6:6

地 6:37, 7:43, 8:10, 10:24

在 Place 7:12, 10:14

在 Verb 7:43, 9:7

如果 X, 那么 Y 7:30, 12:5

尽管 X, 但 Y 9:13

则 Y 11:26, 12:5

【七画】

把 Object Verb 2:28, 3:45

时 3:7

却 Y 4:8, 11:4, 12:19

决 Negative 9:13

即 X 11:30

【八画】

的 Noun 3:12, 5:11

X使Y Vp 4:26, 5:31

到 X (为)止 4:45

Verb到 5:18

些 5:6, 9:10

所 Verb 5:19, 10:27

X和 Y 6:9, 8:9

Verb 於 7:9, 8:12

Index: Characters (Simplified)

Vocabulary from the texts are entered below in stroke count sections in order of the total number of strokes of the first character of words and terms. Groups within each section are based on the first stroke of the first character in the order of 丶 , 一 , 乛 , 丨 , 乚 , 丿 , and 乛 . Different words which share a first character are listed together in the numerical order of their appearance in the lessons. The first number refers to the lesson, the second to the text (M = the main text) and the last number to the line number given in the vocabulary glosses. @ indicates that the word also appears in the full-form character sub-index at the end of this index.

Index: Characters (Full Form)

Vocabulary are also entered here if the first character of a word was originally presented in a text in the full character form. Characters are grouped according to the total number of strokes in the first character and ordered by Word Group affiliations in the numerical order of appearance in the lessons.

【八劃】

兩岸	7.M.24
長期	7.M.46
長期化	8.M.40
爭端	7.M.53
狀態	8.M.40
糾紛	9.M.20
	12.5.2
亞洲	13.5.13

【九劃】

約見	7.2.1
計劃	12.M.48
結紮	12.2.36
軌道	12.5.11
訂	12.5.23

【十劃】

島內	8.M.46
連用	9.M.13
陳姓	12.4.25

【十一劃】

國務委員	7.M.5
國務卿	7.M.12
國際化	8.M.37
國民黨	12.4.21
進展	7.M.8
異同	7.M.29

異常	8.M.47
現代化	7.M.44
現狀	8.M.24
堅持	7.M.48
堅定	7.M.75
參	7.2.5
產生	8.M.27
區別	8.M.29
區分	8.M.30
貪污	9.M.10
貪瀆	12.M.2
牽涉	9.M.16
偵察	9.M.22
從事	9.M.27
專訪	9.M.35
專論	12.5.3
貨品	12.M.17
貨幣	12.M.35
鄉間	12.2.24
販賣	12.2.45
設施	13.21.4

【十二劃】

發展	7.M.2
發表	7.M.72
發揮	7.M.80
發賑	8.M.18

順利	7.M.38
開誠布公	7.M.66
眾	7.2.5
無	13.1.8
無權	7.2.13
無異	8.M.5
無法	12.M.48
無不	14.1.8
飲鴆止渴	8.M.5
統治	8.M.23
惡化	12.M.2
達	12.2.11
報導	12.3.13
報失	13.7.10
詐騙	12.5.17

【十三劃】

會晤	7.M.67
	12.5.9
會親	13.9.9
損失	7.2.18
頑固	8.M.30
傾向	8.M.28
準確	9.M.9
違法	9.M.16
業余	9.M.30
搶購	12.M.2

272